ZERO
ALTITUDE

ZERO
ALTITUDE

How I learned
to fly less
and travel more

HELEN COFFEY

For Sara and the Smoo: the wind beneath my
(metaphorical) wings

First published 2022

FLINT is an imprint of The History Press
97 St George's Place, Cheltenham,
Gloucestershire, GL50 3QB
www.flintbooks.co.uk

British Library Cataloguing in Publication Data.
A catalogue record for this book is available from the British Library.

ISBN 978 0 7509 9572 6

Typesetting and origination by The History Press
Printed and bound in Great Britain by TJ Books Limited, Padstow, Cornwall.

Trees for Life

Contents

Author's Note

When I had the idea for this book – to attempt, as a travel journalist, to go flight-free for a year – the world was set on one obstinate course from which there was seemingly no turning back: growth. Growth, growth and more growth, ever expanding, no slowing down. This was true of world economics, of consumption – and, of course, of flying. Despite promises about reaching carbon neutrality by 2050, airlines were doing little to curb that growth. Rather, with pound signs in their eyes, they were set on further expansion and better connectivity; more bums on seats and more seats to put bums on.

It felt like a giant, unshiftable weight, the momentum of which was too great to contemplate. Some people were contemplating it, of course, and arguing loudly for reduction in response to overwhelming climate science that said we needed to change our habits *now* – yet these courageous dissenters were an outspoken but tiny minority.

Then along came coronavirus.

Things that seemed impossible happened. Planes stayed on the tarmac. Airlines cut down and cut down and cut down until there was nothing left of their schedules. The world stood still for a moment. The world held its breath.

The pandemic did what decades of campaigning could not – it forced everyone to go flight-free. I was no longer alone in my project of trying to stay grounded; the rest of the planet was joining me, whether they wanted to or not.

This huge, world-altering event did several things. Firstly, it put airlines already on the brink out of business. Flybe was the first to topple, but others followed suit, with Virgin Australia and Colombia's Avianca both filing for bankruptcy in spring 2020. Virgin Atlantic was forced to come up with a complex restructuring deal to stay afloat, while British Airways, easyJet and Jet2 axed great swathes of their staff. Government bailouts were dished out to airlines across the globe – to the tune of $58 billion in the US. By the time we globally got more of a handle on Covid-19, the aviation industry had been changed irrevocably. It's why, when I refer to stats about flying in this book, I will often take numbers from 2019 – the data from 2020 in no way reflects the 'norm' about our flying habits, and is therefore only of limited use.

Secondly, people themselves had changed: they'd had to become creative to stay connected without leaving the house. Video apps like Zoom and Houseparty exploded in popularity, virtual pubs were created with virtual quizzes, people 'met' for dinner and drinks from their own kitchen tables and even went clubbing in their living rooms. Humans are incredibly sociable, yes, but also incredibly adaptable. We realised we could easily hang out with someone on the other side of the world without going to the other side of the world. More than that, an entire market, that of business travel, was proven practically obsolete overnight. Why pay for an employee to take an expensive flight across continents for a meeting that could take place on Microsoft Teams for free?

All that is to say, we've seen a future now where we *could* fly less. A lot less. We've experienced a world in which we use the brilliant technology at our disposal to hold meetings with people in different time zones, attend conferences and workshops online, and spend intentional, meaningful time with friends and family who are far away. We haven't quite mastered creating a virtual tropical island paradise in dreary suburbia yet, but it can't be far off.

And yet, despite all this, we already saw things reverting to the status quo in 2021. Airlines gradually ramped up their schedules, demanding even more tax breaks and incentives to get people flying again. There's a real possibility we have learned nothing from our brush with the apocalypse; there's a real possibility that, in our desperation to feel secure and normal again, we will give up all our insight and, more importantly, the potential for real change. Because now is the moment when we could rebuild a better, cleaner, greener industry.

It's not to say we should completely live our lives without flying – but this latest crisis has shown us that perhaps we don't need to do it as much as we thought.

Travel, in all its mind-opening glory, is still my bread and butter. Part of this exploration was to find out how bad air travel is for the planet in the grand scheme of things, and whether there's a possible sustainable future for aviation. The other goal was to discover just how diverse and exhilarating travel can be when you stay grounded. In some ways, the positives people took from lockdown – time to pause, quiet to reflect, a gentle slowing down of pace – are perfectly mirrored by the slow travel experience.

Now that lockdowns have lifted and life has begun to revert to its old shape, my biggest hope is that we become more intentional with our time and money when it comes to travel. That, having pressed pause on life for a little while, we're able to stop and take stock of what matters to us: the dream trips we'd like to carefully, painstakingly curate, with the way we get there forming just as big a part of the planning as the 'there' itself. Mindful travel, you could call it.

Who knows, maybe more people will join me in this experiment (voluntarily this time) – not because they have to or feel guilted into it, but because, after the pandemic, they want to experience the world from a different perspective. Flight-free 2020 may have been an accident; let's make the next flight-free years intentional.

Acknowledgements

If it takes a village to raise a child, it takes a disparate but vast community of beautiful people to birth a book.

First up, a huge thank you to my agent at Northbank Talent Management, Martin Redfern, and my editor at Flint, Simon Wright, for believing in this project right from the off and never faltering (even when my own enthusiasm waned due to the minor stumbling block of a global pandemic).

I am hugely indebted to Anna Hughes, the founder of Flight Free UK, and the British contingent of flight-free pledgees for their unwavering passion and deeply inspiring brand of evangelism – this book simply would not exist if they hadn't presented such compelling and compassionate arguments for staying grounded.

Massive thanks to every scientist, activist, campaigner and expert who gave up their time to patiently explain the complex issues of climate change, offsetting, transport and tourism as if to a small child so that even my tiny brain could process them. Stefan Gössling, Jo Dardenne, Mark Smith, Susanna Elfors, Julian Ekelhof, Duncan McLaren, Roger Tyers, Sarah Leugers, Zina

Bencheikh, Tom Barber, Sam Bruce, Tom Power, Ben Lynam, John Fletcher, James Higham, Ellie Harris, Norman Baker, Jools Townsend, Cait Hewitt, Alethea Warrington and Roger Geffen: thank you, one and all.

Gratitude must be expressed, too, for the most glorious band of friends, all of whom collectively kept me sane during long months of no-travel-frustration (and short, stressful ones of squishing in back-to-back trips alongside non-stop writing): Ruth, Ellie, Corin, AJ, the Codmother, Bee, Manoogle, Rivera and Oglethorpe.

To the best family in the world – Mum and Robin, Sara and James, Susanna and Jessica and all the Coffey clan – thank you for being unfailingly supportive of me in all my endeavours. I love you, forever and always.

And finally, thank you for reading this book – including the acknowledgments, never the most compelling part. I hope you have found inspiration for your next flight-free adventure, wherever it may lead you ...

Abbreviations

AEF	Aviation Environment Federation
APD	air passenger duty
BECCS	bioenergy with carbon capture and storage
BMV	Brasil Mata Viva Standard
CAGNE	Communities Against Gatwick Noise Emissions
CCB	Climate, Community and Biodiversity Standards
CCC	Climate Change Committee
CCU	carbon capture and utilisation
CDM	Clean Development Mechanism
CO2	carbon dioxide
CO2e	carbon dioxide equivalent
CORSIA	Carbon Offsetting and Reduction Scheme for International Aviation
DAC	direct air capture
EFA	Education For All
eVTOL	electric vertical take-off and landing
GGR	greenhouse gas removal
IATA	International Air Transport Association
ICAO	International Civil Aviation Organization

ICCT	International Council on Clean Transportation
IMF	International Monetary Fund
IPCC	Intergovernmental Panel on Climate Change
NGO	non-governmental organisation
RCF	recycled carbon fuel
RFNBO	renewable fuel of non-biological origin
RPK	revenue passenger kilometre
SAF	sustainable aviation fuel
TSVCM	Taskforce on Scaling Voluntary Carbon Markets
UNESCO	United Nations Educational, Scientific and Cultural Organization
UNWTO	United Nations World Tourism Organization
VCS	Verified Carbon Standard
VOS	Voluntary Offset Standard

Introduction

Hello. My name's Helen and I'm a frequent flyer. It's been ... two and a half years since my last flight.

Boy, does it feel strange to write that.

How did I get here? I suppose I could blame my job. Being a travel journalist isn't exactly conducive to keeping both feet on the ground. But heck, it wasn't all for work – what about those minibreaks to Mallorca, the weekends in Rome, that anniversary jaunt to Edinburgh (taken by plane because the train cost three times the price)? I have to take some responsibility here.

By the end, I was flying almost once a week. Twenty-four flights in six months, with no plans to stop or even cut down. Moscow to Malaga, Ljubljana to Lisbon, Doha to Dublin – I was insatiable. My toiletry bag was permanently packed; I could quote the EU261 air passenger rights regulations in my sleep.

But then, just like that, something inside me changed.

It's May 2019 and I'm scrolling through my news feed looking for travel stories when I stumble across a word I've never seen before: *flygskam*. It's a funny-sounding word. Clunky. Inelegant. Vaguely comical. Not the sort of word you'd suspect was about to kick you arse-first down the rabbit hole and into one of the biggest adventures of your life.

Flygskam, it turns out, literally translates to 'flight shame'. Like many of the best things, the concept was invented by the Scandinavians and is the de facto name of the flight-free movement in Sweden. Yes, I quickly discover that a heap of prominent Swedes – including teen climate activist Greta Thunberg and her mother, opera singer Malena Ernman – have simply stopped flying for environmental reasons. Corresponding new vocab has sprung up around it, from *tagskryt* ('train brag', denoting when people share pictures of their train journeys on social media) to *smygflyga* ('flying in secret' – presumably done due to the aforementioned shame).

I read and read and read some more and decide, like any good journalist, to investigate further in the name of #content. *Why don't I talk to some of these nut jobs?*, I think. Maybe we have some of our own? Maybe the Swedish movement has made its way across the North Sea (by boat, or perhaps Zeppelin) to produce some homegrown, dyed-in-the-wool weirdos right here in the UK?

At no point do I suspect there is even the slightest possibility I'll end up becoming one of them.

A quick internet search yields several names, one of which is Anna Hughes. She's the founder of the Flight Free UK movement, set up to encourage Brits to commit to giving up flying for a year. What, really give up? Like, totally give up? Like, not-even-allowed-a-cheeky-last-minute-city-break-to-Prague give up? Bit intense, that.

An hour later I'm dialling her number. An hour after that, I'm putting the phone down. An hour after *that*, I'm still reeling from what feels akin to a religious conversion: my aviation epiphany, let's call it.

Spring 2019 was a time when the UK's Extinction Rebellion protests were in full swing, David Attenborough had stopped beating around the bush and pretty much admitted the world was on fire and our actions were murdering all the lovely animals, and Greta Thunberg had become an established household name, gracing the covers of magazines and touring Europe by train to speak on the coming climate catastrophe (all while being mercilessly trolled by prominent right-wingers – including the actual president of the United States – who thought it completely appropriate to hurl insults at a child). It was becoming increasingly apparent that without wholesale, radical change driven by the world's politicians, business leaders and wealthy, agenda-setting elite, we didn't have a hope in hell of achieving even the least ambitious target of the 2016 Paris Agreement: to limit global warming to *well below* 2°C more than pre-industrial levels.

Although I was on the periphery of it all, I wholeheartedly supported these campaigners – I remember feeling empowered and excited that people were taking a real stand, alongside an unformed yearning to join them somehow. And yet, despite it all, I hadn't for a second considered how flying contributed to the whole climate change picture, nor even once reflected on how my actions as an extremely frequent flyer might be having an impact. I spent considerably more time debating which was the worst London airport (Stansted, obviously) than I ever did thinking about my personal carbon footprint. It wasn't until that one conversation with Anna that I could see how it all joined up – how putting my 'need' to travel cheaply and easily before everything else might not be completely ... OK. Not now. Not the way things were going.

This was supposed to be the story of how I, a travel journalist – someone whose job it is to travel the world – managed to go flight-free for, as it turned out, more than an entire year.

(Lockdowns sucked but they sure did cure me of my initial air-travel FOMO.) But it's not just my story. It's the story of every unsung hero who has sacrificed their own pleasure, convenience, time and, inevitably, money – all because they believe the planet is worth more. I'd never have taken on the challenge if it weren't for their example; I'd never have discovered the true extent of the damage caused by air travel if it weren't for their patient re-education.

Kicking the flying habit isn't easy. It's challenging and frustrating and – yes – can be bloody expensive. Yet, for all that, it's so much more than a sacrifice: it's an opportunity. One that offers the chance to stop, to stare, to breathe in and view the world anew. Forgive me a moment of toe-curling earnestness; 'it's about the journey, not the destination' may be the biggest cliché in the book, but sometimes clichés are clichés because, well, they're true.

Hello. My name is Helen, and I *was* a frequent flyer. But not anymore. And, hopefully, never again.

1

Is Flying All That Bad?
Stacking Up the Stats

I was the grand old age of 12 when I first set foot on a plane to go on holiday. I don't remember feeling anything in particular about it – surprising as it may seem, considering my later career path. I suppose I must have had some degree of excitement but, if so, it got firmly squashed under my all-consuming tween desire to appear 'cool'.

Back then, flying was emphatically not the norm for the people I knew. This was the late 1990s, a time before the proliferation of low-cost flights, before the stratospheric rise of Ryanair, before the birth of the £10 flash-mega-bargain-basement sales that made flying more cost-effective than catching a train to Scunthorpe. EasyJet's Stelios was just an intrepid entrepreneur with a few planes and a big dream; UK airports handled a mere 100 million passengers a year,[1] less than a third of the number they dealt with before the pandemic hit.[2]

It wasn't all about price, though. It was about mindset. Growing up in a middle-class family (Dad was a civil servant, Mum a translator), I was lucky enough to never feel like money was an issue. Presents may have been rationed, clothes purchased

on a strictly need-to-wear basis and pocket money capped at £1 a
week, but there were no discernible financial worries. I'm pretty
sure we could've splurged on a once-yearly migration to somewhere hot and exotic – but I don't think it ever even occurred
to my parents. It just wasn't what you did. Destinations were
limited to coastal Devon, rural Wales or, to really up the ante,
northern France, reached by car while listening to the same three
tapes on a loop for five hours straight (Paul Simon, Neil Diamond
and *Themes and Dreams*, a compilation that included the *Inspector
Morse* theme tune). Holidays meant grey skies and grey seas and
scrambling across pebble-strewn beaches to discover rock pools
teeming with life; this, too, being mostly grey-coloured. We were
freezing but happy.

This was pretty much the experience of all of my peers at that
time. Flying somewhere was an unusual enough occurrence
that it bagged you a feature-length presentation at show and
tell; I still think back, with something akin to envy, to Stephanie
Hunt's 'My Two-Week Trip to Disney World' talk, coolly delivered from behind a pair of new Minnie Mouse shades.

Cut to a quarter of a century later and the world of holidaying
has changed beyond all recognition. Today, we Brits take more
flights abroad than any other nationality, including Americans.
Some 126.2 million passengers were British in 2018, roughly
one in twelve of all international travellers.[3] Far from it being a
noteworthy event, kids are likely to be as well travelled as you or
me; families with children under 5 take the most holidays abroad
of any demographic, averaging 1.8 a year, according to data from
the holiday association ABTA.[4]

The age of the low-cost airline, which properly got going in
the early noughties, democratised flying in a way that no one
could have anticipated. It transformed travel from the preserve
of the elite to something anyone could do, provided you didn't
mind forgoing a complimentary meal and a comfortable seat.
This seemed like a Very Good Thing – both for tourists and, in

many cases, locals. More visitors equals more money equals more jobs; a whole new supercharged industry to revive flagging communities. But, like everything in life, change comes at a cost. There's the human cost – residents displaced in Barcelona because soaring rents have forced them out; Amsterdammers feeling like strangers in their own city as badly behaved stag parties take over – and then there's the environmental cost.

In 2019, just shy of 40 million flights took off worldwide.[5] Passengers flew a total of 8.1 trillion kilometres, a number so staggeringly big as to be practically meaningless. This was an increase of 5 per cent from 2018 – and more than 300 per cent higher than in 1990.

For a while, the impact of all this exponential growth on the planet we inhabit was lost on most people, me included. The world was getting smaller, and that was fine by me – all those places you could previously only dream of going were now not only tantalis-ingly accessible, but practically on your doorstep. Five minutes on the internet could mean you'd soon be jetting off to Borneo, Barbados, Bolivia. It changed travel journalism, too: writers were no longer the gatekeepers, magnanimously (read smugly) sharing a glimpse of the exotic to help readers imagine far-flung places they'd never have a hope in hell of visiting. That age is over. Now, the aim is to inspire, to convince would-be travellers that this par-ticular corner of the globe is the Next Big Thing: 'Go now, NOW, before it's ruined by all the tourists!' we shriek into the void, with a somewhat endearing lack of irony.

Once upon a time, pointing out the negative effects of all this flying was something only offbeat outsiders did. The same people who went vegan ten years before it was 'cool', because farming livestock is responsible for 14.5 per cent of greenhouse gas emissions globally;[6] the same killjoys who were banging on about recycling when no one wanted to know; those same Debbie Downers who, when you railed against the cruelty of child labour, would politely ask where you thought your mobile phone battery came from – and your £3 Primark dress. Overly earnest do-gooders whose greatest gift was bringing down the mood at a party, you understand – not normal people.

But they saw what the rest of us were far, far too slow to catch onto.

According to a report by *The Guardian*, taking one long-haul return flight produces more carbon emissions than the average citizen in more than fifty countries will account for in a year.[7] Aviation industry emissions, which currently contribute 2 per cent of all global emissions, look set to double by 2050. (And even that's an optimistic prediction, as it assumes that future aircraft could be more efficient based on technology that doesn't actually exist yet.) The International Air Transport Association (IATA) predicts passenger numbers will double – *double* – to 8.2 billion by 2037.[8]

I find these numbers just the tiniest bit frightening. The sky already feels damn near full. Pre-pandemic, if you went and stood at Myrtle Avenue, the famous plane spotter's point near London Heathrow, you'd quickly realise just how full, as jet after jet after jet landed every ninety seconds, without pause, for eighteen hours a day. It was mesmerising in its relentlessness. Imagining double that makes my brain hurt. It makes me feel like this whole flying business is slipping out of our collective control.

But am I, along with everyone else, just getting hysterical about the latest cause célèbre? Is flying really so terrible when stacked up against the alternative ways of getting around? Let's crunch the numbers.

Plane vs. the rest

While there's a lot of talk about how bad flying is, it's not always backed up by something tangible we can get our heads around. The calculations are tricky, for a start, because not all aircraft are alike. The newer they are, the more efficient they are, as a general rule – just as not all cars are alike and not all trains are alike. We're therefore always talking in generalities when it comes to comparisons – taking the average emissions of a mode of transport, for instance.

In this book, we'll often be looking at emissions on a per person basis – it's how you calculate an individual's carbon footprint, by looking at the total amount of CO2 produced during their journey and dividing it by the total number of people who are on that particular mode of transport. This way of calculating doesn't take overall emissions into account – it's purely a way to see what's most efficient.

Obviously, there are some problems with using this method – the main one being that 'efficient' doesn't mean 'non-polluting'. Take Ryanair, for example. At the end of 2019, it released an ad campaign claiming to be the greenest airline. Technically, on the parameters it was using, this wasn't inaccurate: the airline has one of the youngest fleets and highest load factors (aviation-speak for bums on seats) in the business, making individuals' carbon footprints lower than if they flew on rival airlines. But this is the same Ryanair that, according to EU data, was one of the top-ten polluting companies in Europe in 2019 – and the other nine were all coal plants.[9] Claiming to be a 'green' company in this context seems like a teensy bit of an oxymoron.

Bearing all that in mind, here's a broad overview of the main modes of transport purely based on CO2 emissions (per passenger per km travelled):[10]

Diesel car:	*171g*
Domestic flight:	*133g*
Bus:	*104g*
Long-haul flight:	*102g*
Domestic rail:	*41g*
Coach:	*27g*
Eurostar:	*6g*

Now, if you're surprised to see a bus beating a long-haul jet, you're probably not alone. But hold your horses before you start booking long-haul flights like it's going out of fashion – the story these numbers tell us isn't as straightforward as it seems. Most importantly, this just shows CO_2 emissions. If you add in secondary effects from non-CO_2 emissions – water vapour, aerosols and nitrogen oxides, for example – which have been proven to significantly impact the climate, domestic flights contribute an extra 121g per km, while long-haul flights are responsible for 93g more, putting them both solidly ahead of motor vehicles. And it's crucial that we do include these – back in 1999 a special report by the Intergovernmental Panel on Climate Change (IPCC) estimated that the total historic impact of aviation on the climate when factoring in non-CO_2 emissions was two to four times higher than when looking at CO_2 emissions alone.[11] Jo Dardenne, aviation manager at European sustainable travel NGO Transport & Environment, tells me the impact of flying 'is much greater than carbon – a lot of warming impacts are being linked to contrails, which have twice as much impact as CO_2 emissions'.

Including the warming impacts of non-CO_2 emissions, then, our table looks more as we'd expect:

Domestic flight:	*254g*
Long-haul flight:	*195g*
Diesel car:	*171g*
Bus:	*104g*
Domestic rail:	*41g*
Coach:	*27g*
Eurostar:	*6g*

There are other factors to consider too – the 'per passenger' number is based on the plane having an average load factor, that is, most seats are filled. Sometimes this might be the case; sometimes it might not be. The car you have will also make a difference – the average hybrid, for example, will emit 113g per km, totalling around 28g per person if you have a full carload, making it technically more efficient than the train.

It's also important to think about the bigger picture. On paper, travelling on a long-haul flight might not look that much worse than driving. But, realistically, are you going to be travelling to Sydney by car? By looking at just the km per passenger number, we can be in danger of overlooking the fact that a long-haul flight goes much further, and therefore produces a load more emissions, than a mode of transport that's never going to travel that far. Likewise, although a long-haul flight is technically more efficient than a domestic one, the very fact you're flying much further means more emissions overall. So, although the per passenger per km number is useful, it's certainly worth also looking at our overall journeys, rather than just breaking them down into their component parts.

Looking at the bigger picture again, aviation accounts for about 12 per cent of transport emissions worldwide,[12] with all flights producing just shy of 1 billion (915 million) tonnes of CO_2 in 2019.[13] If it helps, you can picture 100,000 Eiffel Towers, 6.6 million blue whales, or just under three times the amount of CO_2 the entirety of the UK emits annually.[14] Meanwhile, emissions from trains make up just 1 per cent of transport emissions and, unsurprisingly, road travel accounts for a whopping three-quarters of all transport emissions, most of which come from passenger vehicles. So, cars are clearly a big problem too. But one big difference is that the technology already exists commercially that can help decarbonise the automobile industry; electric cars are on the market. The technology that could revolutionise aviation remains more pipedream than reality, while the desire for uninhibited growth shows no sign of abating in the meantime. Right now, aviation accounts for 2 per cent of all global CO_2 emissions but, if it continues on the same track, its impact is projected to rise by 200–360 per cent by 2050.[15]

There's no getting around it: although other modes of transport aren't perfect either, flying usually trumps them when you add other harmful emissions into the mix, and the industry has barely scratched the surface of decarbonisation while continuing to expand (at least until Covid-19) at an increasingly rapid rate. There's a reason scientists say the quickest way to dramatically slash your carbon footprint is to simply stop flying.

How much is too much?

Part of the problem is that, for many of us, we've never even tried to calculate our emissions from flying. We might eschew plastic straws, be gung-ho about recycling and carry our reusable coffee cup with pride, all while compartmentalising the part of our life that includes travel – because who wants to ruin the excitement of gearing up for a holiday with dreary old climate change?

I'll hold my hands up and say it: I've flown so much in my life I'm not even sure I could calculate my total emissions from flying. I'm not a list maker – I've never written down all my journeys or scratched off countries on one of those special gold-leaf maps. And while the first twenty-five years of my life might be fairly straightforward to track, the last eight are not. When I became a travel journalist, that's when s*** got real.

Taking just my last year of travel before going flight-free, then – the year I took twenty-four flights in the first six months – I used an online calculator to work it out.[16] You pop in your from/to airports, and the calculator gives you a number (frighteningly big in my case), in tonnes, of your CO_2 emissions.[17] I encourage you to go ahead and try it yourself – if only to look that number squarely in the eye and acknowledge its existence for the first time. Then feel free to go and hide under the bed.

My number? Some 9.3 tonnes in one year. To put that into perspective, the average UK citizen's annual carbon footprint

– so not just flights, but all the carbon they produce from every single thing they do – is 5.65 tonnes. I'm also more than double the world average (again, just for my air travel) of 4.35 tonnes, and almost six times greater than India, which is a saintly 1.57 tonnes. Even the biggest carbon offenders, the US, have an average annual footprint of 14.95 tonnes per person.[18] I can't be far off that when you factor in the rest of my carbon-guzzling life.

Now, that year was a particularly travel-heavy one. They won't all have been like that. But say I only took half the number of flights the preceding seven years (4.65 tonnes): that's still 41.85 tonnes in total during the time I've been a travel journalist. If it helps you to visualise it, that's about the same weight as a Boeing 737 plane.

It means that, a) I have a lot of making up to do, and b) I can never cast judgement on anybody for their decision to fly. I wouldn't have a leg to stand on. The flight shame movement has been consistently mistranslated as 'flight shaming' in the media, but it was never about shaming other people, or castigating them, or looking down on them. It was only ever about looking at yourself; it was only ever about changing your own habits.

Can I fly at all?

The big question: is flying really so bad that I can never do it again? Or is there a number I could aim for that would be OK – once a year, say, or one big long-haul trip every few years? Life is rarely black and white. Yes, a lot of us fly purely for pleasure. But what about those of us who fly to see family? In a globalised world, we move around, we migrate, we build lives halfway around the planet from our birthplaces. It's one thing to suggest not flying. It's quite another to suggest people commit to never seeing their parents/children/siblings/long-distance partners ever again.

One statistic that suggests you probably can fly, just not as much, was calculated by Possible – a climate-action charity that tries to create positive, practical ideas to encourage people to become part of the movement. They say that 70 per cent of all flights in the UK are taken by 15 per cent of people, which points the finger squarely at the frequent flyers – the people like 2019 me – and not at those who take a two-week holiday once a year. Get the former to change their lifestyles and reduce the number of flights they take, and we could be onto something. Bear in mind, though, that you don't need to jet off as much as you'd think to wind up being classed as a 'frequent flyer' in this equation: just three return flights a year thrusts you into this category.

Aside from the Flight Free UK pledge, there's another campaign called Pledge to Fly Less, founded by CAGNE (Communities Against Gatwick Noise Emissions). This acknowledges that people might not be able to go completely cold turkey, but that if everyone took fewer flights – in particular those of us who already take a lot – that would go a long way towards improving things.

Globally, it's a similar picture. Stefan Gössling, a professor at the Linnaeus University School of Business and Economics who specialises in sustainable tourism, co-published a study in November 2020 that found just 1 per cent of the population worldwide caused half of all aviation carbon emissions in 2018.[19] To be included in this group of 'super emitters', you had to have flown 35,000 miles (56,000km) in a year – the equivalent of either three long-haul return flights or one return short-haul flight per month. 'We think everyone's on the move, but in reality, just 4 per cent of the world's population fly internationally in any given year,' he tells me. 'When we talk about flying, we are really talking about an elite activity.' He's not wrong – even in the UK, less than half of the population will take an international flight each year. In Germany it's only about 35 per cent of people.

'What we are really talking about is a small group of people who might have to change their behaviour – it's not "normal" behaviour when the majority of the world's population aren't doing it,' says Professor Gössling.

When asked if there's a certain amount we could fly sustainably, he says restrictions and quotas usually aren't feasible:

> Personally, I don't believe in budgeting or restrictions – not because they're not valuable, but because many attempts to restrict, limit, or budget have never made it politically. People don't even need to be involved in a certain activity, such as flying, to still feel like their personal freedoms are being challenged if there's a limit imposed.
>
> Whether we should stop flying or fly once a year isn't the right question, in my opinion. With the right market mechanisms in place, people will decide for themselves. If we saw a big increase in the cost of flying – which is justifiable because aviation in the UK and EU currently doesn't pay VAT, doesn't pay fuel tax, doesn't have an inbuilt carbon cost, and it carried coronavirus around the globe – a huge chunk of frequent flyers would disappear. People wouldn't even notice too much – because it's not curbing their personal freedom by telling them not to fly, rather, it's a personal choice they've made.

Part of the problem is price. Over the last sixty years, the real cost of air travel has reduced by 60 per cent. And although cranking up the cost of flights might feel elitist – and like it's penalising the poorer end of the market – other studies would suggest that is not the case. In debating whether a third runway at Heathrow would really benefit the UK, Professor David Banister, Emeritus Professor of transport studies at Oxford University, outlined that the evidence pointed to the same people flying more, rather than more people flying, as the price of flying has decreased.

'Some might argue that low-cost airlines have helped rebalance this inequality, but the evidence would suggest that cheaper flights have enabled those already flying to travel more frequently and possibly to save money,' he wrote in *The Conversation*.[20] He continued:

> On grounds of inequality, environment and spend, building additional airport capacity at LHR does not add up, as it will enable the richest 10 per cent to fly even more and spend their money overseas. It will be the poorest 10 per cent that stay in the UK, and they will suffer from even higher levels of CO_2 emissions and poorer levels of air quality.

However it's done, experts agree that reduction is essential for the aviation sector over the next twenty years. Transport & Environment's Jo Dardenne says it's best to look at it in terms of short-, medium- and long-term action. 'Short term, we need to reduce demand, because the impact of flying is much greater than the carbon emissions,' she says. 'In the medium term, we have to develop sustainable fuels for as many flights as possible, and long term we're looking at breakthrough technology that could let us fly with zero emissions, such as electric planes.'

According to Professor Gössling, to meet targets stipulating that by 2050 all sectors have to be carbon neutral, emissions across the board need to be in sharp decline. 'We'd like to see a 5 per cent reduction in emissions year-on-year,' he says. But translated to an aviation industry that's been rapidly growing by 6–7 per cent year-on-year, this looks more like a 13 per cent decline each year in order to achieve those targets. Which certainly doesn't fit in with the aviation sector's plans – and which, in the wake of colossal financial losses caused by the coronavirus pandemic, will be fiercely contested by an industry trying to claw its money back.

When all's said and done, scientists are reluctant to give a number of 'appropriate' or 'sustainable' flights because, behaviour-wise, humans simply don't like being told what to do.

If reduction is key, perhaps this should be the goal for each of us as individuals. Sit down and work out how many air miles you flew per year for the last few years. Calculate it as a number and then challenge yourself to reduce that number next year. If it's choosing a holiday, consider short haul instead of long haul. If it's a conference or business meeting, consider whether you need to be there in person. If it's travelling within the same continent, consider whether there are viable alternatives by train or by boat. Work out what your non-negotiable travel looks like – seeing family, going to a friend's wedding abroad – and go from there.

Travel saints

So, we've established that air travel equals 'not so great'. Now it's time to look at which forms of transport are the least impactful. The lowest, of course, are walking and cycling. These aren't accessible for everyone – but if they are for you, one of the easiest ways to bring down your carbon footprint is to swap car journeys for using your legs wherever possible. Even the UK driving theory test now acknowledges this, and has a whole section on reducing emissions (revving your engine is a no-no, FYI).

For longer journeys, rail travel is usually the most carbon-efficient bet, but there's an argument to say even this is beaten by hitchhiking (as my colleague at *The Independent* Simon Calder is always eager to point out). Think about it: it's a journey the car would already have been making, whether you hitched a lift or not. Therefore, by travelling this way, you're not contributing any extra carbon emissions (for more on this see chapter 6). The logic might seem strange, but it does check out, I promise.

For instance, one of the saintliest ways of travelling long haul is by cargo ship. Cargo ships aren't green by any stretch – they're massive polluters. But, like hitchhiking, this way of travelling can be seen as 'carbon neutral' purely because you aren't creating any demand. The ship is making the journey anyway, taking its cargo between ports; you're simply hitching a ride.

People will often make the point: 'What use is giving up flying? You think the plane won't still go without you on it?' It's a fundamental misunderstanding about supply and demand and how the aviation industry works. Airlines exist to make money. They do this by taking people from one place to another. If I stop flying, not much changes. But if lots of people do? Everything changes. Say something happens in a tourist-friendly country in Southeast Asia – a terrorist incident, for example – and people are scared. Demand drops dramatically; planes are taking off less than half full. You think that route will just continue as normal? Hell no! The service will fly less and less frequently, and, if there's never really enough demand to justify it, it might get cancelled altogether. Airlines do this all the time. They are good at making money because they constantly adapt their routes in response to customer appetite.

The coronavirus outbreak is a perfect practical example of this. When it first broke out in Wuhan, China, in late 2019 and started spreading in early 2020, certain Chinese cities were put in lockdown. Governments worldwide started responding, including the UK government, telling citizens not to travel there. But crucially, airlines were not 'forbidden' from flying there – they were free to continue their schedules as planned. Aside from the top-down response, people did not want to go there regardless – they were understandably hugely anxious. Obviously, this had a significant impact on demand for flights and airlines took a machete to their China routes.

The result? Almost 100,000 flights were cancelled during the first month of the coronavirus outbreak, according to data from between 23 January and 18 February 2020. The grounded flights accounted for over two-thirds of China's originally scheduled services.[21] Of course, we all know what happened next – travelling was pretty much off the table, full stop, for most of the following year – but before it was officially banned, consumer behaviour had already massively changed the landscape. It neatly demonstrates the way that airline schedules are not set in stone – they are completely formed and shaped by consumers' choices, which are in turn formed by the bigger picture.

Cargo transportation companies also exist to make money. They do this by taking cargo from one place to another. The difference between flying and travelling by cargo ship is this: if people stopped booking to travel on the latter, precisely nothing would happen. It is not the primary reason the ship is making the journey; passenger behaviour has zero bearing on it. Whereas if lots of people stopped flying ... well, the airlines would be terrified, that's for sure.

Are airlines changing?

There is already some mad energy being put into making airlines look 'greener'. A lot of this is pretty standard greenwashing – the practice of falsely making products or services seem 'eco' or 'environmentally friendly' through marketing and spin, when they're merely paying lip service to the concept of sustainability. The problem is, without targeted government intervention when it comes to properly taxing aviation, there is little incentive for airlines to go through the expensive business of amending their operations in a genuinely meaningful way.

But PR stunt or not, it is important to note that until a couple of years ago, carriers wouldn't have even bothered to make the effort in the first place. Why are they doing it? Because they're scared that the Greta-effect will permeate and that people will start flying less as a result of climate guilt; they're scared that the writing is already on the wall.

Airlines don't really do anything unless there's something in it for them. If they're bellowing loudly about their green credentials, it's because they believe that's what consumers want to hear in order to buy. So, when people say individual decisions don't make a difference, they're only right up to a point; when things reach critical mass, businesses are forced to react to meet the demands of consumers. And some of the technology airlines are investing in *is* impactful, as we'll find out later on in this book.

Veganism is a great illustration of reaching a critical mass that prompted businesses to change. For a long time, vegans were an insignificant enough minority that there was no need for restaurants and supermarkets to cater for them. Then the movement expanded, helped by stunts like Veganuary, and seemingly became mainstream overnight. Demand grew, and smart companies met this demand head on: all of this coming to fruition in the UK in that paragon of loveliness, the Greggs vegan sausage roll.

Do individual actions even matter in the climate fight?

This is the big question that often comes up in terms of sustainability. What on earth is the point in changing our behaviour as individuals when big oil companies and the like – and safe to say we could probably include airlines in this – still aren't bothering to decarbonise? It's even been claimed that the idea of 'doing your bit' and the concept of an individual's carbon footprint is 'one of the most successful, deceptive PR campaigns maybe ever', promoted by the likes of BP to shift blame and focus from them to consumers – the ultimate distraction technique.[22]

We know that the real problems lie at a big-business and governmental level; we should not let corporations wriggle out of their obligations to reduce emissions and take on that guilt for them. But I think this argument also misses the essential point outlined above: that pressure for those above to change comes from below, from the grassroots, critical mass of ordinary people demanding better of their politicians and the businesses they choose to patronise. Change comes when the tide of opinion turns, and that often starts with ourselves.

After all, our own behaviour is the one thing we have control over. It doesn't mean we let the real culprits off the hook – but it means we stop expecting improvement to be a top-down affair, and put pressure on those in charge through our own expectations and demands. In the words of Michael Jackson, 'I'm starting with the [wo]man in the mirror', in the belief that individual behaviour change has a much wider ripple effect than just my own actions.

If you still don't believe me, let's turn our attention back to Sweden – the place where the flight-free movement first took off (pardon the pun). Has *flygskam* had any tangible impact on flying habits? The simple answer is yes, it has: domestic air travel dropped by 9 per cent in 2019 compared to the previous year, according to Sweden's airport operators, Swedavia.[23]

Never let anyone tell you that you don't have power as a consumer – you're voting every time you get out your wallet. Your spending decisions can, quite literally, change the world.

2

This Green and Pleasant Land
Mastering the Art
of the Staycation

Having looked my own flying carbon footprint in the eye – and discovered that aviation really was as bad as all those activists made out – I decided that my first flight-free forays should prioritise the domestic. Yes, I was going to swap the far-flung destinations of yore for my home turf, the UK, making the most of glorious local landscapes that didn't require a passport to visit.

It coincided with being released from lockdowns during the pandemic, meaning any escape from my home city of London was imbued with an intense sense of the exotic. I wasn't alone in this staycation spree – hundreds of thousands of Brits were doing the same. Prevented from heading off to their usual international haunts by draconian travel restrictions, holidaymakers were forced to rediscover the beauty that lay within their own borders. It was a trend reflected around the world, too, as citizens were encouraged to spend their hard-earned cash on domestic trips – Australia's tourism campaign tagline even being 'holiday here this year'.

Well, I may not reside in Oz, but there was no reason I couldn't take up their mantra. Wanting to make the most of my new-found freedom, I planned two trips – one north, one south – on the UK's two sleeper train services, to explore this green and pleasant land for myself.

A highland's life for me

You know that feeling, when it's getting properly dark and you're in the middle of the Scottish Highlands and you're walking down a woodland path strewn with obstacles and over the side is not-quite-a-sheer-drop-but-almost and you haven't encountered anywhere to wee in seven hours and it looks like you still have another eighty minutes to walk before you get to the next town but now it's all got to be done in the pitch black?

No? Well, I do.

We'd set off on the first section of the Loch Ness 360, a fairly new walking and cycling trail that goes all the way around the world's most famous loch, almost as soon as we'd reached Inverness on Saturday morning on the Caledonian Sleeper (the overnight train that trundles all the way from London to various Scottish destinations). We strolled through town – itself a gorgeous proposition, complete with pedestrianised streets, a brooding castle on a hill and that stone that Scotland specialises in, the type that seems to radiate light through the gloom. And all of it carved in two by the mighty River Ness, its clear-looking waters surging through the landscape at breakneck speed. Next, to our hotel for the night, to drop off the bags. And then out we went, setting off at around 9.45 a.m. for what had been described to me as 'a walk of around four hours' by a person who shall remain nameless, who'd helped me organise the trip.

My companion Oli and I are amateur-level but enthusiastic walkers, and so four hours had sounded like a fine distance. Not long enough to worry too much about provisions – we didn't even pack any water, like the optimistic fools we are – or to think about what facilities there might be en route. We had good footwear, layers, hats, phones – but not much else. Luckily, I also had tissues (not a whole lot of toilets in the Highlands, as it turns out).

Off we set, hearts lifted by the winter sun that occasionally deigned to peek coquettishly out from the churned-up cloud and illuminate the world with fresh touches of beauty. The River Ness was set all aglimmer; the distant hills looked bright and inviting. We steadily made our way out of the city, buoyed up by the immediacy of everything. The evening before we'd been in London. Now, here we were, somewhere completely different, without having lost a single day. In fact, by travelling overnight on the train, it felt like we were living on stolen time – there'd been no leaving work early or getting up at the crack of dawn to get to the airport. The whole thing was a world away from flying, where the stress of the journey taints the first eight hours of nearly any trip with mild exhaustion.

We clambered our way up through Dunain Community Woodland at a leisurely pace, stopping to sit on benches and look out over the handsome city we'd left behind. After all, we didn't need to rush. We would reach our destination, Drumnadrochit, by mid-afternoon for a late lunch; neither of us was particularly hungry, so there was no need to curb our natural pauses. Or so I thought.

After walking for a couple of hours, I checked Google Maps, just to review our progress. Drumnadrochit was five hours away, it told me. Hmm. Right. I tried not to panic. Maybe the map was wrong? (The map wasn't wrong.) Maybe we'd gone the wrong way? (We hadn't.) Maybe we'd walked so slowly we'd actually gone backwards? (Obviously not.)

I looked back at the walking instructions – and there at the top, three little words sat clear as day, as if mocking me: 'Route: 20 miles'. Ah. So, yes, about seven hours then. The woman from the Scottish tourist board team who'd told me it was four, I deduced, had typed 'Inverness to Drumnadrochit' into an online route finder, and it had shown her the most direct way to get there along the road – not the official footpath.

Now, an extra three hours might not sound like a lot, but anyone who has done much walking will know it makes *quite* a big difference. Especially when you haven't taken any snacks. Still, we were young(ish) and nimble and we'd just slept on a train, for crying out loud! What couldn't we do?

Walk seven hours before the sun went down, as it turned out.

One night prior, I was tucked up in bed, breathing in a lavender-scented pillow mist. Exhausted from a long week, I patiently waited for sleep to take me into her clutches – but she struggled to oblige. I was way too wired to go gently into that good night. Well, it could have been that, or it could have been the fact that the bed in question was rattling back and forth as we blazed along at 80mph.

It was my first time on the Caledonian Sleeper – in fact, it was my first time on any sleeper train. I defy anyone to not be overcome with childlike excitement when they step on board one. The tiny rooms with their tiny bunk beds! The nifty toilet-slash-wetroom! The little bag of assorted miniature toiletries left on the bed!

Every activity feels fresh and fun in a way that it simply does not in a hotel, from plugging in your phone to charge in the purpose-built wall-mounted holders, to filling in the breakfast card and hanging it on your door (if you forget to do this within half an hour of the train's departure you WON'T GET BREAKFAST, we were told multiple times, imbuing the task with a thrilling sense of urgency).

The Caledonian Sleeper got a much-publicised upgrade in 2019, and we were ensconced in one of its new suites, the most luxurious room type, complete with double bed. Our procurement of superior digs was less to do with the fact that I am a fancy journalist lady, and more to do with the fact that the bed in my original bunk room had been sopping wet due to some unspecified leakage issue.

Curled up in an actual double bed really did give the impression we were sleeping in a hotel room, albeit one in a noisy, moving hotel. But, as much as anything, it was the pure novelty that kept my brain from slowing down and switching off. 'I'm on a train, I'm on a train, I'm on a train!' kept hurtling around my head in time with the rattling carriage. I did get stretches of slumber here and there, but every time I came to I'd feel a sucker punch of excitement in my gut all over again as I remembered 'I'm on a train!', before sighing contentedly and rolling over.

The next morning, after a bracing shower over the toilet, enlivened by the free toiletries, we shuffled blearily along to the breakfast car to gobble down eggs royale – which were, in my travelling companion's accurate description, 'the best eggs royale I've ever eaten on a train' – and surprisingly good coffee. And then, the part I'd been waiting for: we watched the sun slowly creep over the Highlands in all their bleakly majestic glory. The far-off dull blue of Loch Moy; the green, russet, brown, sand-coloured blurs as we clattered past fields and rolling hills, all eerily quiet but for the rat-a-tat-tat of the train on the track. I considered it more than a fair trade for a mediocre night's sleep.

I haven't seen nearly enough of the British Isles. I'm always painfully aware of this when I get sent lists of new openings and events in the UK, and my eyes skitter down the list, alighting at one place in ten that I've actually been to.

Perhaps this is true of everyone, no matter their country of origin – that we're always looking for greener pastures. Why stay at home when you could bugger off somewhere different (and, crucially, hot)? But Britons are surely more susceptible to it, purely because of our island status; we've always looked to the sea, searched beyond our confines to discover the new.

Given this outward-looking quality, it's hardly surprising we embraced aviation with such gusto. For a long time, going on holiday has been synonymous with hopping on a plane. But that is starting to change, according to the various UK tourist boards – especially amid the coronavirus pandemic, which turned foreign travel into a kind of Russian roulette.

In 2019, British residents spent just under £11 billion on 46.4 million holiday trips in England – a 3 per cent increase compared to 2018. Taking Britain as a whole, spending in 2019 was £14.5 billion on 60.5 million holiday trips, up 4.4 per cent from the previous year.[1] Far from being a win for Little Englanders everywhere, this could actually be a positive step in reducing our reliance on aviation; travelling closer to home doesn't have to mean you're closed off to new ideas and experiences. Far from it.

And this is a nation that deserves to be explored. What it lacks in dramatic scenery – towering mountains, insanely hot deserts, raging rivers – it makes up for in sheer loveliness. Don't worry, I'm not going to burst into an impromptu recital of 'Jerusalem', but the more I do see of Britain, the more invested I become. For a small island with an un-extreme climate, we pack in a hell of a lot of diversity, although the whole 'green and pleasant land' bit is undoubtedly our strong suit.

When you're a travel writer, people will often ask you the 'best' place you've ever been (impossible to answer) and, next, the most beautiful. I can tackle this second question more easily, but I know the asker will never be happy with the answer. They want to hear it's somewhere far-flung, untouched and – cliché of clichés – 'off the beaten track'.

'I once saw this pod of dolphins dancing in a hidden waterfall in Tibet, and it was the most ... powerful moment of my life,' I can feel them willing me to say in a quiet, serious voice while gazing broodingly off into the distance.

The real answer is the Lake District. It's such an obvious one that it feels embarrassing to even admit to. I mean, Wordsworth even wrote *that* bloody poem about it. There were no international flights involved, no jetlag, no 'exotic' locals (well, not in a good way). But when I spent a few days in Keswick, next to Derwentwater – in my opinion the prettiest of the lakes – I fell so deeply and utterly in love with the landscape that I kept trying to hug it. I would stroke the bark of trees and the undersides of leaves as I went, like an infatuated lover, stopping every thirty seconds just to stare. It was like when you fancy someone and you just can't stop looking at them – my eyes tried to pull away but kept getting drawn back to the water, a pair of iron filings to a magnet.

I've had similar experiences elsewhere in the UK and Ireland too: the lush green banks of the River Wye; the remote wildness and pristine beaches of the Aran Islands; even the low-key charm of the bluebell woods at Ashridge in my home county of Hertfordshire.

But I'd never been to the Highlands before. In fact, to my deep shame, I'd only been to Scotland twice, once on a swift city break to Edinburgh, the second time to Paisley to watch a bagpiping competition (don't ask). Given my total lack of exposure, I've always carried a special place in my heart for Scotland based on nothing more than an instinct. This time, I wanted to go as high as I could get in a single weekend. All aboard the Caledonian Sleeper: last stop, Inverness.

The interesting thing about the Highlands is that there really is nothing there. People say it's 'wild' and 'remote', but it's hard to visualise what they really mean by that until you experience it for yourself, especially if you hail from a city. Well, let me tell you – they ain't lying.

By 'wild', they mean you'll find yourself picking pine needles out of your pants because you squatted for an al fresco wee and the rotten tree stump you were using for stability snapped off and sent you rolling around in the undergrowth on your bare arse. By 'remote', they mean you won't see another living soul for six straight hours and will seriously wonder if the apocalypse has already happened and *28 Days Later*-style zombies will start lumbering out from the trees.

Yet that is part of its attractiveness: the emptiness; the stillness that blankets the landscape, save for the screeching wind; the subtle differences in the million shades of brown, ranging from mocha and café au lait through to burnt orange and umber tinged with dusky purple. The stark peatlands and moors give way to softly undulating hills rendered dark green by their coverings of pine trees. It's not pretty, exactly – rather, it's striking, hauntingly so. Bewitching in its lonely grandeur.

The wind pummelled us as we went, but the sun occasionally shone too, and the expectation of adventure hung heavy on the horizon. There's an intangible magic about walking – the steady rhythm of it, the fact you can't distract yourself with Netflix or Twitter – that means you feel the rare pleasure of being wholly present. It opens up your mind to the now, and allows you to talk to someone – really, properly talk to them – without your attention being snagged by something digital every thirty seconds.

Over the course of the day, our conversation roamed wildly from issues of life and death to first kisses and dreams for the future. At one point, I described the entire storyline of an unfinished teen-fantasy novel I've been working on for the last decade in painstaking detail (and identifying at least three gaping plot holes in the process). But the topic we came back to most frequently was how much we'd like a mug of something hot – a drink to wrap our hands around as a buffer against the biting cold. And maybe some chocolate. Or a sandwich. Or crisps. Or just a lump of sugar. Anything at all, really. And then, the most amazing thing happened.

I don't think you can fully appreciate the miraculous nature of what occurred next unless you've been walking for six hours without coming across so much as a Londis. For 24km all we'd seen was the very occasional house or sheep wandering the barren landscape. Then, all of a sudden, a flurry of hand-painted fluorescent signs appeared in the woodland.

'Hot chocolate, this way!' they read. 'Cheese toasties!' 'Homemade cake!'

I thought I must be hallucinating – this, surely, was a mirage, the Highlands equivalent of seeing an oasis in the desert. That, or we were about to be abducted by the White Witch from *The Lion, the Witch and the Wardrobe*. Perhaps I wouldn't have sold out my entire family for a Turkish delight, but I almost certainly could have been persuaded in exchange for a brownie and a nice sit down.

We kept following the signs, in a state of near hysteria by the time the arrows pointed us through a wooden archway into a clearing set up with picnic tables and benches adorned with charmingly mismatched teapots. Two other tables were occupied – one by a man with his bike, the other by a mother and her toddler.

A man who had the look of the Highlands about him – an unkempt, russet-red beard and wide, pale eyes – made his way over slowly.

'I'm sorry to keep you waiting – I'm run off my feet today!'

I looked, puzzled, at the two other tables of customers, before it dawned on me. *Ah, we're on Highlands time now.* This was the busy period.

'Do you have any menus?' I asked. A shake of the head.

'Just tell me what you'd like.' A pony? Gold-flaked profiteroles? A lift to bloody Drumnadrochit?

'Hot chocolate?'

'Coming right up. Would you like a piece of my wife's homemade cake, too?'

We answered in the affirmative before he'd even finished speaking.

Off he ambled, returning some time later with two steaming mugs and a generous wedge of sponge cake delicately flavoured with lemon. It was all I could do to refrain from ripping the plate out of his hands and sinking into it, face first.

Presented with our bill, I was unsurprised to find it a little steep – £4 for an instant hot chocolate made in his kitchen, £5 for the cake – but I couldn't blame him. Talk about a monopoly: he could have charged five times that and still had customers. It turned out he was an enterprising farmer who had taken advantage of the walking trail running right past his land by offering a few treats and drinks to hikers and cyclists, which I can only applaud him for. Heck, he was offering a public service.

'Leave the money on the table,' he said, inadvertently sounding like a hooker in a movie. 'I know in London you just wave a bit of plastic and they move the numbers around in Zürich. But you're in the Highlands now.'

Move the numbers around in Zürich?

Still, I rather enjoyed the idea of being a fancy Londoner, with my fancy London ways, and a private banker on call in Switzerland to tinker with my investments. We left the money on the table. I'd have to speak to Klaus about it later; get him to transfer some funds from the Cayman Islands account. But it was worth it.

Onwards and downwards. By the time we actually saw the fabled Loch Ness the sun had almost ducked behind the horizon. We only caught glimpses of her through the trees, the blue-grey vastness just hinted at. And then she was gone, her inky depths hidden by the coming night.

Whenever I've gone walking in the dark before, I've been properly prepared, with my trusty head torch on hand (well, head) to guide me. All I can say is, thank goodness for smartphones. They all come with built-in torches these days – you can rail against big tech all you like, my friend, but you can't tell me that's not useful.

We soldiered on in the pitch black, trying to stay upbeat when faced with the fact that Oli's mobile was almost out of battery and we still had ninety minutes to go. The woodland path we were on was uneven and treacherous; I kept thinking about what I would do if I slipped and fell down the steep verge over the side of the path as a 'fun' way to pass the time.

The benefit of playing this mental game was that it helped distract me from the overwhelming terror of being in the middle of the woods at night. It was a kind of primeval fear – I couldn't even say what I was scared of, exactly. Perhaps it's inbuilt from our ancient ancestors being ambushed in the woods by predators and rival tribes. Or maybe it's the rather more modern fear imbued by the *Blair Witch Project*. All I know is, trees make weird creaking noises in the dark and it makes me want to curl up in a ball and wait for death.

But, just like watching a horror film, there was a tang of exhilaration beneath the paralysing fear. I could feel my heart pumping in my chest, strong and urgent, my senses heightened so that every rustle of leaf, crack of twig and expletive of Oli as he tripped over a tree root seemed ten times too loud. The second we got clear of the trees, the words 'that was *spooky*!' tumbled out of my mouth, unbidden. It's not a word I use often, and thank goodness.

Thoughts turned to what we would drink when we reached Drumnadrochit, so close it was palpable now: definitely a whisky or two, something peaty with the taste of liquid smoke, to warm us up from the inside out. I had visions of a cheery, cosy pub, aglow with lamps and filled with beaming locals who would instantly befriend us. Maybe there'd be a fire! And music! It was Saturday night, after all.

We finally crossed the bridge into Drumnadrochit, the promised land, the hallowed place we had made an eight-hour pilgrimage to reach. We walked down the dark, silent street to the Fiddlers Highland, a pub with food that had come recommended. Its windows were black; its door locked. A sad little sign informed us that it was closed for the winter: 'come back in March!' Oh.

We gloomily trudged our way back up the road to the only place in town that was open: the Loch Ness Hotel, which had a café-bar out front. We were the only customers.

Still, this was Scotland, and so even a mediocre café with red plastic seating boasted a whisky selection better than you'd find in most London gentlemen's clubs. The hospitable barman, clearly about as rushed off his feet as our bearded friend had been earlier, let us taste as many as we liked before committing, and we sat down in a daze of tiredness and ecstasy that our labours were complete. We massaged our feet back to life; cheeks grew rosy from the sweet warmth of alcohol. I looked back on our day and felt a flicker of, yes, it could only be described as *pride*. There's a masochistic pleasure in doing something slightly difficult and uncomfortable, if only for the luxury of stopping and rewarding yourself afterwards.

Clearly, we weren't going to find much else in Drumnadrochit; sustenance would have to be sought in Inverness. We boarded one of the excellent but diabolically infrequent buses back, and found ourselves returned to civilisation in a mere half-hour. Yes, after walking for eight hours, the journey by motor vehicle took thirty minutes. It was a touch disheartening.

Thankfully, things could only get better. That cosy pub I'd been fantasising about, all fire-warmed and filled with beaming locals? We found it. And it was every bit as good as I'd imagined.

Scottish nationalists are very different from English nationalists. Wander into a pub of the latter by mistake, and you might try to make yourself seem smaller, avoiding looking anybody directly in the eye lest they interpret it as a challenge and hit you with a blunt instrument. Wander into a pub of the former by mistake, and they'll most likely buy you a drink and give you a blue and white flag to wave while you all sing along to the Proclaimers.

That's what happened to us, at any rate. We were firmly installed in a warm nook of MacGregor's bar, sipping on Thistly Cross cider and cheerfully heaping steaming forkfuls of vegetarian tatties and neeps pie into our faces while a guitarist and singer worked their way through covers of Scottish bands. The owner had told us that there had been a Scottish independence rally in the area during the day, so things might get a bit 'lively'. What this translated to was a lot of full-throated singing, cheery, non-discriminatory flag-waving and some impromptu chants of 'f*** Boris' that we happily joined in with.

We ate, drank and screeched that we certainly would walk 500 miles and then, quite possibly, walk 500 more (accompanied by flashbacks of our day's never-ending hike). But soon even the creaking trees became a distant memory as two new musicians took to the floor, one of them being the bar owner, Bruce MacGregor. He had mentioned that he 'played a bit'. It turned out he was actually one of the most gifted Highland fiddlers in the world, storming through traditional Scottish tunes as if the violin were an extension of himself – an extra body part he just happened to be able to pick up and put down at will.

Accompanied by a skilled guitarist with a deep, resonant singing voice, he segued effortlessly between languorous ballads and fast-paced jigs. On the former, the audience joined in, misty-eyed, singing along to songs they'd clearly known since childhood; the latter prompted them to jump to their feet and dance in whatever space they could find. It made me feel a little wistful. These were old Scottish folk songs, passed down for generations – what was the English equivalent? Chumbawamba's 'I Get Knocked Down'? 'Three Lions on a Shirt'?

I came to from my reverie to discover Bruce was telling the entire place that there were 'two special guests up from London' and that they were to make us feel welcome. The pub fell deathly silent for a moment; all heads swivelled towards us. A beat passed. And then a cheer went up.

People came over to introduce themselves and ask about our visit; a woman insisted we get up and dance with her as the musicians started up again.

All of this is not to say that Scottish nationalists are perfect or that there aren't any issues with the movement – just that no one wearing an England flag as a cape has ever invited me to jig or asked with genuine interest how my day was. And that's a crying shame.

After the excitement of Saturday, Sunday was a rather pedestrian affair (albeit without the walking). A day of mooching, if you will, spent wandering Inverness town in pleasant aimlessness amid the unrelenting drizzle. At some point we decided to start drinking because, hey, Scotland! And a lazy, meandering pub crawl ensued, which took us from more down-at-heel establishments (at one, a round of three drinks cost less than £3), to the more sophisticated Malt Room, where battered leather sofas and dim lighting were the perfect backdrop to perusing its hundred-strong whisky menu.

Slightly swaying, we fought our way back through the biting cold for a final dinner at our hotel. Scallops with black pudding; blackened miso cod: we ate ourselves into a stupor, all the better to fall asleep on board a moving vehicle.

On the return journey, we were back in our bunk beds, adorably tucked and cocooned. It was like being back in the womb – if the womb had come with a constant rattling soundtrack loud enough to wake the dead. I even resorted to reading the painfully obvious tips from a sleep expert helpfully provided in the Caledonian Sleeper literature ('don't have a coffee just before bed' and 'limit your screen time' – most enlightening). Once again, my body had other plans. But it didn't matter. Every time I woke up, I remembered 'I'm on a train!' Every time, I felt overcome with childlike excitement all over again.

Sleep is overrated. Sleeper trains are not.

Carbon comparison
230kg of CO2e for a return flight London Gatwick–Inverness[2]

74.6kg of CO2e for a return train London Euston–Inverness[3]

Carbon emissions saved: 155.4kg of CO2e

No man is an island

Train tickets in the UK can be some of the cheapest you've ever seen – but only if you know exactly when and where you want to travel in advance, preferably so far in advance you haven't even been born yet. For those of us who are less prescient, the price can leave you peeling your jaw off the floor ten minutes after purchase.

Such was the case when I bought tickets to try the second of Britain's two sleeper trains: the fetchingly titled 'Night Riviera' service from Paddington to Penzance, operated by Great Western Railway. I was desperate to get away after months of going nowhere thanks to Covid-19 restrictions. And where better for feeling like you're 'away' in the UK than the Isles of Scilly, a little archipelago nearly 50km off the Cornish coast with, thanks to the Gulf Stream, a temperate microclimate, white-sand beaches, palm tree-lined paths and seas a shade of aquamarine more closely associated with a Caribbean-inspired Instagram filter?

A well-meaning woman from GWR I'd been emailing about the upcoming trip had made me a reservation, so I pootled along to the station to pay for and pick up the tickets. I wish I'd asked her how much they would cost beforehand, if only to spare the National Rail customer service rep the embarrassment of having to watch a grown woman holding back tears.

'How ... how much?' I croaked in disbelief, my throat doing that tightening thing that makes your voice go all wibbly.

The man looked uncomfortable and tapped the screen again. The journey came to nearly £200.

Now, Penzance is a long old way, I'm not disputing that. What I *am* disputing is that the outbound journey, booked a month in advance, cost £146. For a seat. Not a fancy deluxe berth, just, y'know, a chair. The strange, hard-to-understand rules of British rail tickets mean there are a certain number of cheap fares and, once they're gone, you're at the mercy of the ticket-pricing gods. Unlike with flights, where you can shop around for the best deal, the nature of trains means you generally don't have this option. Don't like the price? Don't travel. There is usually no competitor to give your business to instead, swanning out of the metaphorical shop like Julia Roberts in *Pretty Woman* while shouting, 'You work on commission, right? BIG mistake. Big. Huge!'

It is hard not to compare train prices with air fares when you're new to the flight-free life. I chuntered to myself all the way home from the station: 'I could've gone to Mallorca for that price. To Morocco. To New York (well, in the heyday of Norwegian's super-cheap fares). I'm not even leaving the country!'

But part of the shift in mindset needed to stop flying long term is to nix the comparisons. No good can come from it. Flying is almost always cheaper – it's why so many of us do it – and it will continue to be so until governments start taxing aircraft fuel and make a concerted effort to truly encourage terrestrial travel. This actually happened in Luxembourg – the government made all public transport (trains, buses and trams) free in 2020 to 'alleviate heavy congestion and bring environmental benefits'.[4] Unbelievable scenes. But until change is more widespread, it's best to steer clear of flight comparison sites and just look at rail prices as their own stand-alone (and, at times, inexplicably expensive) thing.

The rest of the process did not go smoothly either. There was a mix-up with the ferry, meaning I would have to stay an extra day. There was talk of staying a night in Penzance. I was forced to take another trip to St Pancras station and change all my train tickets on one muggy, sweaty evening, as the queue behind me grew and I felt twenty pairs of eyes on me, all belonging to people who wished me dead.

I say all this not to put you off, which may indeed be the end result, but to illustrate a potential difference between travelling by land and sea and travelling by air. Although the former can be much more difficult, by the time I set off, I cannot stress enough how invested I am in this trip. I am more than just excited – I feel the desperate need to enjoy every second of the experience, having already put so much time, money and energy into the whole affair. I'm the guy at the roulette table who's already lost his car, remortgaged his house and used up his child's university tuition fee fund, and now has no choice but to push all his chips into the middle of the table and declare he's 'all in!' on black fifteen. I'm in too deep; *not* having a good time simply isn't an option at this stage.

It's in stark contrast to flying for work, when I'd book months in advance and then totally forget I was even going away until the day beforehand. There was no jeopardy; I never felt I had much to lose if the trip was a little lacklustre. And where's the fun in that?

I depart on a Thursday night, arriving at Paddington station at the thrillingly late hour of 11.30 p.m. – the train sets off at quarter to midnight. The Night Riviera (which I keep prefacing with 'Murder on the …' in my head, an excellent title for a never-written Agatha Christie novel) is a proper sleeper train, with sleek little berths, complete with individual beds all trussed up with duvets and pillows, sinks that double as nightstands, charging points and a range of lighting options.

They do look nice and cosy as I trundle past all the carriages, with train staff popping their heads out like benevolent sprites offering to help me find my cabin at regular intervals. I shake my head grimly. There is no cabin ahead of me tonight. Only seat.

After all the hoo-ha changing the tickets, I decided, out of respect for my dwindling bank balance, to forgo comfort and embrace a life of spartan endurance on the outbound leg. I'd surmised that, on board a sleeper service, they wouldn't just be any old seats – they must surely be special ones, extra comfort-able and reclinable, maybe with a footrest, possibly with a natty reading lamp.

On all points I was sorely mistaken. It's just … a seat. Hard, unyielding, upright. The one gratifying feature is that the entire carriage contains just a handful of passengers when I travel, meaning there's an entire row to lie across, provided you don't mind the occasional 'excuse me' as people come up and down the aisle.

I don't usually think of myself as a high-maintenance travel-ler, but after I've taken out my neck pillow, executive moulded blackout eyemask and wireless headphones, I concede that, actually, I might just be. I decide I can make my peace with it. You have to embrace life's luxuries once you're past the age of 30 and accept the fact that there are no prizes for 'who spent the most uncomfortable night'.

One fun thing I quickly learn is that they leave the lights on in the carriages the whole night through, like it's some kind of Vegas casino. It is a fitting punishment, I suppose, for being too stingy to shell out for a cabin.

And yet, for all this, for all my grumbles, for all my regret that I hadn't stumped up the readies for a bed, I feel the stirrings of ... could it be ... exhilaration? Call me a masochist, but after years of working as a travel writer, when the concept of 'slumming it' was so alien as to be from an entirely different galaxy, there is something inherently adventurous in setting up camp in my little corner of the carriage. And, you know what? I only go and sleep. I wake to find the sun slowly rising over the Cornish countryside, pastorally pleasing in the half-light, and treat myself to a blueberry muffin and iced coffee.

We pull into Penzance and I'm off along the harbourfront, ready to carpe this diem like nobody's business.

The Vomit. That's what locals call the *Scillonian III*, the ferry that makes the three-hour journey between the mainland and the islands. It's an ... *accurate* nickname. I do not partake in the festivities, but I can tell that several other people do based on the harassed-looking staff members running around with mops and buckets, and the sharp tang of antiseptic in the air.

It's all part of the boat's design; it has to have a shallow hull in order to avoid running aground when it docks at the islands, and the result is a vessel that is more 'go with the flow' than any boat has a right to be. The 'flow', on a stormy day, being a bucking broncho ride tossed unceremoniously from wave to wave. I pride myself on my strong stomach and, at first, I rather enjoy the rolling sensation, the rise and fall as we dance across the peaks and troughs. In fact, it has a soporific effect, and I find myself merrily drowsing for the first few hours. Then, forty-five minutes before we're due to dock, the rollicking churn becomes rather more serious. I engage in some deep breathing that makes it sound like I'm in the early stages of childbirth; I try to distract myself by watching episodes of *The Durrells* on my phone and sternly tell myself that I have never been travel-sick in my life and *I am not about to start today, pal*. Somehow it works, and I manage to step onto dry land with my breakfast still in my stomach, a feat so Herculean I am somewhat surprised to find the local community aren't waiting to applaud me as I arrive.

Again, this tale may make you think, 'Why on God's green earth would I do that rather than flying?' And again, I say that, strangely, this mode of transport comes with unexpected benefits. It bakes into the traveller such a deep relief to be standing on solid ground that Scilly seems even more of an absurdly idyllic paradise than it already is. It inspires the feeling that you really have travelled somewhere – that you are far from home, about to intrepidly explore somewhere fresh and unknown. And, most importantly, it instils a very real sense that you have somehow earned your right to be there.

The place is sublime. My mum tells me before my trip that she and my dad had visited, just once, as newlyweds, and had planned to return. 'But it's not easy,' she warned. 'People go back every year, and they book their accommodation twelve months in advance. You're basically waiting to fill dead men's shoes.'

It's a morbid thought, but it only takes me an afternoon to see what all the fuss is about. Even in the rain, the pale sand seems to glow as if illuminated by an internal light source; flowers the colour of flaming sunsets and flamingos pop even brighter against overcast skies. I scramble around St Mary's, the main island and my base for the trip, marvelling at the way the weather changes on a dime, from incessant drizzle to eye-watering sunshine and back again, and at the tropical-looking vegetation on succulent- and palm tree-lined paths that make me feel I've stepped into a *Jurassic Park* sequel. *Yes*, I think to myself sombrely. *I could wait for someone to die to come back here.*

And then there's the sea. When the sun peers out, bam! – the water becomes the piercing turquoise of a chlorinated pool. Shut your ears to the south-west accents and you really could be in the Bahamas. Until you dip a toe in, at which point the fantasy promptly unravels.

'It's colder than it looks,' says Bryony Lishman of Adventure Scilly, who's kindly agreed to accompany me on a brief swimming tour from Porthcressa Beach. She is sensibly trussed up in full wetsuit, as is her husband Nick, while I stand shivering in a swimming costume. 'A lot colder. It's the gulf stream – it means our waters are chillier than Cornwall's.' It shouldn't make sense, but it's true: as we make our stately procession into the big blue, the icy zip and zing of the water dances around my ankles. I've done enough outdoor swimming that I take a perverse pleasure in the pain of this experience: the gasp as the cold first hits you; the shock that somehow jolts the landscape into laser-sharp focus.

The hard part is always ducking your head under, but the rewards are instant – I find myself squealing with delight at the uncanny clarity, feeling like I'm exploring an underwater gallery as we paddle. 'Look at that!' one of the three of us will cry every few minutes upon spotting a fish, an anemone or a weird, translucent worm, and the others will join them, taking in wide lungfuls of air to prolong our stay beneath the waves. I'm as happy as a seal pup, ducking, diving and rolling as my limbs waft free as seaweed and forget they were ever numb to begin with.

Part of the joy of Scilly is island hopping, and I follow my porpoise instincts to two of the other options, St Martin's and Tresco. Speeding across the Celtic Sea in one of the transfer boats is like the ocean equivalent of an Uber – just slightly damper from the spray. Each island has its own distinct personality, everyone tells you, and they're right. St Martin's has a quiet, rugged elegance. She's shy yet charming, reserved yet blessed with an unfussy, untamed beauty. The main street naturally winds its way from Lower Town to Middle Town to Higher Town (displaying a very literal approach to place naming), all within the space of twenty minutes on foot. But for such a small strip there are all the essentials – the Seven Stones pub with an expansive terrace offering unblemished sea views, the Island Bakery serving up doorstep baps stuffed with local crab – and plenty of non-essentials too, from a workshop making bespoke Scilly-inspired jewellery to a tiny art cooperative selling homeware created by craftspeople on the islands.

With each new enterprise I make a nuisance of myself by asking the owners the tiresomely inevitable question: 'How did you end up here?' It's something I find endlessly fascinating about island living, as if the inhabitants had all accidentally washed up on shore, like flotsam and jetsam after a shipwreck. The population here are modern-day pioneers – most of them upped sticks and moved to what feels like the edge of the world, the last populated place to the west of Britain until you hit America, in a community so tight-knit it could end up feeling as much like a noose as a safety net.

What amazes me most is how many residents' origin stories are totally and unashamedly mad. The owners of the pub, Emily and Dom Crees, were locked into the London commuter rat race until about seven years ago. They loved coming to Scilly on holiday, saw the local boozer on St Martin's was up for lease and just ... went for it.

'Were you in the pub business before?' I ask.

'Nope,' says Emily. 'Well, we were experts at drinking in them. That's got to count for something.'

Knowing no one on Scilly and nothing about the industry, they abandoned their lives on the mainland, threw themselves into life as part of a 150-strong community, and taught themselves the business along the way. They now have a toddler, who bimbles around the terrace merrily chuntering to herself. By all accounts, they don't seem to regret their decision to execute a life swap of epic proportions.

The other place to get a drink on the island boasts a similarly bonkers tale. Having dug my toes in vanilla-coloured sand and submerged myself once more in the freezing aquamarine sea,

I warm up with a tour of the island's very own vineyard. I learn about grape varieties and terroir as I amble up and down vine-strewn hills, before new owners James and Holly Falconbridge treat me to a tasting of their red, white and rosé wines while their black cat curls and uncurls contentedly in a patch of sunlight.

'We came here on holiday last summer and loved it,' says Holly. 'The owners of the vineyard were planning on retiring, and asked if we knew anyone who'd be interested in buying a winery. And we thought … why not us?'

Again, they had no connections to the islands. Again, they had no background in wine. When I meet them, they've been on St Martin's for less than a year, having moved over just before Covid-19 swept the globe, plunging them into a winter of self-isolation while living out of a teepee onsite. Yet they're two of the most upbeat people imaginable. 'It was a strange start, but it's going really well now,' enthuses Holly. 'We've pretty much sold out of the rosé!'

Like I say, the place attracts pioneers. As I whip back across the waves on the return boat to St Mary's, the late-afternoon sun setting the sea ablaze with twinkling lights, I wonder whether I could ever be that brave – or that crazy.

'It's nice. It's very … manicured.' This is the most common response when I tell locals I'm visiting Tresco, the one Scilly Isle that's privately owned. I instinctively feel the sting beneath the choice of word. The unsaid implication is that it's not *truly* wild, like its peers. It's not rugged. It's not *authentic*.

At least, that's how I bitchily interpret it. The islanders are far, far too polite to say such things themselves. 'Manicured', as it turns out, is incredibly apt. There's a full team of staff here to manage the land, to prune, to pare back, to maintain. It has the same ecological make-up as the other islands – peroxide blonde beaches, sea-blasted heathlands peppered with plum-hued blooms – but the feel here is like stepping into another world. Tresco is essentially car-free, and so the smooth paths encircling the island are populated only by bikes, pedestrians and electric buggies, used by employees to get around or transport well-heeled guests hither and thither. I opt to cycle, trying and largely failing to use the prettily illustrated map to navigate by, and eventually just settling for following my nose.

The place is as quiet as the other islands – visitors have a way of magically melting into the scenery after they get off the boat, and I sit on one expansive beach, so wide I can't fully see where it ends, without encountering another soul for over an hour – and yet there are perhaps more spots where guests congregate, creating a holiday-resort vibe. In fact, the island is largely given over to luxe holiday cottages and accommodation, and I start to notice certain commonalities between the guests: hale and hearty families, ruddy-cheeked and flushed with good health as they bike along in uniform lines, dressed in identikit 'Isles of Scilly'-branded rugby shirts that look vaguely nautical. As the day goes on, the more the impression galvanises that Tresco, more than anything, resembles a very, *very* fancy Center Parcs.

It doesn't come as much of a surprise to learn that this is the island most frequented by celebrities – Amanda Holden is a regular, often spotted pausing to take frequent selfies while on her daily constitutionals, while Kate, Wills and their royal offspring all came for a break just before my visit. Judi Dench, too, is allegedly a fan. I can certainly see the appeal; it is impossible to imagine any celebrity, no matter how famous, getting mobbed here.

The island also holds one truly magical attraction you can't find elsewhere: the Abbey Garden. Presided over by curator Mike Nelhams, who strolls about the grounds like a proud peacock, the site takes visitors all over the world, gathering together 20,000 species of plant from eighty different countries, including Brazil, New Zealand, Myanmar and South Africa. The effect is a bombastic yet well-ordered mix of flora. 'We've introduced red squirrels, too,' Mike tells me. 'There are no grey squirrels on the islands, so we thought, why not?' Twenty were delivered by helicopter to much fanfare in 2014; there's now an estimated population of more than a hundred.

We climb to the top of the gardens for a view of lofty palms backed by the sea in the distance, and he tells the story of how the garden came to be. Augustus Smith, a man who has been described as 'the saviour of Scilly', turned up on the islands in 1834, bought the lease from the Duchy of Cornwall and set about creating all sorts of infrastructure that would revolutionise the place. His reforms weren't always popular – a good deed never goes unpunished – but he was the first in the UK to introduce mandatory schooling for children up to the age of 13, alongside setting up a magistrates' court and repairing and building new roads and quays. He set himself up in Tresco Abbey and somehow managed to find time to establish the garden, ordering plants from Mediterranean climates all over the world. Another example of a pioneer forging a new path. There must be something in the water.

Back on St Mary's that evening, I follow up a few G&Ts by chomping down on perfectly salted chips on a bench by the beach at sunset. The sky is aglow with marmalade streaks and my eyes swim with unbidden tears that splinter the light into 1,000 kaleidoscopic colours. The overwhelming beauty meets my booze-addled soul and I come loose at the seams a little. I muse that, although you have to be a little crazy to move to the edge of the world, perhaps you have to be even crazier to live the life that most of us are prisoner to – concrete-laden, hemmed in, grey and jaded. Surely we're really the mad ones? I wonder if I'm onto something.

Or if, far more likely, I'm just pissed.

The days pass fast in paradise. I go from touring a high-welfare duck farm with a family so warm and hospitable that I consider begging them to let me set up camp in their herb garden and live off the land, to horse riding on the beach, the swoosh of tails and grind of hooves on shingle the only sounds; from learning about the islands' bronze- and iron-age heritage while standing in the remains of a 2,000-and-something-year-old village now covered in grass, to chowing down on exquisite smoked seafood pâté, seared scallops, and so much fresh Scillonian crab that I feel I might start growing pincers.

There is a feral and unbridled majesty to Scilly and, although I've not left the UK, I certainly feel like I'm in another country, if only because each new person I meet is bursting with a friendliness that is the most foreign thing of all. That's the thing about small communities. There isn't the option of anonymity; you cannot go unnoticed. And so they breed openness and tolerance, excitement for new faces and affection for old ones. The people here truly rely on each other, even without the extra pressures of a pandemic – relationships are forged in fire and must be trusted upon to hold fast when things get tough. If no man is an island, then who could understand that better than those who inhabit them?

The journey back catches me off guard, like I've slipped into a parallel universe where everything is just a degree off kilter. The Vomit is there in all her flat-bottomed glory, waiting to be boarded – but she lilts gently on a sea that's calm as a millpond. I take a seat on deck this time, and marvel at the cornflower blue of a sky that's mirrored by the water, the sun warm on the back of my neck. The boat barely moves, bar a slow, drawling kind of rocking, like a woman swaying her hips in time to her favourite song. I oscillate between trying to read my book and scouting for pods of dolphins, which often jump alongside the boat during clement weather. Unlike the endless outbound leg, now the time seems to elapse at double the frame rate. It's such a pleasurable passage that I feel a pang of disappointment when the mainland drifts into view.

Still, there's more journey to come and, after a hefty meal and large goblet of red wine in Penzance, I'm ready for the final stage. I've finally been kind to myself and booked a bed on the sleeper; the type that's soft and flat, with a pillow and duvet, and comes in a room with a little sink and a place to put your things. I cannot tell you how luxurious it feels after my previous stint in cattle class – only that I fall asleep smiling and I wake up still smiling in London, where the train has been pulled in for ninety minutes. The Night Riviera is just so darn accommodating that they let you stay on and kip, only asking that you vacate your berth by 6.45 a.m. I float across London on a cloud of fine memories; at 8.30 a.m. the same morning I'm back at my desk, ready to work, the islands already feeling like a distant, technicolour dream.

Every time I close my eyes, I see dizzying flashes of turquoise sea and porcelain sand projected across my lids. Every time I close my eyes, all those pioneers seem less and less mad.

Carbon comparison
180kg of CO2e for a return flight London Gatwick–Newquay;
60kg of CO2e for a return flight Newquay–Scilly
= 240kg of CO2e[5]

39.9kg of CO2e for a return train London Paddington–Penzance;[6]
22.6kg of CO2e for a return ferry Penzance–St Mary's[7]
= 62.5kg of CO2e

Carbon emissions saved: 177.5kg of CO2e

Why Would Anyone Do This to Themselves?
Tips and Tricks from the Flight-Free Experts

Now that I'd got a taste of my first sleeper trains in the UK, I felt emboldened to flex my travel skills further afield, transporting them across the Channel and onto the Continent. But, still a long way off being able to call myself an experienced terrestrial traveller, I wanted to check in with the experts first – those flight-free grand masters whose wisdom would become the pillars of my new slow-travel 'lifestyle'. How had these people been not sleeping on night trains for decades without having a nervous breakdown? And had they ever perfected the art of vomiting elegantly on a turbulent sea crossing? There was only one way to find out.

I meet Mark Smith at London St Pancras – ranked the world's best station in 2020– which is as fitting a place as any to quiz the UK's most prominent rail expert.[1] I feel a little giddy, as if I'm meeting an A-list celebrity. You may never have heard of

Mark; and, to be fair, until my flight-free journey began, I had only come across him in passing. But now ... now he is my guru, my guide, the Yoda to my Skywalker. The man who can tell you how to get from Tirana to Tashkent by train without breaking a sweat.

When I first asked for tips on giving up flying on social media, one name came up again and again.

'The Man in Seat 61,' people would say in hushed, reverential tones. (I mean, I couldn't hear them as they were replying on Twitter, obviously. But let's go ahead and assume they were hushed and reverential.)

'He will be everything you need. He will be your guiding light. Your moon and stars. Your gateway to another world.' (They may not have been quite this poetic.)

I started to hear his name so much I wondered if he was paying some of these people. And then I went onto his website, and everything started to make sense.

If you are planning any international trip by train and haven't done so already, go to seat61.com. IMMEDIATELY. I insist. It is a thing of pure wonder. Not only will it tell you how to get between pretty much any two places by train, but it will also let you know the timetables, the prices, how to book it and, crucially, give you exquisite extras like, 'I recommend lunching in this little place in Barcelona just down the road from the station before continuing on your journey. The croquettas are particularly good.'

Mark's absolute adoration of travel comes across in these little tips – they conjure up the excitement of the journey in a way that is the polar opposite to buying plane tickets in under a minute on some soulless price comparison aggregator.

'I love travel, and trains and ships are real travel, romantic travel, where the journey matters, where you see where you're going,' Mark tells me over coffee to an exhilarating sonic backdrop of train horns and Eurostar announcements, evoking the anticipation of a hundred journeys all about to begin. 'Airlines sort of suck the joy out of travel. But trains and ships are civilised and humane. You sleep in a bed; you eat in a restaurant; there are no seatbelts; and you can stand up and walk around. It takes you from the city centre to the city centre. It shows you the countryside – countryside that hasn't been destroyed by virtue of the motorway you are travelling on tearing through it.

'The journey can be as fun – and sometimes more fun – than the destination.'

And I can see it, as he says all this and his eyes light up – I can see the excitement of it all. I catch a glimpse of an idea that is, as he says, romantic: me, impeccably dressed while lounging in a train dining car somewhere, glass of the palest rosé in hand as lush greenery whizzes by the windows. Perhaps there's a debonair stranger with a whisper of sadness in his eyes who strikes up a conversation in the bar car later and he ... Ahem. Sorry. Lost focus there for a moment.

But, for all that, it's not always easy to do. Not the pulling a stranger on a train bit – the actual booking of the train bit. Yes, you can put a journey into the likes of the Trainline app and it might come up with something. But, equally, it might not. Because Trainline isn't a person; it uses data and algorithms, but not always logic.

'If you want to go from London to Florence, and let's assume you want the day train, not the night train, you can't just type London–Florence into a journey planner because you need an overnight stop,' says Mark, with the kind of gusto that comes from talking about your very favourite subject:

Instead of the journey planner coming up with an answer for you, you have to tell the journey planner exactly what you want; you have to know in advance how to do it. A very simple example is, if you want to go from Paris to Moscow, there's one train a week and it leaves on Thursday night. You have to *know* that it leaves on Thursday night before you open the journey planner, because if you look at Wednesday and Tuesday and Sunday, you're not going to find it.

That suggests you need something that actually explains it all, rather than just a journey planner where you can put in anywhere to anywhere. Of course, I can't explain everywhere to everywhere, but hey, if I explain most places to most places … I'm always trying to fill the gaps.

That was the motivation for Mark to set up his site, way back in 2001. He spotted a gap in the market – one that, rather incredibly, still hasn't really been filled by anyone else. There is still no one to rival his knowledge, skills, meticulous research and unquenchable passion for breaking down train journeys. And, let me tell you, they need breaking down. Booking long-distance train travel is the furthest of cries from typing a destination into Skyscanner. Of course, from one perspective, that's all part of the fun. Mark continues:

> Booking flights is easy. Nightmare to do and it doesn't give you anything back when you actually do it. Booking trains is hard – it's a challenge. But when you actually do it and make the journey, it's wonderful. And it's like everything else in life: if you put more effort in, you get a lot more out.

It definitely needs some actual thought, rather than three clicks and you're done. A journey planner, for instance, might put together your itinerary of trains without knowing that there's quite a lengthy platform change at such-and-such connecting station, or that you need to add in more of a time buffer at X interchange because one of the trains is often tardy. The buffer is important because, unlike with flights, consumers have very few rights when it comes to connecting trains. If you miss one, you're pretty much on your own – the train company doesn't care why you missed it. The previous train company whose service was late, which is why you missed your next train, also doesn't care. No one is compelled to take responsibility; if you're stranded, no one has a duty of care towards you.

It's one of the issues Mark Smith is most fervid about, in fact – that there should be parity between EU air passenger rights, which are comprehensive and protect the consumer, and train traveller rights, which are a different kettle of fish altogether. Under EU regulation 261/2004, if your flight is cancelled at the last minute, you will, at the very least, be entitled to food, drink and accommodation paid for by the airline, plus they are duty-bound to get you to your destination as soon as possible – even if that means booking you a ticket on another airline. (For those of us in post-Brexit Britain, these consumer protections remain identical.) If the flight was cancelled due to a fault of the airline (rather than circumstances outside their control), passengers are also entitled to compensation ranging from €125 to €600, depending on the length of the journey.

Train companies have no such responsibilities. Your train was cancelled and you're stuck somewhere overnight? Sucks to be you. 'Europe needs to address passenger rights for a world where there are no through-tickets,' says Mark:

> When I worked for a train company in the university holidays, I would issue through-tickets in biro on blank ticket stock, from London to Istanbul, London to Rome, London to Barcelona, London to Lisbon. That was very Old World; it doesn't exist now. Everything's computerised and yield managed and dynamically priced, controlled in a different ticketing system for each operator, and through-tickets are rapidly becoming the exception, not the norm. And technically, your connectional protection, same as with air travel, doesn't exist when you buy separate tickets, or even where separate tickets get added together by Raileurope or Trainline.

Mark champions reform in this area, and has even spoken as part of the transport committee at the European Parliament in Brussels on the subject. The parliament passed provision for better protections a couple of years ago, but Mark thinks the council is 'likely to reject that decision'.

Although the EU would say they're trying to create a level playing field between train travel and air travel, their focus is on the wrong issues, according to him:

> They're obsessed with delay compensation. They haven't realised that people are making through-journeys on multiple tickets because they have to. And the biggest issue is not getting back 20 per cent of your €29 ticket, it's what happens when you miss that €29 train because the preceding train is late, and they want you to buy a €130 full-flex ticket to get you to your destination. That's a much bigger issue.

Fierce lobbying from train companies, who are vehemently against enhanced regulation, is part of the problem – even though greater protection might be in their best interests commercially. 'I think it would stop bad publicity and it would stop people being afraid,' says Mark. 'Once you've had a bad experience where you've missed a train and paid through the nose, you'll be afraid to do it again.'

So yes, there are pitfalls; many more than with flying. But Mark would say it's definitely worth it, and maybe I would too once I've found that glass of rosé and the handsome stranger. Here are his best tips for staying grounded.

Go direct (or don't)
'There isn't one website that does everything, so don't believe anyone who tells you their website sells all European train tickets,' says Mark. For example, the only place you'll get Prague–Budapest tickets for €20 with print-at-home delivery

is the Czech Railways website – nobody else connects to them. Sites like trainline.com and raileurope.co.uk connect to France, Italy, Germany, Spain, Austria and the UK. They're easy to use but charge a fee – if you want to avoid that, go straight to the operator to book instead.

But, equally, sometimes it's worth the extra money, according to Mark:

> Some of the operators are a bit quirky, [Spanish rail company] Renfe being an obvious one. By 'quirky', I mean not always user friendly: switching back into odd bits of Spanish when you've changed it to English. So even if you're booking a Madrid–Lisbon sleeper in English, you need to know the difference between a Turista and a Cama-Turista and, if you don't, you'll end up in a seat all night.

Which is why it's sometimes worth paying the booking fee: because at least then it's in plain English and you can book several trains together all in one place.

Don't rely on the connection time

People in the know talk a lot about 'padding your connections'. It means including generous pockets of time between trains so that, if one is late, it doesn't have a knock-on effect and ensure you miss every other train on your journey. Mark advises:

> Use some risk management. Booking engines don't do risk management; they apply the same theoretical ten-minute armchair connecting time whether you're connecting into a half hourly local train – 'oh I've missed it, there's another one thirty minutes later' – or it's a sleeper train – 'oh I've missed it, I'm stuffed'. You pad – you create firebreaks where, if you're making a really long journey, you can catch up, even if there's a delay and you end up on the following train.

Prioritise journey over destination
A key tenet of the slow-travel movement is to see the journey as being as much a part of the holiday as the destination. In which case, the journey itself should be high up in the decision-making process when it comes to booking your next holiday.

As for Mark's top picks?

London to Fort William on the Caledonian Sleeper. It would take me away from London after work on a Friday on a little travelling hotel, with private rooms and a lounge. And then you wake up in the middle of the west Highlands, with a complete contrast from speeding along a four-track electric mainline at 80mph through Hemel Hempstead and Tring and places like that, to waking up at 30mph on a single track with a diesel struggling at the front in the middle of the west Highlands. Fabulous train, never get tired of that.

His other favourite is the Bernina Express from Chur to Tirano in the Swiss Alps – you can use it to get from Zürich to Italy too:

It's obviously a lot slower because it's narrow gauge and it goes very slowly, but you won't care because it's fabulous. It runs over an UNESCO-listed railway and it's probably the best Swiss-Alpine train you can take. And on the website you'll find a clever way of doing it for €29.90.

Don't worry about sleeping
Anyone who starts to travel more widely by train will soon realise that booking sleepers is the only way to go if you want to save time. But not everyone finds it easy to drop off on a moving vehicle. Mark advises:

The trick is not to worry whether you do or don't. When I first took a sleeper train, and we're talking the 1980s, I didn't know if I got the best value by going to sleep and using it or staying awake and enjoying it – I was pulled both ways. Just don't worry about it. If you worry about it, you'll lie awake worrying about it. Don't worry and you'll sleep when you're ready. And it's lovely snuggling between crisp sheets, reading by the glow of your berth light and listening to the steel wheels swishing on steel rail.

There's that train romanticism again; oh, to hear the swish of wheel on rail!

His final tip, of which I fully approve: 'A good nightcap helps.'

The way Anna Hughes talks about travel makes me want to ease off the gas and go lie in a hammock some place. It sounds so gentle, so low impact, so ... relaxing. In fact, it gives me a flashback to my last time in an airport – Singapore's swish Changi Airport to be exact – where, nauseous and disorientated, I struggled across its shiny-floored acres desperately searching for somewhere to buy a bottle of water. When I finally did, I realised I hadn't been through security yet and would have to chuck it or chug it, which almost brought me to tears.

The founder of Flight Free UK stopped flying more than a decade ago and doesn't seem to have had any regrets about her choice in that time:

I prefer slow travel anyway – feeling the ground beneath my feet. I don't like the artificiality of planes. I feel like jetlag is your body's way of saying, 'please don't do that!' It's unnatural. I enjoy the slow life.

There are instances where she has to say no to opportunities – social events abroad, for example – but these are infrequent enough that it seems a small price to pay. There is wistful talk, too, of blowing all her carefully accrued carbon credit on one big trip after a lifetime's dedication – 'I could fly to Indonesia and stuff myself with street food!' – but this, too, is spoken of in much the same way I talk about buying a run-down chateau in rural France and moving there to write. In short: it ain't going to happen:

> I don't really think I would. I've lived so consciously up until now. And, when I'm retired, I'll actually have the time to go by boat! I'll probably never get on a plane again. Unless carbon neutral planes are invented.

Until that day, Anna is on a one-woman mission to get people in the UK to sign up to take a year off flying. It all started when she was asked to contribute to an aviation discussion on a radio show, during which Maja Rosen, who'd started the Flight Free 2019 campaign in Sweden, was also being interviewed. 'I thought it sounded amazing,' says Anna. 'Given the situation we're now in, I felt like it was no longer enough to reduce my own carbon footprint – I needed to open it up and do more. And it took over my life.'

Asking participants to commit to just one year of staying grounded is all part of the game plan:

> It's to hook people in – telling people to give up flying forever is unlikely to appeal. But if you challenge them to take a year off, that short-term change can lead to long-term change. It's the same principle as veganism and challenging people to try Veganuary.
>
> We humans are very adaptable but very reluctant to change our habits. If you take on the challenge, you'll probably adapt really well. In a way, it's easier to say to yourself you're cutting something out completely for a while than trying to reduce.

She tells me this long before the Covid-19 pandemic took over the world, but her words seem strangely prescient as I recall them now. Because one thing it proved irrefutably is that, yes, we may not like change – but we're awfully good at it. The unthinkable happened – life as we knew it came to a standstill – and five minutes later we were hosting Zoom dinner parties and taking virtual cooking classes. And, of course, not flying.

One of Anna's tips for the flight-free life is, naturally, checking out the seat61 website (told you, everyone knows about it). But what else?

> It's perfectly possible to still travel even without flying. Be prepared to look a little harder than you would for flights – and be prepared to make the most of the journey. It will probably take longer to get there, but you can really do things with that journey: look out the window, read, catch up on your emails, make a phone call. It entails approaching travel in a whole different way; there has to be a slight shift in mindset.

That unholiest of portmanteaus, 'staycation', is back on the table too. 'You don't have to travel far at all – the UK is amazing. It's about not overlooking what we have here and reconnecting with local treasures. Don't look at it as a sacrifice. It's an enriching experience.'

There's a lesser-known idea that took hold in Sweden off the back of the *flygskam* movement, and it's less about shame and more about hope. At the same time that some campaigners were focused on warning people off flying, others were shaping the conversation around what we should be doing instead: taking the train. People started posting pictures and descriptions of their train journeys on social media; they were creating excitement around it, building each other up, inspiring each other. And thus the '*tagskryt*' – 'train brag' – concept was born.

Its de facto founder, Susanna Elfors, was really just trying to find a way to travel more sustainably herself when she set up the Tågsemester (Train Holiday) Facebook group in 2014. She wasn't looking to start a global movement. Just get a conversation going, share some tips, be a resource for others who wanted to fly less:

> For a long time, I knew flying wasn't a sustainable way to travel. Colleagues who work in transport told me. Plus, I think most people have known for the last ten to fifteen years – but they didn't *want* to know. You want to pretend it's not true, because flying is easy and fun. Even those who are environmentally conscious can ignore it: research shows they are likely to fly further than other people. They're more likely to get on a long-haul flight to Vietnam or Guatemala, go on an eco tour, stay at an eco lodge. While flying halfway around the world!

Research even shows that climate change researchers can be blind to the issue – they fly more than any other group of academics.[2]

Working in sustainable housing at the time, Susanna didn't want to become just another person paying lip service to a green lifestyle while not following through. So she took a train holiday to Lake Garda in Italy with the Swedish arm of Thomas Cook, and what ensued was a huge disparity between her expectations and reality:

> I thought the journey would be great. I'd imagined there would be lots of things to do, a bar with a welcome drink, a nice dinner, a talk about our destination before going to your nice sleeper carriage ... but it wasn't like that at all! We had to change trains several times.

Susanna followed it up with a train trip to Berlin, which again proved more difficult and uncomfortable than she had expected. And that's when the idea for a Facebook group was born, to get people sharing their tips, their favourite journeys and their recommendations for how to book. It started small and then, four years later, Greta Thunberg had her big moment and train bragging took on a life of its own. The group swelled to more than 100,000, Susanna was invited to the European Parliament to give her views on sustainable travel, and she somehow appeared on Japanese TV (the ultimate dream).

Along with a colleague, she decided to harness this energy and appetite and start up a company. They've organised group train holidays for members of the Tågsemester group, a meet-up event that had more than 1,000 attendees, and now they're pivoting towards helping train companies promote themselves:

> We are more for train brag than flight shame. There should be a tension between despair and hope when it comes to climate change. If people think there's no point and it's too late to do anything, they'll continue flying. And the same thing happens if you're told you can't travel at all. But if you're given an alternative – that you *can* still travel, but more sustainably – you feel hope.

The group has never been about telling people they have to give up flying; it's about inspiring people via the beauty of rail travel. 'Then you get people on the fringes,' says Susanna. It means that members broadly fall into two categories: environmentalists and, in Susanna's words, 'train nerds'. The latter 'hate Greta' but they have the kind of useful knowledge about timetables and itineraries that everyone benefits from. And who knows? They might just become converts to the cause, given enough time and persuasion:

There's an important social component about the group. Before, people bragged about going on flights. They'd put their pictures on Facebook. But what about if people could do the same thing going by train? And have other people commenting on their post saying, 'this looks great!'? If you want to change people's habits, it's very important that they feel like they're doing something good and that they've found their tribe. You do what your neighbours do and what your friends do.

Susanna quickly came to the same realisation as Mark Smith – that the appetite for slow travel existed, but there was a huge knowledge gap when it came to booking trains. She lays the blame for this squarely at politicians' doors:

It used to be quite usual to travel by train, but then something changed. In the 1930s, politicians wanted people to go by car – so they built big motorways everywhere. In the 1980s, they wanted people to go by plane – so they gave subsidies to airports to make it cheap to fly. By comparison, it's much harder to go by train these days.

Her best advice for getting on track – pun very much intended – is to shift your mindset. 'Philosophically, you have to change your idea of what travelling is. You have to change your idea of distances.'

So, if you have a weekend, go to a city that's not too far from home. If you have a week, go a little further (but don't kill yourself spending forty-eight hours non-stop on modes of transport, unless you're into that). 'And you can do your big trip, but you need a lot of time,' says Susanna, 'like in the old days, when people did the grand tour, and they went for six months to really see the world.' Clearly, this isn't possible for many of us – unless we're lucky enough to be able to take a sabbatical or an adult gap year. But some countries' annual leave policies can help make a pared-back version a reality – for instance, Austria offers twenty-five days' statutory holiday, plus a further thirteen public holidays, totalling thirty-eight days, or seven and a half weeks. (In stark contrast, the US doesn't have any legal minimum allowance when it comes to paid time off.)

Susanna cites a truly fabulous-sounding family trip, where taking their time meant they got to experience several holidays in one: a three-week jaunt to Croatia, stopping off in Budapest, Prague, Vienna and Ljubljana on the way. 'We went to cities but also went swimming at the beach and walking in the mountains. You can mix vacations.'

Her more practical tips include tapping into your inner Boy/Girl Scout and being prepared for any eventuality: take games, take snacks. Heck, take some crafts. Slow travel goes a lot more slowly if you're hungry and bored.

You've also got to ignore the little voice that says getting to your destination as fast as possible is the goal. Unless you're competing in the BBC's *Race Across the World*, there's absolutely no need to be in a hurry. 'Try not to sit for too many hours on a train,' Susanna advises. 'Break up the journey. See other places and take your time.'

I speak to her during lockdown – at a point when, in the UK, we could only leave the house to exercise or shop for essentials. The idea of seeing a friend in person, buying a coffee or even sitting alone in a park was still a distant dream. Small things, once taken for granted, were the stuff of deepest yearning. And so Susanna's parting advice resonated all the more:

I think being satisfied is all about your expectations of what your life should include. If you expect you will fly a lot and see everything, you will be disappointed if you switch to slow travel. If you expect to sit in an apartment for years on end, you will think a walk in the forest is something wonderful.

As she spoke, I looked out of the window, misty-eyed, and fantasised about just such a thing – stepping between light and shade, green giants all about me soaring into the sky, the feel of rough bark under palm, the play of wind through the branches. Maybe, just maybe, our individual worlds shrank so much amid the pandemic that we really could appreciate the wonders found closer to home. Now that would be something to brag about.

Tips from a non-expert

I can hardly put myself in the same category as these hallowed flight-free experts; to them, I am but a child, taking my first faltering steps into the world of zero altitude. As I write this, it's been just over a year since I decided to clip my wings; a year in which the travel industry as we know it came grinding to a halt. My 2020, so full of grand terrestrial plans, consisted of just three trips, with those pencilled in for the following year looking increasingly uncertain.

And yet, somehow, I feel like I've picked up some helpful habits along the way. I know little about booking sites or algorithms, and I think other people are probably better placed to wax lyrical about the whole 'it's about the journey, not the destination' philosophy thing, but I do know something of the journey itself – and what I need as, it turns out, an incredibly fussy traveller. Here are my top tips; all of them are tailored to my particular neuroses, but hopefully some are more universal.

Download before you go
Here's the thing about flight-free travel – it is looooong. The time can be passed easily in myriad creative ways: take a good book, a laptop, a notebook and pen for if you get inspired, some knitting if you're into that. Regular intervals will be spent just

gazing out of the window at the views while your mind wanders in pleasant aimlessness.

But, for me, there's always a point in the journey when I no longer want to make any effort whatsoever in terms of entertaining myself – when I want to, as a friend refers to it, 'put my brain in the ashtray'. It means doing something mindless, where you're just passively consuming, rather than actively participating. When this moment comes, it is key that the need can be met, and that it doesn't rely on potentially dodgy Wi-Fi. My pre-travel checklist now features downloading multiple episodes of both something light and fluffy and something absorbing and dramatic to fit whatever mood I find myself in. Episodes beat films in my experience; they feel like light bites, small plates if you will, that you can dip in and out of without being too upset if you, say, accidentally drop off in the middle of one.

Pack the snacks

Being hangry on a train, boat, bus or any form of transport is no fun. I mean, it's also no fun on a flight – but either they are short enough that it doesn't matter too much, or they are long enough that the airline feels obliged to feed you. The same cannot be said elsewhere. There is no guarantee that a train, even one going a long distance, will have a proper restaurant carriage, bar car or little shop. They may not even have a cute snack trolley. Always go armed with more than you need, and enough food and drink that, if you couldn't buy anything to eat for the entirety of your journey, you'd still be OK.

Food is one of my favourite things about travel, so I probably think about this more than is entirely normal. Regardless, I like to build my travelling sustenance out of things I'll look forward to, treats that will punctuate the day with extra joy. Oh, and remember to opt for snacks that aren't too pungent – no one wants to be *that* passenger – and that preferably don't require you carting around dirty Tupperware for hours on end.

Accessorise your sleep

You'll read about this in other chapters of the book, but it's always worth saying it again – if you're staying overnight on a form of transport, don't shy away from being a high-maintenance traveller. Whether it's a sleeper train or an overnight ferry, catching zzzs on the move can be harder than you think, even with stellar facilities and an actual bed. Getting your kit and routine down can really help.

Top of my list is a really, really good eye mask. Mine is moulded so that it blocks out the light. I've also heard good things about the Ostrich Pillow, a mask and pillow in one worn over your head. If you can suck up the judgemental stares (which you won't be able to see from inside your giant, alien-like head cocoon anyway), the reward might be the nap of a lifetime. Other failsafes include a quality travel neck pillow that can also be used as a regular pillow; a micro-towel that can be used as a blanket; bed socks and multiple bedtime layers (trains and the like can get pretty nippy); and wraparound wireless headphones to listen to calming music as you drift off (I am not responsible enough to be trusted with extremely losable ear buds). Select your soundtrack with care: Max Richter's *Sleep* album has been my go-to for every overnight trip during the last eighteen months.

I also like to pop a melatonin pill, which gives you a natural dose of the hormone responsible for making you feel sleepy. It's not for everyone – and, sadly, you can't buy these delightful sleep aids over the counter in the UK. But a Nytol or other herbal sleeping tab might just give you the final shove needed to stumble over the border and into the land of nod.

Seats are OK

Some people will tell you to only travel in a berth or couchette on a sleeper train, which comes with a proper bed. I'm mostly with them – obviously, it is approximately 1,000 times nicer – but life doesn't always work out that way.

Maybe you're strapped for cash. Perhaps all the beds are taken. I've been in this situation a couple of times and believe me when I say I was *terrified* of sleeping in a seat. I do not sleep well when not horizontal. And I take my sleep seriously – it would be my religion if I hadn't already found God. I talk about it an unnecessary amount, I look forward to it, and I worry when it looks like I'm not going to get enough of it. But, as it turns out, with some good prep and winding down, even I managed to drift in and out of slumber. I'm not going to pretend it compares to the quality of sleep you get in a bed, but it's not as bad as you might think. The main thing is to build in some time to nap the day you arrive at your destination – around 3–4 p.m. is my crash point. And don't feel guilty about it either; you've saved money, you can afford a couple of hours between the sheets.

Analogue itinerary

We are digital animals these days, especially when it comes to travel. Timetables, tickets, connections and platforms can all be accessed at the click of a button. But things can go awry. Namely, your smartphone could run out of battery with no access to a plug or battery pack, or you could find yourself with no internet signal at a critical moment (both of which have happened to me). I am an old-fashioned cat, and so I always like to be prepared should I be stranded in a tech-free wasteland. Call me crazy, but I write down or print off a full itinerary – including key contact names and numbers, transport and hotel details and whatever else I can think of – plus physical print-outs of my tickets, and carry them somewhere accessible at all times. As much as I love my phone, my phone doesn't love me back. I never want to be so reliant on it that I can't survive without it.

Sea off sickness

Getting travel sick wasn't something I thought about until I boarded a boat to the Isles of Scilly and surfed upon a giant wave of nausea all the way there. It shouldn't put you off the flight-free life though – you've just got to strategise. If you know you're susceptible, look into medication before you go. Sea bands can help, as can timing when you eat: board a vessel feeling neither hungry nor full, meaning there's less scope for agitating your stomach.

For some, being out on deck in the fresh air can help. For others, descending to the lowest level of the ship, which is actually the most stable point, can be best. Find what works for you – but also find and familiarise yourself with the route to the toilet and locate a sick bag. I'm sure seasickness is what the Scouts were referencing when they came up with that 'Always be prepared' motto.

4

At a Rail's Pace
All Aboard a Train Tour of Europe

With my new bagful of tricks and tips from the flight-free sages at the ready, it was time to put them into practice somewhere new – namely, the European destinations I'd have thoughtlessly jumped on a kerosene-guzzling short-haul budget flight to reach in my previous life as a frequent flyer.

And, while the prospect of embarking on a journey that involves twenty-four hours on trains might not normally fill me with joy, after spending the entirety of 2020 in Blighty I felt a tingling anticipation before my first-ever interrailing experience. Yes, a full ten years older than most people who would engage in this sort of travel – people with young, lithe bodies that require a mere two hours' sleep to keep functioning – I was going to be riding the rails across Europe for the first time.

Not only was this going to be an adventure, it was also to be an adventure at a time when almost no one else was having adventures – thanks to the pandemic – thereby securing me bragging rights for at least a month. I boarded the Eurostar at 10.24 a.m. on a Thursday in the knowledge that, if all went to plan, I would be in the sun-warmed port city of Rijeka, Croatia, the same time the following day.

Connections are key; it's amazing how far you can get in a day by train if you time it right. The first part is easy – London to Paris, a hop so swift that I have never once done it without saying, 'wait, are we in France?' twenty minutes after coming out the other side of the Channel Tunnel. Before you know it, we've arrived – and I set foot on foreign soil for the first time this decade.

It's a brief walk from Gare du Nord to Paris Est to pick up my next train, but I find it strangely disorientating. There are so many people – many more than I've been accustomed to seeing in London while Covid restrictions reign. It is hot, and I am carrying three pieces of luggage, and my laptop is very visibly peeking out of the top of my tote bag as if to say 'bonjour!' Skittish and sweaty, for some reason I feel like I am going to be mugged, especially with my phone in my hand and my eyes glued to Google Maps – the epitome of a wide-eyed, idiot tourist. I seem to have morphed into one of those people I hate: convinced that 'abroad' isn't safe, that foreigners aren't to be trusted. Is this what happens naturally after ten months without travelling? Have I already become so close-minded?

I feel much happier once aboard my second train of the day, whizzing its way from Paris to Karlsruhe in south-western Germany, where it's a quick change for the onward service to Munich. I've opted to spend the day working to make the most of the fallow time and am struck by just how delightful an experience this is when ensconced in an airy, well-ventilated carriage on a wide seat with shockingly decent Wi-Fi and a tray table expansive enough to fit my hulking laptop. I wish I could tell you that I spent the time looking out upon the frankly lovely views of rural France and Germany, but there really is nothing to prevent me from actually doing my work – no 'dog ate my homework excuse' that will allow me to bunk off for the day.

On the third train of the day, Karlsruhe to Munich, there are little carriages big enough to hold six passengers apiece, with a sliding door to enter. I feel like I'm riding aboard the Hogwarts Express. There's this to say about German trains – they really do appear to run with staggering efficiency. On the second leg the train leaves a minute early, which is just bad manners in my book (I picture a harried, unkempt passenger sprinting through the station, relieved that they've *just* managed to make it on time, only to find their chariot very much does not await).

I arrive at Munich on time (of course) with two hours to spare before my final train, the big one: an epic ten-hour overnighter all the way to Croatia. I take a leaf out of the Man in Seat 61's book – the rail travel expert offers impeccable dining suggestions near stations alongside all the practical train info – and head to the *Bierhaus* and eatery Augustiner-Keller, a ten-minute stroll from the station. It is, as expected, a marvellous decision: speedy service, a convivial atmosphere and reassuringly hefty German fare that sticks to the ribs – the perfect pre-sleep cuisine. I order myself a *Käsespätzle und Radler*, which comes out in around ten minutes, ideal for anxious travellers desperate not to miss a connection. I've got ample time, and yet my eyes keep twitching back to my watch every thirty seconds or so. It's perhaps a sign of my inexperience as a train traveller; Greta probably swoops into the station with five minutes to spare like the cool, clued-up Gen Z-er she is.

Sated and increasingly sleepy, it's back to face the Nightjet. Side note: I simply adore the names they give to sleeper trains. They always sound romantic, selling you a story that is so much more appealing than, say, the 13.24 fast train to Norwich. I have yet to find one that fails to stir something in the soul: the Night Riviera, the Berlin Night Express, the Euronight, Hellas Express, Intercités de Nuit and, best in show, the Santa Claus Express, which winds its way from Helsinki to Lapland.

Sleeper trains used to be de rigueur across Europe – the natural way of traversing the Continent in comfort and style. Then low-cost aviation arrived, heralding a new era of easy travel, and these services were stripped back as travellers increasingly picked plane over train. But the promising news for those dabbling in the flight-free lifestyle is that sleepers are very much back in vogue: numerous new European night-train routes are slated to launch in the next few years.

Austria's national railway company, ÖBB, will kickstart its new programme with an overnight link between Vienna, Munich and Paris, plus a sleeper connecting Amsterdam and Zürich with a stop at Cologne. A new Nightjet train from Zürich to Rome, via Milan, is also planned, alongside routes between Berlin, Paris and Brussels, plus one between Zürich and Barcelona. Meanwhile, Snälltåget will run night trains from Sweden and Denmark to several Austrian ski resorts, as well as a sleeper from Stockholm to Copenhagen, Hamburg and Berlin. And new operator European Sleeper, working with Czech company Regiojet, is set to launch an overnighter from Brussels to Prague, via Amsterdam and Berlin.

The more these networks get expanded, the broader the horizons become for us terrestrial travellers, enabling us to cross multiple nations while unconscious and wake up somewhere entirely new.

The way to do night trains, as anyone will tell you, is to book a couchette – a sleeping berth with a bed. That way, you can tell yourself you're not spending the night on a train – goodness me, no! – but, rather, a sparse yet comfortable travelling hotel. The way *not* to do them is to book a seat. But I am left with little option – I'm travelling on an Interrail pass, and when they go to make the reservation, there is no room at the couchette inn. I try to convince myself that I am getting the full Interrail experience this way: I am Julie Delpy in *Before Sunrise*, drifting around Europe on the cheap seats while still looking impossibly sexy in a dishevelled sort of way and chatting up Ethan Hawke. That's plausible, right?

Signs are looking good – it's just me and a lone man in our six-seater cabin. However, this potentially suave travelling companion can only speak Slovenian and German. I can only speak English and *un peu de français*, so our love story gets as far as conveying where we are getting off the train and ends abruptly there.

Unlike Julie Delpy and all manner of other budget rail travellers before her, I do not view the fact that I've only got a seat as some kind of impediment to doing things properly. While my fellow passengers attempt to get some kip using rucksacks as pillows while still fully dressed, I brush my teeth, cleanse, tone *and* moisturise, and change into loungewear as a stand-in for full flannel pyjamas. My Slovenian looks at me in utter bewilderment as I reverently unpack my sleeping mask, neck pillow, melatonin pills, cashmere socks and travel towel, which doubles as a blanket. (I draw the line at spritzing my White Company lavender sleep mist on the grounds that it might just be too much for him to handle.) I pop on my wireless headphones and start up my best-loved ambient melodies.

Well, Mr Slovenia can smirk all he wants – it works. We're lucky enough that the train is half empty, the result being that we can each spread out on our respective rows of seats. With armrests up and the neck pillow transformed into a regular pillow, it's not so far off the experience of sleeping in a bed. I drift in and out contentedly, floating on a haze of excitement that I will wake up in a foreign land.

The biggest disturbance, in fact, comes courtesy of the train guards, who seem to change after each stop and have therefore concluded they must recheck everyone's ticket at regular intervals. The interruptions feel incessant. The first time it happens I am understanding, the second time, perplexed, the third time, irked, the fourth time, just plain angry. *Surely there must be a better way!* I want to wail, but I am too tired to figure out how to say this in German/Slovenian/Croatian, so settle for grumpily going back to sleep instead. That'll show 'em.

The other intrusion comes on the border between Slovenia and Croatia. Embarrassing as it is to admit for a travel journalist, I had somehow forgotten that the latter wasn't part of Schengen, meaning there are passport checks either side of the border, undertaken by police who board the train and make their way along each carriage. It's fairly disconcerting, let me tell you, to be awoken by an officer carrying what appears to be a gun and demanding to see your ID in the middle of the night.

What makes it so jarring is that I've just spent an entire day on trains in different countries without ever once being asked to show my passport. It highlights just how gloriously liberating the concept of Schengen is – that, once I've boarded the Eurostar, I can whizz across France, Germany, Austria and Slovenia, all without having to prove who I am or why I'm there. It's such a smooth, joyful and inherently welcoming experience for the traveller. More than anything, it makes me feel keenly the loss of the UK removing itself even further from this delightfully convivial concept of open borders thanks to Brexit. I hate the thought of suddenly being subject to questioning upon entry to any EU country. 'What is your business here?' they will be fully entitled to ask. 'How long are you staying? Where are you staying? Do you have enough money for that length of time? Where are your euros? Do you have six months left on your passport?'

We have lived for so long without such restrictions, that I think most people will have forgotten – or, like me, aren't old enough to remember – what life was like before. Our world is shrinking just that little bit more, and I am already in mourning.

Despite the aforementioned incursions, I wake at around 7 a.m. feeling, if not quite perky, well rested enough to greet the new day with anticipation. I change, brush my teeth and hair and watch the sun rise over misty fields, tinging the sky a delicate shade of rose-petal pink. The train meanders its way through northern Croatia at an unhurried pace, and I look out over landscapes far greener than I'd expected. Then, suddenly, there it is – the sea! The deep blue of the Adriatic twinkles at me flirtatiously, and I feel fabulously far from home.

Finally, the Nightjet trundles into Rijeka station, where I wheel my suitcase across the tracks and look up in wonder at the sign that tells me I've made it, five minutes later than expected. Some twenty-three hours after setting off from London, I am in a Croatian city by the sea. It is 30°C. I am deliriously excited.

Everyone I tell that I travelled to Rijeka by train is surprised. Wait – make that utterly dumbfounded. 'What? Are you crazy?' they ask, looking at me as they would a phantom, or a cow with two heads. I got the exact same response when I previously shared some of my travel plans on social media; native Croats kept popping up in disbelief, telling me unequivocally that I should avoid the train at all costs and that overland transport in Croatia was, in no uncertain terms, shite. When I explain that the Nightjet isn't in fact a Croatian train at all – that it's operated by an Austrian company and had made its way from Germany – there is at last a glimmer of understanding. 'Ah, it's *international*. That's why you're here on time.' And with that, order is restored to the world.

It's why Rijeka makes one of the best destinations in Croatia for non-flyers – it's the end of the line on the Nightjet (along with Zagreb, the final stop on the other branch of the service). Want to carry on to more popular coastal spots – Split, perhaps, Šibenik or Dubrovnik? The transport options become domestic and, therefore, infuriatingly slow and unreliable, according to locals. But it's not the only reason I was drawn here.

I love me an underdog. When it comes to travel, give me your second cities, your third cities, heck, your fourth and fifth. It's what's so worthwhile about the European Capital of Culture scheme: each year, it plucks two usually lesser-known cities from obscurity and thrusts them into the limelight, gifting them a wodge of cash in the process for legacy venues that last long after the year itself. In return, the cities lay on a rich programme of cultural events encompassing art, music, theatre, dance and literature, all of which draws in higher than usual numbers of tourists and helps put the place on the map.

That's what usually happens, at any rate.

The recipients of the 2020 accolade, Galway and Rijeka, had just enough time to announce their heady year of performances before coronavirus muscled its way in and shut everything down. The northern port city of Rijeka at least managed to fit in an opulent opening ceremony before everything went south; pity poor Galway, on the west coast of Ireland, which was forced to cancel even that.

Rijeka is Croatia's third-largest city, and when I tell people I'm coming here, nobody has ever heard of it. Despite its plum position by the Adriatic Sea and its convenient rail links, it is not a place that traditionally attracts too many holidaymakers. The city itself is an alluring blend of contradictions: pretty, dilapidated, open, stubborn, charming, gritty, laid-back, hardworking. Rijeka's tagline for its 2020 bid, Port of Diversity, could scarce be more apt.

You might not think it from the wide, pedestrianised Korzo main street, where everyone strolls at a leisurely pace – stopping to greet familiar faces every 10m or so in an expressive and melodious Croatian that sounds almost Italian – but this was always a city built on industry. Dirty, noisy industry at that: paper mills, sugar refineries, torpedo factories – the modern, self-propelled variation of the weapon was invented in the city – and, of course, the shipping business, still going strong today. You also wouldn't think it from the temperament of the locals, an intriguing combination of extreme friendliness and contrariness with a propensity to complain ('if the rest of Croatia goes right, we go left' my guide, Sandra, tells me), that it was the very first fascist state, set up by Italian poet and army officer Gabriele D'Annunzio in 1919 at the end of the First World War. He and a band of nationalist intellectuals staged a curious coup, striding into the city unopposed and claiming it as their own. Initially humoured by Italy only because it was, understandably, a wee bit preoccupied after the war, their independent state became something of a unique social experiment, where intellectuals, artists and political oddballs gathered to ... well, have a good time and do whatever the hell they liked (D'Annunzio's motto became '*Me ne frego*', which roughly translates as 'I don't give a damn'). Amazingly, it survived under his rule for around fifteen months before he got the boot by the Italian government.

It's hardly surprising the residents themselves didn't put up much of a fight – the city has passed through so many hands that inhabitants must have been hard-pressed to keep track. Much easier to go about their daily lives and let others worry about governance. Sandra tells me that her grandmother lived in the same house for her whole life – and in that time lived in seven different countries.

For a long time the city fell under the rule of the Austro-Hungarian Empire, and was of supreme strategic importance as a means for landlocked countries to reach the sea; Rijeka was the jumping-off point for the rest of the world. Then came the French. Then Austria again. Italians. Briefly the Germans. Then it was part of Yugoslavia. Finally, in 1991, it became part of independent Croatia. For various periods in its history it was declared a free and independent state too, and was frequently caught in the middle of international turf wars in which rival empires laid claim to it.

Apologies for the impromptu history lesson, but I've always found that a city's past, besides being interesting in and of itself, helps shape its present character. To the casual observer, modern-day Rijeka seems scrappy and resilient. Its people may carp and complain, but they'll always put up with the next thing that's thrown at them with a wryly smiling stoicism because, despite being fiercely independent, the city has had to endure countless interlopers over the years. They're survivors, all of them, who've retained a heartening openness to and tolerance of visitors born of being a port city: facing the sea, welcoming the rest of the world in.

Each new regime has left its mark in a fascinating way, the architecture being a case in point. Wander down a street with coloured shutters, Juliet balconies and cypress trees lining the way, and you could be in the middle of Tuscany. Turn the corner and you might see an ornate former theatre painted in pastel shades that is unmistakably Austrian. Round the next bend, a brutalist office block is straight out of former Yugoslavia. The mixture creates something completely unique.

Unusually for a city by the sea, Rijeka is not a tourist town. Industry has always been the main money-maker here, meaning it's never been a destination that had to pander to visitors. It doesn't mean that holidaymakers aren't welcome – just that the place has a refreshingly authentic life to it that doesn't revolve around newcomers. The sea feels strangely hidden away, too, due to the layout of the city. And yet the nearest beach, Sablićevo, is a mere fifteen-minute walk from the city centre. It may be September, but the sun feels summer-like and scorching, and I alternate between lying on a wooden platform shaded by steps and taking dips in the glass-clear Adriatic. I'll tell you how clear the water is – mere metres from the shore I look down to see fish shimmying around my calves. I duck under to ogle them in awe, a shoal of hundreds suddenly flashing electric blue as they all turn at once on an invisible cue.

But culture is what I'm here for, and culture is what I get once I manage to peel myself away from the seductive pull of the water. The city managed to keep an impressive amount of its 2020 programme going, even though it was mainly only enjoyed by locals. The big-ticket items are two exhibitions, housed for the year inside a trendy-looking waterfront warehouse. One is all about the modern history of Rijeka and its place in a fast-changing world.

But it's the upstairs exhibition that really wows: 'The Sea is Glowing' is a range of mainly video installations, ostensibly exploring invisible economics linked to the sea, but somehow managing to encompass the increasingly confusing digital world we find ourselves in. I spend hours there in the soothing half-light, semi-delirious from lack of sleep. Glassy-eyed, I finally follow my feet outside to find a stage has been erected by the quay, on which a band is playing aggressive rock. More unexpected culture from the little city that could. I stay and listen for a spell in the bath-warm evening air, before I realise I could be asleep at my three-star digs, the Hotel Continental, and hightail it outta there.

The city's legacy building from its Capital of Culture year is a total renovation of the old sugar refinery, now rather grandly dubbed the Sugar Palace. The next day I'm privileged to get a sneak peek inside the building, where the finishing touches are being added to what will become an extensive and permanent city museum detailing Rijeka's complex history. The interiors are suitably majestic, with sweeping staircases and high-ceilinged halls. The curator tells me that throughout its turbulent history, Rijeka's main problem was that it was 'the wife that everyone wanted' – a very badly translated version of a Croatian expression that basically means everyone fancied a piece of her. I may have only been here for twenty-four hours, but I can already see why.

It turns out that, while it may not be the most tourist-focused of Croatia's coastal cities, Rijeka has plenty to suit visitors. Fresh seafood abounds, with squid-ink risotto, fresh calamari, shark and ray adorning plates at much lower prices than in the other coastal darlings; the coffee is excellent, having become a staple during the city's time under Austro-Hungarian rule, with a lazy café culture to match. The cultural offering continues at the city's new modern art museum, its maritime museum and Peek and Poke, a quirky little museum where I lose at least an hour playing Pac-Man, Space Invaders and Street Fighter on old games consoles. Phenomenal views are on offer, too, for those bold enough to venture up the hill to Trsat Castle. From its lofty height 138m above sea level, you can drink in a new perspective, seeing how the river cuts through the heavily wooded valley to make its way, glinting, back out to sea.

Guide Sandra says you can follow the river bed, which dries up after a couple of kilometres, inland on a hiking route that leads you into the middle of the wilderness within an hour or so. It's one of many things I won't have a chance to do – two days is 'NOT ENOUGH' to truly experience Rijeka, she tells me repeatedly. But, sadly, it's all I've got. There's just time for a final Aperol spritz at a seafront bar as I watch the sun set over the harbour before it's back to the station, where I'm plunged into darkness, stumbling my way down the platform to find my return chariot to Germany.

I don't know what's happened to me over the last thirty-six hours, but when I ask a train guard whether there are any available beds on board, and he says yes, for the modest upgrade fee of €60, I baulk and politely turn it down. Perhaps the very fact of interrailing reintroduces the natural thriftiness of student days. I return to my cabin, which is hotter than the sun but, as yet, unoccupied by any fellow passengers, and think about what I've done. I'm still not sure I've made the right decision as the train trundles off into the night and the air-con finally kicks in; I'm even less sure when a well-built German woman in a leather waistcoat and huge work boots (which she *doesn't take off*) gets on at some point in the middle of the night and proceeds to spend the entire journey slowly moving the zip on her bag back and forth, possibly to soothe herself, possibly to drive me insane.

Either way, it is something of a relief to pull into Munich station at 6.10 a.m. – although it's admittedly a less-than-ideal time to arrive anywhere. What is open at 6.10 a.m. on a Sunday in Munich, you ask? Bugger all. I head to my hotel in hopes that they might look kindly on me and let me check in early, but that also incurs an extra charge, and my inner student once again stubbornly folds her arms and gives a sideways look to camera. OK, fine. Time to get creative.

After some flustered bag repacking, I leave behind my monster of a suitcase (one of the lesser-spoken benefits of travelling by train rather than plane – the unlimited luggage allowance) and head out, back on yet another train, in search of an activity unaffected by the earliness of the hour. This time it's a local S-Bahn service that thankfully only takes fifteen minutes. I alight at Fasanerie, exiting the train into what appears to be some kind of rural idyll – I can hear birds singing and little else as I stroll past the level crossing and out to the main event: the Fasaneriesee lake. Nature thankfully doesn't keep Sunday opening hours.

It is beautiful. The kind of beautiful you try, and fail, to capture on your not-really-good-enough camera phone, so when you show people later they don't *quite* get it. There is a hazy, pale amber hue to the sky as the sun slowly rises, but I'm not the only early bird – there are joggers, walkers, mums in hi-tech work-out gear pushing sleek, expensive prams. All of which leads me to the ultimate conundrum: how to avoid flashing strangers while changing into a swimsuit in public? Oh yes, I didn't come here just to take in the view – I'm getting in that water, even if it means risking public nudity. If I were German it would be fine, of course; I'd simply strip down where I stood without the merest hint of shame. But I am British, and therefore my only option is to scramble into some bushes and do the ungainly 'naked dance' while praying no one comes past at that exact moment. Embarrassed about being so embarrassed, I shuffle out of my barely hidden changing area, still feeling hideously exposed. It's

97

a strange sensation to be striding forth in a swimming costume, cap and goggles while all about me are clad in expensive athleisure wear.

I take my first few steps into the water, still feeling foolish as I stumble slightly over the uneven ground, the only swimmer in sight. And then I plunge in, soft as a sigh, arms taking lazy strokes through cool, clean water, and I don't care what I look like anymore. As I swim, the sun draws itself higher in the sky and my cheeks warm. I pass ducks and swans, who glide past, haughtily indifferent, but no one else. I feel like if I could stop time and just live in this one moment – far from coronavirus, far from the threat of climate crisis – I would.

But I can't, so I paddle back to reality, do the getting changed dance all over again, and sit on the banks of the lake, contentedly munching on a stale but tasty breakfast brioche that I'd purchased the day I left London – a lifetime ago now. My lake-cooled skin tingles in the warm glow of the sun, and I feel like I am glowing too. The next twelve hours in another new city lie ahead of me, brimming over with potential and promise.

By the time I get back to the city centre, Munich is just about waking up. I take myself for coffee and waffles at Bean Batter, a café near Central Station recommended by a friend; I cruise the Marienplatz and am standing in front of the *Rathaus* (town hall) in time for the endearingly out-of-tune glockenspiel for the midday show; and, as it's a knockout of a day, with the last hints of Indian summer in the air, I head off in the direction of the *Englischer Garten* (a public park which derived its name from the informal landscape style popularised by Capability Brown in England in the eighteenth century). On the way, a not-unattractive young man matches my stride and strikes up a conversation: what am I doing here in Munich? I immediately assume he's trying to rob me rather than, say, chat me up, and I cling onto my rucksack a little tighter. It's not that this kind of thing never happens to me anymore, just that it rarely happens when I've spent the night trying to sleep on a train seat before going for an outdoor dip, and neglecting to shower, brush my hair or apply make-up. There is still pond scum between my toes. I answer him politely nevertheless, chirping, 'for tourism!' and wonder why English suddenly sounds like my second language.

'But Germany is awful. Why would you come here?'

'What do you mean, it's "awful"?'

'It's just the worst place for a holiday. You could go to Italy, Spain, Greece ...'

Now, I don't completely dispute this young man's point. If I were to pick a top holiday destination, it certainly wouldn't be Germany. There's nothing inherently wrong with the place but, when you have the whole world at your disposal, it would be pretty far down the list for most travellers – and so when you fly, you usually don't choose it. You plump for the top-tier, strictly A-list destinations, and bypass all the bits of the world that aren't considered the 'best'. But, as my suitor grumbles on and on about his 'lacklustre' home nation, I have a sudden Damascene moment: *this is where train beats plane.* If I were flying, I'd never have come to Munich and had an extra day of delightful discovery. I'd have gone straight to Croatia and back, no dawdling, no distractions. But travelling by rail, when my journey took me through the city not once, but twice, it would have been churlish not to stop off and explore. Travelling by train meant I got to see somewhere new that I might never have got around to visiting otherwise; and that is a beautiful thing.

Rant over, he makes his move: 'Would you like to sunbathe with me?'

'Um ... No thanks.'

Perhaps I should have embraced the adventure and said yes. But it was so long since I'd slept – and making small talk with a stranger who wanted to badmouth the lovely city I was exploring with fresh, unjaded eyes was about as appetising as most German food (I'm sorry, but I won't be dying on that particular hill).

The English Garden is simply magnificent. It's one of Europe's biggest urban parks, and a high point is the freezing-cold River Eisbach – literally meaning 'ice brook' – that runs through it. This fast-flowing channel gets big enough waves at one junction that people go there to surf; at other spots, they come prepared with giant rubber rings and hop in, using it as an all-natural river-rapid ride. Others dunk and leave, using it as a cooling-off point on a sunny day.

I set up camp on its banks for an exquisite form of people watching bordering on the absurd. At one point, a group of grown men enter the current atop hot-pink unicorn inflatables, beers in hand. At another, an extremely fat, extremely naked man with tanned skin the colour of a polished conker strides in, hands on hips, submerges himself, and strides out again (rather neatly proving my point about Germans' comfort level with nudity).

The sun flashes off the teal-coloured water as lovers, friends, children and families all come to take a turn about the park using the Eisbach's fast-flowing current. I'm tempted to join them, stopped only by the fact that my passport, phone, purse and all my train tickets are in my bag – the heart-stopping anxiety of leaving them by the water's edge while I head off to who-knows-where would most definitely outweigh the enjoyment of doing so.

Having sampled a few of the city's highlights, my gaze is pulled more and more frequently to my watch, as I await the hallowed hour of 3 p.m., when I can check into my hotel with impunity and, I'm not ashamed to admit it, take a nap. I wish I was still young and energetic enough to 'push through' the exhaustion barrier but, alas, I know myself. I have reached a stage in life where a bad night's sleep can't just be brazened out – it is a debt that must be repaid, swiftly and in full. I head back to my crashpad, nonchalantly breezing in at 3.01 p.m. as if I hadn't been waiting outside for five minutes, counting down the seconds. I'm directed up to a chic, modern room where, once inside, I only have eyes for the expansive bed. *Hello, big boy.* I fall upon it, fully clothed, and only wake when my alarm tells me it's time for dinner.

It may be touristy but, heck, I *am* a tourist, and so I make a beeline for Hofbräuhaus, an iconic beerhall where there are huge steins aplenty and oompah music plays relentlessly in the background. Due to my aforementioned aversion to bratwurst served in various ways, I instead order two pretzels the size of my head and spend the evening eating my own bodyweight in salty bread washed down with *Weissbier*. The atmosphere is lively and convivial, and I feel the blissed-out, tired contentment of flying – or should that be train-ing – solo. Sharing experiences with someone else is all well and good, but the feeling of freedom that accompanies the lone traveller, master (or indeed mistress) of your own destiny, picking and choosing what you do and where you go without consultation or lengthy debate, is truly liberating.

The following morning, Munich proves itself a worthy tourist destination once again: there is a real-life breakfast buffet at the hotel. Yes, in days gone by this would hardly be worthy of comment, but during a pandemic? I thought I'd never see one out in the wild again. There's a one-way system in place and mandatory gloves and masks, but I'm free to construct my own carefully curated plate filled entirely with beige foods – croissants, pastries, waffles, pancakes and muffins – with no one to judge my life choices. I could not be happier.

With that, it's time to get back on the rails. The journey to Paris would be entirely uneventful were it not for one key element: the second leg is on board a double-decker train. Is there anything more exciting? Well, yes, if you're from a country that has double-decker trains. But when you hail from a place where the term 'double decker' exclusively applies to chocolate bars and buses, it is a thing of wonder. I sit atop the second tier, at the height of trees and giants, and, looking down upon the world with a smug benevolence tempered by mild disdain, wonder if this is what God must feel like ...

Damn, I love Paris. It is the only city in the world where I feel giddy as soon as I arrive, with the thought 'I'm in Paris! I'm in *Paris*! I'm in PARIS!' running circles in my head. I feel like I've snuck into a celebrity party whenever I visit, all glamour and champagne and great lighting, and at any moment someone's going to realise I don't belong there and throw me unceremoniously out the door.

The French even manage to make face masks look chic, and in September 2020 they are wearing the heck out of them – inside, outside and everywhere in between – with a diligence that makes me realise just how lax we've been in the UK. They only seem to take them off to smoke (this is still Paris, after all).

I wind my way to the once-seedy-now-cool Marais district and check into Sinner, a hotel so sexy I feel like I need a cold shower five minutes after entering. The dark-lit lifts have glowing red ceilings in a pattern reminiscent of confessional booths; the blackout corridors lead to uplit red doors with black iron fists for knockers; there is free perfume to spritz and complimentary lube in the bathroom. Everything about the place screams, 'Go on, have some sex!' and I feel the shine is taken off my whole solo traveller bit, just a little. Still, I make use of all the amenities (barring the lube), even listening to the in-house hotel radio station as I primp and preen, ready for a Big Night Out *à Paris*.

A red button-up blouse, red lipstick and shades – hell, the only things missing are a string of onions, baguette and beret. I take myself for a stroll to the Louvre, where I join the well-dressed set for a drink opposite the famed glass pyramid as the sun sinks low in its reflection. One of my favourite bits about travel is the ability, just for a day or two, to pretend you are an entirely different person with an entirely different life. Right now, I am sampling 'carefree woman in red who sips gin cocktails on a late summer's eve, and orders in impeccable French from behind giant sunglasses'.

It's a good fit, but not one I can keep up for long. Despite eighteen months of diligent Duolingo lessons, it turns out my *français* is just fine until anyone asks me anything even vaguely unexpected, whereupon I crumble into dust.

But I soldier on regardless, giving up my pescatarianism for the first time in years to order steak frites at Bouillon Chartier, a restaurant where the waiters exude a kind of gruff charm comprised of giving every impression they would rather be anywhere else while simultaneously scribbling orders on the tablecloths and serving up your dinner within minutes.

Half a bottle of wine in and I'm feeling a rosy glow when I make the questionable decision of finishing up with a baba au rhum. They don't mess around when it comes to this booze-filled dessert – it is literally some cake, swimming in eighty-proof rum and, after two spoonfuls, I note I have tipped over from warmly tipsy to quite possibly drunk. I'll only really know once I get outside.

I weave myself through the tables, feel the fresh air hit me and, giggling uncontrollably as I spot a cat in a shop window, conclude that, hey, drunk it is. But what a city to be drunk in! I stumble my way back to the Marais, smiling at everyone I see and forgetting that the gesture is completely meaningless, hidden behind a face mask.

Slipping into my hotel, I note it has somehow become even sexier in my absence – incense-like smoke is pouring forth from the restaurant, setting the tone for either an orgy or a child sacrifice. In fact, they've used the same incense you get at Catholic churches to complement the whole 'sinner' theme, and having spent every Sunday of my childhood dragged to mass on pain of death, the smell evokes a heady mixture of boredom, nausea and the sensation of busting for the loo but having to wait. Maybe not so sexy after all.

The following morning, it is 34°C. The Indian summer and/
or irrevocable climate change-induced temperature is a little too
spicy for my tastes – especially while having to wear a face covering
for most of the day – but I gamely kick off my tour early with a trip
to the Picasso Museum. From there I pop in for an obligatory but
lacklustre macaron at Ladurée, feeling more basic than an episode
of *Emily in Paris*, before wandering along the Seine, where it's so
quiet that I finally take my mask off and let the breeze airdry the
sweat from my face (a sensation that's a lot more enjoyable than
it sounds). Striking out east, I make my way to my most hotly
anticipated activity – a dip at the Josephine Baker, an outdoor pool
slap bang on the Seine. You can look out over the river in between
lengths, and then sun yourself on the upper deck – all for €4.

Where else to go in the City of Love when the mercury rises
and you are very much alone? A quiet and shady idyll, cooled
further by the icy hand of death, is what I plump for. Morbid as
it sounds, the Père Lachaise Cemetery is the perfect place to wait
out a heatwave; in the shadow of majestic trees and, well, yes,
mausoleums, I wander pathways of the dead, perfectly at peace.
Not dissimilar to Highgate's famed cemetery in London, the
place has its own fair share of famous incumbents: Jim Morrison
is probably the weirdest celeb corpse, but less unexpected
residents include composer Frédéric Chopin, singer Edith Piaf,
playwright Oscar Wilde and novelist Honoré de Balzac. Despite it
holding the title of 'most visited necropolis in the world', attracting some 3.5 million visitors a year, it is blissfully quiet.

Joining the land of the living again for my last ninety minutes,
I stop by a quintessentially Parisian restaurant terrace for tuna
steak and a glass of coldest rosé while I soak up the sun. I am
already experiencing the peculiar internal tension that comes
when the end of a trip is in sight – slight relief to be returning
home to the familiar, coupled with sadness to be dragged back to
reality and, in this case, quarantine, where nothing unexpected
is likely to happen to me for some time.

But such is the life of the frequent traveller. I grab my luggage and head back to Gare du Nord, actually fairly excited at the prospect of looking out of the window at rural France rushing by as evening falls. There'll be a light dinner and, more enchantingly still, mini bottles of wine to choose from. It feels like the chicest of treats in the way a short-haul flight never does.

Making my way up to the Eurostar terminal, I'm a little confused. There aren't a lot of people. In fact, there are just two young men sitting morosely on their suitcases. Hmm. I stride confidently towards the doors, to find they are locked. Now, at this point, the savvy traveller – or just a person with a baseline amount of common sense – would wonder if perhaps the train wasn't running. They might use their phone to take a gander at the Eurostar website, or even settle for asking one of the depressed-looking gentlemen outside the terminal. But none of this occurs to me – the rigid thought *I am going home this evening* refuses to buckle, even under the weight of mounting evidence to the contrary – and so I descend and look for another way up. There are lifts that take you inside the Eurostar terminal, circumventing those pesky locked doors. Ping! I am on the other side, though in truth, there's no one here either: no passengers, no staff, no one manning the border-control check points. I find myself stubbornly wrestling a very large, wheeled suitcase through the cordoned-off security section and press on blindly until I reach another set of locked doors. It is only at this very late stage of the game that my brain finally fizzes half-heartedly into gear, managing to throw up the rogue thought, 'erm, maybe the train isn't happening?'

A very kind French woman finds me in my fevered wanderings and confirms that, yes, she believes Eurostar have been cancelling a lot of the scheduled services. 'But ... but I'm going home!' I say with the guilelessness of a child. It's as if I simply can't comprehend that, after travelling for six days on trains, all the way to the Balkans and back, *this* is the hurdle that's going to stop me from completing the perfect itinerary.

'It happened to my daughter too – perhaps you can get a flight like she did?' she says, the unwitting temptress here to test me. Ha! Not today, Satan.

Still deep in my frugal interrailing mindset, I leg it to the nearest and cheapest accommodation option. As I'm handing over the exceptionally reasonable fee of €25, it hits me that this may be my first-ever hostel stay. And I feel a weird rush of, yes, excitement at the prospect. It's not that I'm some highfalutin traveller who demands all the trimmings – just that, having spent the last eight years in travel writing, I usually get offered rather smarter places to lay my head. Somehow, the whole hostel thing had passed me by.

Well, I'm not ashamed to admit it – I was impressed. A clean bed, enough sockets, serviceable communal showers, and all of it bright, modern and fit for purpose: it was excellent. I realise I sound like someone's mother telling their Gen-Z, tech-savvy kid that you can 'order things online, you know, over the internet!' and you are most welcome to roll your eyes.

There's nothing to be done but embrace my unexpected final night in Paris. I shower, trowel on some make-up over the day's sunburn and head west, with no real plan. After the evening I've had, I fully expect to be disappointed – to come across nothing but seedy-looking places or empty bars with overpriced drinks. But the god of good vibes is smiling on me, and within fifteen minutes I've rounded a corner onto a lively outdoor terrace lit by a neon sign, with a live band playing upbeat swing. It feels like a caricature of a good night out in Paris and, as I grab the last available table and order a champagne cocktail while the music plays and the crowd claps and cheers, I think this, if you could distil it, would be the pure essence of *bonhomie*. The 'bad luck' of having my final connection cancelled suddenly flip-reverses in my mind, feeling instead like a stroke of sweetest serendipity.

The next morning, everything runs like clockwork. There are actual Eurostar staff at the terminal (always a good sign), border-control agents, the works – with the only added hassle being the long and complex passenger locator form, necessitated by the pandemic, that must be filled in by all travellers entering the UK. After the small matter of providing a lock of hair, my dad's death certificate and the rights to my unborn first child, I am allowed onto the train. Big blue skies and wide green fields shimmer past as we race cross-country, and I feel I am returning after weeks away rather than days. The come-down after this exquisite high will be brutal – I'm now duty bound to quarantine for two weeks, missing the last gasp of summer and the first glorious taste of crisp, bright autumn. But, right now, whizzing along Teflon-smooth tracks as the sun filters through the carriage, going off the rails was undoubtedly worth it.

Carbon comparison
200kg of CO2e for a flight London Gatwick–Rijeka;
65kg of CO2e for a flight Rijeka–Munich;
110kg of CO2e for a flight Munich–Paris;
55kg of CO2e for a flight Paris–London
= 430kg of CO2e[1]

31.6kg of CO2e for a return train London–Paris;
38.2kg of CO2e for a return train Paris–Munich;
47.4kg of CO2e for a return train Munich–Rijeka
= 117.2kg of CO2e[2]

Carbon emissions saved: 312.8kg of CO2e

5

Carbon Guilt
Does Offsetting Actually Work?

Getting to western and central Europe by train was all well and good – but what if I wanted to get somewhere ultra-long haul where flight-free travel options just weren't feasible? Could I do so with a clear conscience by embracing the practice increasingly promoted by airlines as a quick fix to counter emissions: the dark art of offsetting? It was time to investigate whether carbon credits could be a legitimate way to hop on a plane, guilt-free.

In 2019, easyJet made a bold statement, announcing with much fanfare that it was going to be the first major airline to operate 'net-zero' flights by offsetting the carbon emissions from the fuel used for every passenger service.

Britain's biggest low-cost carrier was going to achieve this ambitious-sounding goal by 'investing in projects that include the planting of trees or protecting against deforestation and renewable energies'. It added, rather tellingly: 'We know carbon offsetting is not perfect, but right now we believe it's the best way to address the carbon emitted from flying.'

We know carbon offsetting is not perfect was seemingly easyJet's way of anticipating environmentalists' less-than-enthusiastic response to the news. *We know carbon offsetting is not perfect* was a way of pre-empting any criticism about this deeply problematic approach to addressing emissions produced by flying.

Carbon offsetting is one of the most contentious issues when it comes to air travel – and carbon emissions in general. Not so long ago, voluntary offsetting was an incredibly niche concern, adopted by only the greenest of sandal wearers to try to balance the scales. Then, just like that, pow! Like the condemning of plastic straws, the take-up of keep cups and conversions to veganism, it entered the zeitgeist as a way of 'doing your bit'.

While those using it are still very much in the minority, carbon offset company Cool Effect said individual purchases of its offsets rose 700 per cent between May and December 2019; Gold Standard, which certifies carbon offsetting programmes, saw offsets bought by individuals multiply by six from 2018 to 2019. Even royalty have been reduced to using it as an excuse when trying to get out of a tight spot: Prince Harry and Meghan Markle gave carbon offsetting as their primary defence in the summer of 2019 after being hounded by the press for taking multiple trips by private jet.

You didn't have to worry about flying less anymore – now, you could fly to your heart's content, and simply pay a bit more *not* to worry about it. Or, in the case of easyJet, let the airline worry about it for you. For many of us, it's the perfect means of appeasing our consciences without having to sacrifice our desire to keep travelling quickly and cheaply. We can pay some money and balance the scales – if I launched my own carbon offsetting project, I'd call it Guilt-Be-Gone! (exclamation mark included).

And, if it really resulted in carbon-neutral air travel, it *would* be the perfect product. Guilt-free flying on net-zero flights: sign me up. The one teensy, tiny problem? In reality, it's a whole lot more complicated than that.

What is carbon offsetting?

Let's start at the very beginning (a very good place to start).

The original thinking behind carbon offsetting goes like this: if countries are given certain targets to reduce their emissions, as they were in the Kyoto Protocol (a 2005 international treaty that committed industrialised countries and economies in transition to limit and reduce greenhouse gases) and the Paris Agreement (the first-ever legally binding global climate change agreement adopted worldwide, signed in 2016, which set out the aim of limiting the increase in global average temperatures to 'well below 2°C above pre-industrial levels'), that target needs to be reached overall – but there's quite a lot of flexibility around how it's achieved.[1] If a country committed to reducing carbon emissions by 70 per cent within a certain timeframe, for example, some parts of the economy might find it fairly easy to decarbonise – and might even go above and beyond, reducing their emissions by, say, 90 per cent. Another industry may struggle based on the nature of what they do (coal plants, as a rule, are not going to find this easy). But it's the big picture that matters in offsetting, so our coal plant, instead of having to reduce its emissions by 70 per cent, can purchase that first company's 'extra' emissions savings they made on top of the target – they can buy that 20 per cent. In fact, they don't have to stop there. They could buy extra reductions, in the form of carbon credits, from a developing country where an emissions-reduction project has been set up. More than 200 types of carbon offsetting projects have been given the nod by the Clean Development Mechanism (CDM), which certifies emission-reduction projects in these countries.

One of the most common types of offsetting schemes, favoured by many because it's cheap and relatively easy, is to plant trees. Trees absorb carbon – they 'breathe' it in. Therefore, if you plant enough of them it can technically pick up the slack for extra carbon emissions produced elsewhere. But reforestation is just the start of it. There are all kinds of offsetting projects, many with a focus on emissions reduction rather than removal. Renewable energy schemes are common in the offsetting world: for example, investing in wind farms, biomass energy, biogas digesters or hydroelectric dams. These don't absorb carbon in the way that trees do – the emphasis here is on replacing energy produced by fossil fuels with 'clean' energy.

What are the different kinds of offsets?

In general, schemes can be split into one of four categories: the capture of greenhouse gases for use or destruction; the reduction of greenhouse gases by reducing the amount of fuel or electricity needed to perform various activities; the capture and storage of greenhouse gases; or the reduction of carbon emissions by moving from fossil fuels to renewable sources of energy such as solar and wind energy.[2]

We won't stray too deeply into the murky world of carbon emissions trading – where, instead of reducing their emissions in line with what's required, companies can throw money at the problem by buying up carbon credits to offset their output – but suffice to say it's a thriving industry. It turns out our actions as individuals are being reflected on the global stage; just as many of us would rather say 'f*** it', jump on a plane and worry about our carbon footprint at some later, unspecified date, so would many industries.

No, rather than the compliance market, where government regulations require businesses to curb their emissions or buy up offsets by law, we'll be looking at the voluntary market, where regular Joes, like you and me, can buy offsets of our own volition.

This is a market that has blossomed in recent years, though it's still a minority of us who are doing it. Around 2 per cent of all online airline seat sales are offset, according to IATA,[3] while just 1 per cent of flyers use voluntary programmes to offset their emissions.[4] The voluntary market works in a similar way to the compliance market, but the difference is there's no central certification scheme like the CDM. Instead, various certifications and brokers have sprung up in this space to certify and sell carbon credits. While this means there's a tonne of choice – and in fact, in some cases might mean voluntary schemes are actually more trustworthy – it makes the whole thing harder to navigate as a consumer. With no centralised body, the onus is on you to do your homework and find the legitimate schemes.

How does it work in practice?

If I pay a tree-planting scheme to offset my flight, what happens next? Do they calculate how many trees would be needed to absorb my carbon and then get out there with a spade?

I can't be the only one who didn't realise that when you're buying a carbon credit, 'credit' is the operative word. In fact, what you're buying is an amount of emissions that has *already been saved*. This is how it works, in brief: a project is set up, for example, to plant trees. The trees are planted, they grow, the CO_2 reduction is calculated. Ideally some kind of certification scheme checks their work and verifies their calculations (if they're legit). They are awarded a certain number of carbon credits – each one representing 1 tonne of CO_2 that has been removed (or reduced) – which they can then sell, with the money usually going back into the scheme to, for instance, pay for more tree planting, thus creating more carbon credits. Once a credit has been bought, it gets 'retired from the register', meaning it can never be sold again. So, in reality, you're paying for something that has already been done.

'There's a logic behind it,' says Julian Ekelhof, director of CO2OL Climate Solutions, which oversees various sustainable land-use projects including reforestry:

We'd prefer it the other way around, because that's most intuitive. But that wouldn't be robust enough. It's done from a transparency and robustness perspective: you have to prove that the trees have been planted and demonstrate the decarbonisation you've already achieved. Only once it's been proven can you go ahead and sell it as credits.

You have to perform the climate effect before you can monetise it, otherwise it's too high-risk – there's a chance the tree doesn't grow or simply doesn't get planted in the first place.

It means projects have to pay the cash up front in the knowledge they'll make the money back later, which can be challenging. Every few years, projects are audited again, and new emissions reductions calculated, unlocking further carbon credits that can be sold and enabling the project to continue.

The same process is pretty much true no matter what the type of offset, although it's important to remember that there are a limited number of schemes where CO_2 is actually being removed from the atmosphere – trees being one of them – while a large proportion of projects just cut emissions by reducing the amount of fuel or electricity needed to perform an activity or by moving from fossil fuels to renewable sources of energy. Obviously, this is a good thing – but the idea we might have of a straightforward 'I produced *this* many tonnes of CO_2 by flying, and I bought carbon credits that took away the same amount of CO_2' is usually a world away from reality.

And, in fact, experts are keen to draw the distinction. There are carbon *reduction* projects, and there are carbon *removal* projects, and the latter are far preferable, according to the climate scientists I speak to. In September 2020, a team from Oxford University launched the Oxford Principles for Net Zero Aligned Carbon Offsetting (or the 'Oxford Offsetting Principles'), to provide guidelines to help ensure offsetting 'actually helps to achieve a net zero society'.[5] One of the key tenets? Second only to cutting our own emissions first and foremost and investing in high-quality offsets was switching to carbon *removal* offsetting.

'Most offsets available today are emission reductions, which are necessary but not sufficient to achieve net zero in the long run,' said the principles:

> Carbon removals scrub carbon directly from the atmosphere. Users of offsets should increase the portion of their offsets that come from carbon removals, rather than from emission reductions, ultimately reaching 100 per cent carbon removals by midcentury to ensure compatibility with the Paris Agreement goals.

Duncan McLaren, professor in practice for the Lancaster Environment Centre at Lancaster University, agrees that in thirty years the current offsetting model will be obsolete. He tells me:

> Fast forward to 2050: everything seems to be planned around this date for reaching net zero. Once you get to a place of cutting emissions by 100 per cent, the *only* offsets that can be left in a system like that are removals. We can't have the same system as right now.

So ... does offsetting work?

That's the million-dollar question. And, in truth, the answer is yes and no. (Or 'it's complicated' in the parlance of Facebook relationship statuses circa 2008.)

The big point to remember here is that these schemes need to be 'additional' – not existing projects that were happening anyway, but ones that only exist for offsetting purposes. For example, some offsetting projects are classified as 'forest preservation'; i.e., someone can charge money for simply making sure an existing woodland doesn't get the chop. Aside from the fact this is pretty sketchy as an offsetting concept to begin with, in many cases the forest might already have been being protected, funded by an environmental organisation or government grants, and therefore there's nothing 'additional' about it.

In fact, three-quarters of projects are unlikely to have resulted in additional emissions reductions and just 2 per cent have a high likelihood of being classed as 'additional', according to a 2016 study for the European Commission into United Nations-sanctioned offset projects.[6] That's because most energy-related offsetting projects are likely to happen anyway. There's already a strong demand for clean energy and 'a market that will pay', according to Friends of the Earth.

Professor McLaren tells me about a real-life example that sums up the 'additional' issue. A colleague of his got married, and the newlyweds asked all their friends and family to donate to an offsetting forestry project as their wedding present. A few years later, the couple decided to visit the forest; but when they asked the site manager to point out 'their' trees, they were told everything had been paid for by a woodland grant. The trees would have been planted regardless thanks to this money – the project was not 'additional' at all. It's a problem called 'double counting' and is one of the potential pitfalls that come with offsetting.

Clearly, this doesn't apply to all projects; but there are other issues too.

For offsetting to truly work, whatever the scheme is has to *permanently* lock away or reduce carbon emissions – otherwise it just doesn't add up. Balance is not restored. Tree planting, on the face of it, is a simple, effective way of storing carbon; as a tree matures, it can take in 21 kg of CO_2, plus other greenhouse gases, per year. But trees, as we know all too well, are exceptionally vulnerable. Forest fires, pests, deforestation: all these things happen with enough regularity that we know trees are in no way a 'permanent' storage solution. A study in the US found that the number of trees that die from pests per year is the equivalent of 5 million cars' worth of emissions.[7]

Elsewhere, emissions calculators don't always add up. Things can get murky with flying in particular, because a tonne of CO2 from a plane is not the equivalent of a tonne emitted at ground level. Burning fuel at altitude produces a load of other harmful emissions and impacts that also contribute to warming the planet.

In the voluntary sector, at least, there is a pretty good level of reassurance now that, if you're buying through a reputable scheme backed up by a reputable certification, the emissions savings will be accurate and the scheme itself will provide additionality. But that's no longer the biggest issue opponents have with offsetting.

Putting off action

Perhaps the biggest problem of all with the entire concept of offsetting is that it can provide a false sense of security – a comfort blanket that allows us to put off doing the urgent mitigation work that's needed to tackle the climate crisis. On a compliance level, it allows high-emissions industries to delay the point at which they have to hugely adapt their businesses to decarbonise. Industries like the aviation sector, for example. Professor McLaren says:

> This is one of the reasons we haven't made the progress we'd like to with cutting emissions. The pressure from companies in those markets means there's been a lot of latitude – it's easy to buy excess emissions permits and maintain your form of business that involves producing emissions. What offsetting has done is make it easier to move slowly. In fact, offsetting as a market tool is one of the reasons we're now in the hole we're in.

Stefan Gössling, a professor at the Linnaeus University School of Business and Economics and Lund University's Department of Service Management, who specialises in sustainable tourism, concurs that offsetting is at odds with decarbonising air travel: 'If offsetting is your strategy, how are you thinking about the future? How are we going to fly carbon free at some point?'

The plus side

Offsetting can remove the incentive to change. That said, there certainly are reputable projects, and although not viable in the long term, in the short term they can be vital as part of an overall emissions reductions strategy, argues Julian Ekelhof: 'Are offsets the solution? Definitely not. No one working in this field would say that. But it is one measure we can use – so many things need to be combined for us to achieve our targets.'

When asked how we can rely on a project making a real difference, he makes a convincing case:

> Long-running forestry carbon projects, for example, have been monitored over several decades now. It's been proven to be solid. Risk is reduced with assessment, you have measures in place for fire protection and disease control, you have to prove you have the land title so no one cuts down the trees. If there's a harvest, that's taken into consideration. Plus, there are risk buffer systems – you always have to over-produce, to over-perform for what is used as carbon credits, so that you're still covered if one part of the project is lost.

He adds:

> There are certain inherent risks, but it's not like anyone is planting trees and hoping for the best. Not every reforestation

project should be a carbon project. But with the ones that are, the risk is so minimal that the benefits far outweigh the problems.

What about greenhouse gas removal?

Forget trees – there's now a heap of carbon removal tech out there, often heralded as our saving grace.

DAC

First up, there's direct air capture (DAC) or, as I like to call it, the magical carbon-sucking machine. It sounds like pure science fiction: a tool that's capable of absorbing carbon from the atmosphere, which is then stored away underground. A 2019 study published in *Nature Communications* said this technology could help us meet the Paris Agreement's temperature targets at a lower cost.[8] So why are we even bothering to cut emissions at all?

Well, as with all things in life, if it sounds too good to be true, it probably is. The same study outlined that DAC would have to be rolled out intensively and at a breath-taking speed to achieve the required results. And, more importantly, in their modelling of future impacts, the study authors found that the energy needed to run the machines would hit 300 exajoules a year by 2100. That's the equivalent of half of all current energy supplies. Or, to put it another way, the energy demands of China, the US, the EU and Japan combined. Or, to put it *another* way, running 300 internets simultaneously. Even if energy demand goes up as predicted, it would still have to use a quarter of all energy supplies by 2100; and using a quarter of the entire world's energy supplies to get us out of a hole we're still doggedly digging for ourselves instead of, y'know, stopping digging now, sounds a little frivolous.

Even the study's authors warned of the dangers of relying on DAC to do the work rather than cutting emissions. 'Inappropriate interpretations [of our findings] would be that DAC is a panacea and that we should ease near-term mitigation efforts because we can use it later in the century,' said study author Ajay.

Dr Nico Bauer, a scientist at the Potsdam Institute for Climate Impacts Research, told Carbon Brief of the paper:

> Policymakers should not make the mistake to believe that carbon removals could ever neutralise all future emissions that could be produced from fossil fuels that are still underground. Even under pessimistic assumptions about fossil fuel availability, carbon removal cannot and will not fix the problem. There is simply too much low-cost fossil carbon that we could burn.[9]

There's also the issue of what to do with the greenhouse gases once you've removed them. Some schemes build up the amount of carbon in the biological environment, such as planting trees or putting carbon back into the soil: both of which are fairly short-term solutions. Many ideas revolve around trying to get carbon back underground in mineral form, a much more permanent type of capture.

BECCS

One of the most commonly discussed technologies is bioenergy with carbon capture and storage (BECCS). You harvest biomass (e.g. trees), and process it in a way that can be used to produce energy. If, for example, you burn the trees, you then use chemicals to capture the carbon they release as it comes up the chimney and store it underground. As long as you replace the trees, in theory you have a carbon-negative energy-production process: trees take carbon from the atmosphere, you burn it, capture it and store it underground.

CCU

Other techniques have been developed, too, where the carbon captured isn't stored somewhere, but is reused, a process known as carbon capture and utilisation (CCU). It could be used to carbonate drinks; more excitingly still, it could be used to create hydrocarbons, taking hydrogen from water and carbon from the air to create synthetic electrofuels. Why should I give two hoots about synthetic electrofuels, you ask? Well, these are the very kind of fuels that could conceivably be used to power planes at some point in the future. If you got the balance right, you could end up with carbon-neutral aviation using this tech, whereby flights are recycling the same amount of carbon they emit. The possibilities are actually pretty exciting, even for us non-science types.

Is GGR the answer?

Many climate scientists agree that greenhouse gas removal (GGR) technology is going to be a fundamental piece of the puzzle in achieving a carbon-neutral society.

Dr Roger Tyers, a researcher in environmental sociology specialising in behaviour change and public policy, certainly thinks so:

> I have a lot of faith in those kinds of man-made solutions. Natural solutions don't really work. Carbon neutrality will have to involve man-made carbon negative emissions technology. It's going to involve machines. You can't just compensate by planting more trees, nice as that sounds – it's like taking a knife to a gun fight.
>
> In a way it seems counterintuitive – we pollute the atmosphere with machines and then we're using machines to deal with the problem – but Mother Nature doesn't care about what's aesthetically pleasing.

Professor McLaren agrees:

> Almost certainly we've got to the point where it seems highly unlikely to achieve our desired temperature outcomes by simply reducing emissions. Even with the best will in the world, we're not going to step off a cliff and halt all emissions tomorrow. When you take into account the significant amount of emissions that will still be produced between now and 2050, we're going to need these technologies.

What's problematic is when we start to rely too heavily on the idea that future technology can 'save' us, and that we don't need to drastically change the way we live now to make it less carbon intensive. Professor McLaren says:

> The risk is that we collectively do less to cut emissions now, because GGR tech seems to have the potential to roll back time. It means notionally we might assume we can emit now and take it back later. But at the moment, GGR technology does not exist at the scale we would need to do that. We can't just imagine infinite carbon removal to remove infinite emissions.

There's always a cost to these technologies, whether it be massive energy consumption or the requirement for great swathes of land. In one climate modelling forecast, the model highly recommended the mass use of BECCS to sort out the problem of excess emissions; the programme ran the information and decided it looked much easier and cheaper than doing the hard work of reducing emissions. But its modelling required a piece of land *twice the size of India* in order to grow enough biomass to achieve the stipulated targets. There is always, always a cost, and it's usually too high.

This tech needs to be used thoughtfully and strategically, too, for the emissions we absolutely cannot eliminate – not as a catch-all to ensure our lifestyles can remain unchanged. If we have a limited amount of capacity for GGR technologies, due to the constraints of land or energy use outlined above, there's a danger that it could be sold to the highest bidder rather than ringfenced for those who need it most. Professor McLaren continues:

> The thing that worries me is seeing big companies making net zero pledges. Very few are saying they're going to cut emissions to next to zero. They say they'll cut emissions by 30, 50, 70 per cent – and then they're going to use removals. Aviation and big tech could end up annexing all the carbon removal capacity that we have.

So ... yeah. Back to that Facebook status: it's complicated. GGR is a tool that's likely essential in helping us meet our climate targets, just like regular offsetting – but it ain't no silver bullet.

Can I trust the offsetting industry?

Despite the recent surge in interest, voluntary offsetting for flights still has a pretty low uptake. Partly it's down to cost – a bona fide offset won't actually come that cheap – and partly it's down to lack of trust in the system.

'People thought that carbon offsets were not likely to actually deliver what they were reported to and had scepticism about whether the money is going to go to planting trees or fund renewable energy,' said Dr Tyers in a 2018 study he conducted to look at whether 'nudging' consumers to use voluntary carbon offsetting schemes for air travel would work.[10] Using controlled trials and focus groups, the technique was largely found to be 'ineffectual'.

Where does this lack of trust come from? Well, for many years the voluntary carbon market was a sector that felt a little like the Wild West. In its early days, many project developers used 'internal methodologies' to calculate their schemes' emissions reductions. There were no checks, no verifications from a central body – you could just work out your own numbers (potentially rounding up if you felt so inclined), submit them, and there would be no repercussions. The double-counting issue we looked at earlier was a huge problem, as was transparency when it came to trying to research a project yourself as a consumer.

Things have improved considerably since then; today, the majority of projects follow rules and procedures set out by an external certification standard, meaning they have to meet a third party's criteria and work to their methodologies in order to sell carbon credits. Regulation is a lot tighter now than it was even a decade ago. But, even so, it's difficult to navigate as a well-intentioned traveller.

According to Sarah Leugers, the director of communications for offsetting certification scheme Gold Standard, the voluntary market in its current form cropped up 'because of a failure of political will':

> The various standards were created to try to fill some of the gap that national negotiators have left. There's been some good in that organic ability to innovate; different standards have been introduced to fit different needs. We didn't work in forestry at all initially, so another certification cropped up to fill that. It's really about bottom-up innovation.

Gold Standard is one of the most exacting certifications dealing with the voluntary market. It was originally set up in 2003 by conservation NGO WWF specifically because they were concerned that the UN's CDM certification was not robust enough. And for a project to qualify, it really does have to deliver what it says on the tin (and then some). Sarah says:

> A project has to design-in not just climate benefits, but impact for at least two other sustainable development goals in order to

qualify. They have to submit a monitoring plan that's approved. After planning, the project gets design certification, which is reviewed by an independent third party. It moves forward, the impact is measured, and after around a year the project goes through performance certification – a third party again reviews it and does a site visit. That's when our partner says yes, this project should be issued x number of carbon credits.

Projects have to prove their 'additionality' (to dispel those double-counting worries) and provide accurate baselines before going ahead so that there's clear, measurable proof of the climate impact later down the line. It's a lengthy process. Not only that – a scheme can't get certification if it's reducing emissions but to the detriment of the local people. Projects must adhere to a comprehensive set of safeguards, both environmental and social, to ensure local stakeholders are engaged and on board.

As a consumer, there's also a reassuring amount of data available if you're buying credits from an initiative that follows an internationally recognised standard. Sarah continues:

You can go to our registry and look up monitoring reports and verification reports, all publicly available. If someone were to purchase directly from us, they would see credits they bought being retired from the registry in real time, so there's a real traceability connected to the purchase.

Julian Ekelhof, whose forestry schemes are Gold Standard certified, agrees that transparency is built into the process:

The certification includes hundreds of pages of documentation, criteria, independent auditing and monitoring of the project. There's complete transparency – you can look it all up.

There's also a period of public consultation – so if you're being verified, there's a period where everyone can check exactly what the auditor has done. We've had people visiting the project, we've worked with universities, we invite anyone with a question about the project to come directly to us. The projects' locations are public as well – if you want you can even look us up and see satellite images to check the forests really do exist.

Of course, Gold Standard isn't the only certification in the voluntary market. To name but a few, there's the Verified Carbon Standard (also confusingly known as VCS or Verra); the Voluntary Offset Standard (VOS); Climate, Community and Biodiversity Standards (CCB); Brasil Mata Viva Standard (BMV); and SOCIALCARBON. And each has its own list of criteria that projects must meet in order to qualify, plus its own methodologies in calculating climate impact.

Wouldn't it be easier if there was just one centralised body or regulator so you knew which offsets were absolutely worth your money? Well, yes, is the short answer – and it's something that is increasingly gaining traction. Dr Tyers states:

Standardisation would help. The UN is trying to do something about this. Whether I like it or not, offsetting isn't going away – I think if one body came out and said, 'these offsets are good, these ones are not,' that would meaningfully go some way towards helping consumers have confidence.

The former governor of the Bank of England Mark Carney is heading up the Taskforce on Scaling Voluntary Carbon Markets (TSVCM), aimed specifically at increasing the size, efficiency and transparency of the voluntary carbon market; some kind of standardisation might well come out of the taskforce's recommendations.

'We're trying to create a global set of standards that hopefully can influence government policy,' said Bill Winters, chief executive of Standard Chartered and Taskforce chair.[11] 'Part of the objective here is to put clear, transparent standards and benchmarks out there.'

How can you tell if an offset is legit?

It can feel overwhelming to discern which offsets are delivering the goods in a sea of conflicting information and rampant cynicism. First off, it's worth ensuring that whatever offsetting scheme you use is verified by an internationally recognised independent standard. From there, do a bit of research if you want peace of mind: how transparent is the project? Is more information easily available, such as audits, the location, in-depth details about how it operates and the amount of emissions reduced? If it seems in any way opaque, that should be red-flag central. Gold Standard's Sarah says:

> Make sure you look at the fine print. Look at where the money's going, what the underlying standards are, and make sure they disclose the proceeds. It's up to people to do a little more due diligence, like with almost any sustainability claim these days.

Forestry Project Manager Julian Ekelhof is adamant that checking the robustness of a scheme goes 'beyond certification' too:

> Yes, the first stop is absolutely that it's a requirement to be certified. But you have to look further. It's not just, do the trees grow – but was there a consultation with local stakeholders, is anyone else claiming the carbon offset, for example the government, the locals, a company that uses it in their supply chain. Look for the project design document – if it's public, you know it's been peer reviewed and checked. Is there more than a nice picture gallery? Is there information on the location

available, has someone with no vested interest visited the project? These things are crucial.

There's also a distinction between schemes that reduce emissions and those that remove them, as we saw earlier. If what you really want is to restore balance in a more literal sense when you fly, consider opting for something that actually takes CO_2 out of the atmosphere. One example is Climeworks, which uses DAC technology to remove CO_2 and transform it into carbonate minerals stored 800–2,000m underground. If you need more convincing, Greta (yes, *that* Greta) even visited one of their plants in March 2020 to see how the tech could be used in the fight to stop global warming.

Finally, the uncomfortable reality is that any carbon credit worth its salt will set you back a few bob. If it costs £1 to tag an 'offset' onto a flight as an optional extra, for example, there's no way it's anything more than greenwashing.

'You can't trust incredibly cheap offsets,' warns Dr Tyers. 'The only truly meaningful offsets are fairly expensive.' Sustainable transport expert Professor Gössling agrees that a good offset will 'probably cost at least £20 a tonne'. In real terms, this means a round trip from London to New York – which produces, on average, 2.8 tonnes of emissions (in total, including warming impacts other than CO_2) per economy passenger – would set you back an extra £60. Bear this in mind if you're shopping around: carbon credits are a commodity where getting a 'good deal' actually isn't a good deal at all.

How do I calculate my emissions?

In terms of calculating emissions specifically relating to aviation – and therefore taking into account extra harmful gases released when fuel is burned at altitude – Atmosfair is recommended to me by several experts, including Jo Dardenne, aviation manager for NGO collective the European Federation for Transport and Environment. A German non-profit, Atmosfair specialises in using voluntary climate payments from private individuals and businesses to fund renewable energy projects in fifteen developing countries. The best bit about using it to offset flights is that Atmosfair's emissions calculator has been finely calibrated for flights. As its website reads:

> The calculations include the effects of the different pollutants according to the latest scientific knowledge, especially to their impact at high altitude ... flight altitude, aircraft type, the number of seats on board and how many of them are occupied all play a very important role in the calculation of emissions.

What is the aviation industry doing?

While most airlines and various countries' aviation industries are promising to become greener – the global aviation industry says it aims to halve emissions (compared to 2005 levels) by 2050, and the UK aviation industry has pledged to cut its net carbon emissions to zero by the same year – it's really important to note that aviation *was not included under the Paris Agreement*. Yes, you heard me correctly. The Paris Agreement 'does not establish sector-specific goals for addressing potential temperature rise' – and that has largely left it up to individual nations to decide what limits to impose.[12]

In the UK's case, that meant putting off addressing the issue for as long as possible. The 2008 Climate Change Act was supposed to apply to all sectors, outlining how emissions needed to be cut. But international aviation and shipping were both left out of the five-year carbon budgets, seemingly because it was quite tricky to calculate.[13] The government did the equivalent of shoving it under the mattress – out of sight, out of mind – but promised that these industries would be included by 2012. But 2012 came and went, and aviation emissions continued to be kept separate from overall targets. Although carbon budgets for other sectors were set with the aviation issue in mind – allowing for emissions from flights and airports to take up around a whopping 25 per cent of all of the UK's total permitted carbon emissions by 2050 – this was not officially enshrined in law. This led to a situation where the government could both make a lot of noise about hitting net zero by 2050 while simultaneously supporting airport expansion.

Think about it: every sector's getting limits put on it, caps that mean it has to radically change how it operates or invest heavily in offsetting schemes. But not airlines. They could keep flying as much as they like, free from restraint, with no incentive to adapt.

In fact, the UK only included aviation and shipping emissions for the first time in its sixth official climate budget, in 2021 – and even then it doesn't come into effect until 2033. This, despite the UK being responsible for the third-highest amount of CO_2 emissions from aviation globally, behind only the US and China.[14]

The industry is still attempting to skirt the problem by coming up with its own version of what it believes will balance the scales – or at least have the appearance of doing so. Allow me to introduce you to the Carbon Offsetting and Reduction Scheme for International Aviation – more commonly known as CORSIA – a mitigation approach developed by the International Civil Aviation Organization (ICAO). From 2027, CORSIA has stipulated that airlines will have to purchase carbon offsets for all international flights. Michael Gill, IATA's director for aviation environment, said:

> It's mandatory in the sense that it creates obligations on airlines to purchase offsets rather than obligations on individual

passengers. [Airlines] will be obliged for every year after the scheme comes into effect to purchase offsets in respect of any growth in their emissions above the 2020 baseline.

The money will be pumped into reforestation and renewable energy projects, with the scheme aiming to introduce more transparent criteria for offsetting aviation emissions than is currently found in the voluntary market. We're about to have our flights offset whether we want to or not. Does this mean we can relax?

Ha! If only. *Any growth above the 2020 baseline* is the key bit to watch out for here. The idea was originally for 2020 emissions levels to form the baseline for each airline, with the mandatory offsetting ensuring CO_2 emissions are stabilised *at those levels*. So airlines won't actually be offsetting your flight for you – they'll only be offsetting any emissions over and above the incredibly generous baseline. They'll only be offsetting their *growth* as of this point onwards. For the environmentally conscious, it means nothing changes, whatever Mr Gill says – the onus is still on you to buy your own carbon credits on the voluntary market if you want to make sure you're covered for a flight.

In fact, the goalposts for CORSIA have already been moved: 2020's air traffic was deemed not to be a sufficient baseline after the mass grounding of flights during the pandemic, so they went with 2019's emissions instead. And considering how high levels of aviation and related emissions were in 2019 – with almost 40 million flights taking off that year – it could be argued that using this as a baseline is a tad stingy. 'That reduces the ambition of the scheme to zero,' as T&E's Jo Dardenne puts it. 'And airlines won't have to pay for offsets for at least five years, until 2027.' In the meantime, they're still pumping emissions into the atmosphere with no caps and no payback.

According to Jo, offsetting fundamentally cannot solve aviation's climate problems:

In principle, offsetting means you're going on a diet and paying someone else to go to the gym for you. And under the Paris Agreement, every sector needs to reduce as much as possible. We've got other sectors trying really hard – aviation can't just keep coasting.

Specifically, CORSIA doesn't encourage reducing emissions – you can continue polluting and just pay someone else to reduce instead, so we don't think the scheme fits in with our targets. We're focusing on regulators to ensure aviation pollution is reduced, and that means taxing and investing in cleaner fuels.

Gold Standard's Sarah concurs that we 'absolutely cannot rely on CORSIA. It's only taxing growth from 2019, not airlines' whole emissions. They're only responsible for offsetting their increase.'

What are airlines doing?

What about individual airlines that are already offsetting flights off their own bat or offering voluntary offsets? It's a tricky area, and one that's ripe for accusations of greenwashing, mainly because it's almost impossible to know exactly which projects are being funded, how much is being paid per carbon credit, and whether the numbers stack up in terms of accounting for fuel being burned at altitude.

EasyJet, for example, says it is using a combination of Gold Standard- and VCS- certified projects to offset every single one of its flights – an admirable achievement. But the first example it gives of a project it's investing in is 'forest regeneration' – the type of scheme I mentioned earlier where you're essentially paying for a forest *not* to be destroyed. It's such a nebulous shoot of offsetting that Gold Standard point blank refuses to certify these types of projects. It's not to say protecting forests doesn't have any benefit – of course it does – but the idea that this will make your flight 'carbon neutral', as easyJet claims, is simply preposterous.

Mind you, at least they're playing some kind of active role in offsetting. Most airlines simply link to a voluntary contributions scheme, complete with emissions calculators of varying quality. Some, such as Ryanair, offer customers the option to add on a couple of euros to their flight as a 'contribution' towards offsetting projects. As we've already seen, there's no way that €2 is going to legitimately offset your flight. In fact, €2 isn't going to do much more than ease your conscience. And in February 2020, only 3 per cent of Ryanair passengers were doing it anyway; perhaps indicative of a lack of trust that the money would really have an effect.

Even Dutch carrier KLM, one of the market leaders when it comes to making aviation more sustainable, appears to charge half of what it should for offsets in its voluntary scheme. According to its emissions calculator, an Amsterdam–Bogota round trip produces just over a tonne of CO_2 emissions per passenger.[15] The price of the offset is €18.58 (slightly less than the £20-a-tonne price we'd expect to pay for a good offset). Type the same journey into the Atmosfair calculator, and it gives the price as €84 for the same journey. On top of the tonne or so of emissions from CO_2, it adds on an additional 2.4 tonnes for the additional warming impacts of contrails, ozone formation, etc. – those 'CO_2e' impacts that were mentioned in chapter 1. It's clear from this comparison, then, that KLM's calculator doesn't take any of the additional warming impacts from flying into account – an issue that's problematic when it comes to buying carbon credits.

Meanwhile, a joint investigation into the offsetting schemes used by some of the world's largest airlines carried out by *The Guardian* and Unearthed, Greenpeace's investigative arm, found that their credits, generated by various forestry projects, appeared to be based on a 'flawed and much-criticised system' and should not be used to back up claims of 'carbon-neutral flying'.[16]

Perhaps it's unsurprising; with the best will in the world, you can't put your faith in the very industry that is causing the emissions in the first place.

So ... should I offset?

While it's still a small percentage of passengers who are buying offsets, more and more of us are doing it and, if Mark Carney's right, it's going to be a $50 billion business by 2030.

Despite the doom and gloom and handwringing of a lot of the above (my sincerest apologies), offsetting schemes aren't inherently a bad thing – far from it. Like many things in life, they're only bad when they're relied upon too much or used irresponsibly.

When it comes to aviation, the real issue is not those people who take a flight every couple of years and diligently offset using a robust scheme – it's those of us who fly much, much more frequently and think that offsetting truly mitigates our actions (or, in most cases, don't bother with it at all). It's airlines using the practice as an excuse not to inhibit growth in any way or heavily invest in developing alternative low-carbon or carbon-neutral fuels.

Even the projects and certifications themselves do not believe offsetting is the answer. 'Our work ethic is based on the following principle: only compensate what can't be avoided or reduced,' says Atmosfair. 'Offsetting cannot solve the problem of climate change since it does nothing to change the actual source of CO_2. It is a necessary second-best solution as long as the best solution does not yet exist. Individual flight passengers are responsible for examining their actions prior to offsetting emissions. For example, sometimes a video conference instead of a business trip suffices, a longer vacation can take the place of two shorter ones.'

It's the same story I hear from all of the experts I speak to: if you need to fly, offset, but reducing is best. Reduce first, *then* offset: this is the rule we should apply to every area of our lifestyles in order to live more sustainably. Dr Tyers says:

> I do think it should be a last resort. We need to change our behaviour, and the single fastest way to increase your carbon footprint is to fly, while the easiest way to cut your footprint is to fly less or not at all. Anything which diminishes the likelihood of us doing that can be dangerous.

It's the same guiding principle as the one that applies to industries: that they need to decarbonise as much as is physically possible, and offset what's left over only *after* putting the work in.

The reason being that, in theory, if emissions from the Global North were only tackled by offsetting, they would not be lowered enough to reach the targets for 2050 or 2100, according to the IPCC.[17]

Given that it's currently such a small market, the people who choose to offset their flights tend to have already considered the necessity of their journey; they're the ones who are most likely to be doing their bit by cutting back where they can, according to Professor Gössling:

> I think it's a different story when individuals [rather than industries] buy carbon offsets – because they have already considered whether or not they should fly, and they are then trying to bring the best out of the worst. If you buy high quality carbon credits, that can actually make a difference. Given there's only 1 or 2 per cent of people doing it, we shouldn't pick at them; they're probably the ones who have actually thought about whether they need to take their flight in the first place. I think for anyone who has decided to fly, it's still the better thing to do.

For essential flights then, ones where there's no alternative, offsetting can be a positive choice. One of the most important things, as we've already seen, is to do your research – find a scheme that you trust, that's certified, that you believe in. If we're going to use offsetting as a force for good, we have to fight the impulse to use it as a set of blinkers that allows us to disengage from our actions (and our guilt).

All in all, I think I've come around to the idea of offsets as a 'last resort'. The carbon credits market is often presented as something sinister when, in fact, it does a lot of good. It has a bad rep because of the people who *don't* use it responsibly – the schemes guilty of double counting or claiming additionality when there is none, the industries using it as a get-out-of-jail-free loophole to indefinitely put off decarbonising (of which aviation is undoubtedly one). And, as we'll see later, it's not that the technology doesn't exist to make zero-carbon flights a reality – on the contrary. But it's expensive and time-consuming to develop and implement, and airlines currently have little incentive to do so, with no limits put on their emissions or their use of cheap, abundant kerosene.

In the meantime, it's up to us to weigh up our consumption, to question which journeys by air are essential, to go forth and reduce as much as we can. And then, yes, to offset the flights we can't do without. It may be like paying someone to go to the gym for you – but at least *someone's* working out.

6

Drive Me Crazy
Learning to Hitchhike vs. Learning to Drive

Time to turn our attention to the UK's most popular form of transport: the car.

I know what you're thinking: driving isn't that great for the planet either though, right? Well, no – no it's not. Even with technology improving all the time, the sheer number of cars on the road is cause for concern. Transport is responsible for nearly 30 per cent of the EU's total CO_2 emissions, of which 72 per cent comes from road transportation;[1] in the car-mad UK, that second number is even higher, at an alarming 91 per cent.[2] But – and this is a big 'but' – a car travelling the same distance as an aircraft is going to produce 90g fewer CO_2 emissions per km, per passenger (provided you're travelling with a full carload).[3] And – and this is a big 'and' – life is all about compromise. If I'm shutting down options in one area, I want to open them up in another, to feel my horizons expanding even as people tell me going flight-free will never take off. So back off, yeah?

More importantly, the technology to decarbonise cars is already out there – thanks, electricity! And, especially during the pandemic, I felt a creeping envy of friends who could dash off for a weekend away when we were still being advised against getting on public transport for 'non-essential' journeys. There was a sense of wildest freedom – and, honestly, of being a proper grown-up – that I had come to associate with hopping in the car and driving off into the sunset wherever one damn well pleased. I thought back to those wonderful, endless car trips we'd taken when I was a kid as a means of getting on holiday – instead of jumping on a plane – and realised that, in fact, the journey was the only bit of the holiday I could still recall with any clarity, all of us singing along to those same three car tapes on repeat and having the time of our lives.

And so, I decided now would be the ideal opportunity to get to grips with motorised transport in two guises: learning how to drive myself, and learning how to convince someone else to drive for me (otherwise known as hitchhiking).

My experience of learning to drive was supposed to be quick, easy and painless. That's the whole *point* of doing an intensive driving course. Instead, it's not until six months after my five-day course that I am even able to book a test; by which time I have, of course, completely forgotten how to drive. This is what getting behind the wheel for the first time in fifteen years looks like during a pandemic.

I had always assumed I would be able to drive at some point in my life. I did have a stab at it in my late teens – countless lessons with a middle-aged man who bragged about the cost of his koi carp and refused to teach me the parking manoeuvres. Although I wasn't a natural by any stretch, looking back at that year, when I must have had upwards of thirty sessions, I do feel a little like he wasn't all that keen for me to pass, thereby soaking up a steady income stream. That's the tricky thing with driving instructors. There's very little incentive for them to be any good.

I left for university without having taken the theory or the practical test – the only upside being that I still had the potential to achieve the holy grail and 'pass first time' – and spent the next decade thinking little of it. No one had a car at university; not unless they were incredibly minted. The years that followed saw me move to London where, again, driving always seemed a rather foolhardy pursuit, what with the congestion charge and the low-emissions-zone tax and nowhere to park.

I happily got myself around the place via public transport and, later, by bike. But staring down the barrel of a year without flying, I decided that now might be the time to finally get behind the wheel. I would be joining the majority of British holidaymakers; a 2021 RAC survey found that, of the 48 per cent of respondents who said they would try to take a summer holiday in the UK, nearly three-quarters (71 per cent) planned on driving.[4] Although, as we'll see in future chapters, getting people out of cars and onto public transport is the ultimate goal, encouraging people off planes as much as possible in the meantime is a priority. For example, a family of four travelling from London to Cornwall by car instead of flying into Newquay will emit around 258kg less CO2 in total.[5]

And, with the best will in the world, public transport isn't always a viable option as it stands. I'd love to go to, say, Wales, on a whim. I'm always getting invited to Wales for work. All the trips sound brilliant. But every time I ask, 'Could I do it by public transport?' I'm met with an awkward silence.

'I mean, I'm sure we can ... there must be a way to ... Let me check with ... Um ... No, no not really.'

(Trains in Wales are insane, by the way. Take a look at a map and you'll immediately see what I mean. You can't even travel from the top to the bottom of the country along the west coast – instead, you have to catch a train *into England* and then head back out again. Utter madness.)

So, back to learning to drive. First things first, the theory test: it's really hard. No one tells you this. *No one*. Everyone I've ever spoken to about it calls it a 'piece of piss' and says there's nothing to worry about. They're right in some respects. About 80 per cent of it is common sense (what should you do if a driver cuts in front of you? a) stay calm, b) honk at him and shout expletives, c) flip him the bird, d) follow him home and murder his wife and child), but the other 20 per cent is the kind of very specific knowledge that can only come from spending quality time with the Highway Code. The minimum tread depth for tyres, for instance (1.6mm). The precise braking distance if you're travelling at 50mph (38m). These cannot be common sense-d their way out of, friend.

Then there's the hazard perception test, which seems to be less about perceiving hazards and more about perceiving them at the exact moment the test creator deems appropriate.

All in all, for someone who hasn't taken an exam in close to ten years, it is an anxiety-inducing nightmare of an experience – and anyone who tells you it's 'no big thing' is lying.

The stakes were particularly high when I did mine as, in classic journalist fashion, I left it till the very last minute – the Friday before I was due to start my intensive driving course. You can't even book your practical test until you've passed your theory. If I failed the theory, I could do the practical lessons – but there's no way I could finish the week with a licence, somewhat defeating the point of the whole palaver.

After a week of stressed-out studying and paying for extra mock hazard perception tests online, you'll be pleased to hear that I did pass it – but I promise to never make you feel bad if you failed yours. Or say it's a 'piece of piss'.

The first time I meet Neil, my instructor for the week, I'm reassured that it's all going to be OK. Not just driving – life, the universe, Brexit, all of it. He's everything you could wish for in a driving instructor: jovial and calm in a crisis, with a roguish east

London accent. Still, twenty-five hours is a lot of time to spend in a car with a man you just met. In classic millennial style, I'd decided to 'throw some money at the problem' and cram in a five-day course, five hours a day, with a test at the end.

I think it's hard for people who have been driving for years to recollect just how scary it is when you don't really know what you're doing. There you are, in a puny metal box, hurtling along at speeds that could literally kill someone – quite possibly you – just acting as if it is all totally normal. Everyone else in their metal box hates you, because of the big learner sign and your adherence to the national speed limit. People not in metal boxes simply stroll out into the road at will, far from any kind of official crossing; bus drivers brazenly pull out when you have right of way.

Despite all this, by day three I find I'm actually ... enjoying it, maybe? Or it could be I've just got a handle on my fear. Either way, I am doing less stalling in the middle of exceptionally busy junctions and clipping fewer wing mirrors as I go, although I still find it nigh on impossible to change lanes on a fast-moving dual carriageway without making little whining noises like a distressed baby animal who's lost its mother. And I still can't visualise passing my test – it seems like an impossible feat.

The really great thing about an intensive course, though, is that you make a crazy amount of improvement in a short space of time. Under normal circumstances, it would have taken me fifteen weeks – over three months – to achieve the progress I've made by 3 p.m. on Wednesday. Probably more, because each lesson you have to re-remember what you're doing all over again. I've heard some say it doesn't sound safe, but I genuinely disagree: having that much time in the car massively increases your confidence and skill level.

The downside is that, by the end of five hours, you feel that your brain is dribbling out of your ears like soup. The journey back from residential east London is spent staring into space, lightly drooling.

Day four feels critical. In real terms, there would still be ten weeks of lessons to go. In intensive terms, my test is tomorrow, and I still can't quite get the hang of turning right at traffic lights without hyperventilating and waiting for five minutes until there is not a single car on the road while Neil says – calmly and patiently, but with a slight edge to his voice – 'You can go. You can go now. Helen, why aren't you going?'

Today's the day I need to get past that. And the lane-changing thing. And roundabouts. And manoeuvres. At the moment, 50 per cent of the time, they work every time. I think the odds on that might need to improve slightly.

But on day five I get in the car feeling more at home than ever. Everything is second nature now – adjusting mirrors, getting in gear, pulling out and trundling along. I chat happily as we go, and realise that, yes, it is undeniable: I am having a *nice time*. It hits me that I really can drive – that I could pass this thing! – and it shouldn't be such a revelation, but it is.

We do a mock test and, I'll toot my own horn, I am *nailing* it. Every instruction is heeded, my hill start is perfection, my parallel park can't be beaten. But then. Then, the roundabout. I'm driving along thinking what a prodigy I am when we approach it – a big, uncontrolled one, with three lanes of cars hurtling around at speed. I always feel like I'm taking my life in my hands at this one. And so, perhaps trying to overcome my natural hesitancy, I *do* take my life in my hands: I completely lose my head and just keep driving. I'm about to go when my brain finally cranks into gear and communicates that there are a s***-ton of cars coming my way, and at the last moment I pull off something that's not quite an emergency stop but is definitely in the same neighbourhood.

I know immediately that I've failed but carry on with all the grace and dignity I can muster. At least it wasn't the real thing. The bad news is I did, indeed, fail. The good news is, it's the *only* thing I got wrong in forty minutes of driving.

It weirdly puts me in an extremely confident place to take my test. Which is ... when, you ask? On the Friday it transpires there is no test. All the available slots were booked up.

'Oh yeah, it's the busiest test centre in the country,' Neil tells me.

Then why am I taking my test here??? I want to shriek, but I bite my tongue.

'Something should come up next week.'

I'm still vaguely optimistic at this point. Maybe it's a good thing – time for my new skills to bed in. But nothing comes up the next week. It doesn't come the week after, nor the week after that. In fact, it's a full five weeks before I get the call to arms. Not ideal, but I'll have a three-hour catch-up lesson with Neil beforehand; I can totally still make this thing work.

And then ... coronavirus happens. From one week to the next, everything changes and all driving tests are cancelled for four months. Driving should be the least of my worries, and it is. But I feel like I'm back to where I started; I feel like this thing that so many people do so easily is always going to be just out of reach.

I did my course in February; in August I *finally* get a test.

Attempting to recreate the fluid feeling of the first time around, I book two three-hour lessons beforehand. What a difference six months makes – not in terms of driving, but in terms of Neil's physique.

'I've lost three stone!' he says proudly, and I congratulate him, realising sadly that I have lost nothing during lockdown other than my *joie de vivre* and a £50-a-month brunch habit. We pootle around the streets of Wanstead, and I'm pleased to note that, in the words of Celine Dion, *It's all coming back, it's all coming back to me no-o-owww.* Sure, I stall. I hit a wing mirror. But these are minor considerations compared to the fact I can remember where the clutch is.

Lesson two dawns a couple of days before the test and I'm feeling good. But what happens next convinces me that, rather than a random string of unfortunate events that have so far thwarted me, someone or some*thing* is actively conspiring against me. We set off, and I am smooth as silk. You would probably look at me and think, hey, that person is driving a car like a person who knows how to drive a car. Neil makes me pull over to try a hill start. I stall it. I stall it again, though it doesn't feel like it should stall. The engine completely fails to switch back on.

We swap sides and I sit there thinking how you have to see the funny side of life as Neil frantically tries the old classic, turning it off and on again, for a very long-feeling fifteen minutes. It eventually works, and we set off, although the car does a strange bunny hop down the road like a drunken kangaroo. It's making noises like it is very sick and wants me to know it would like to go home now, please. I stop at a traffic light. Attempt to start again. Nada. It is not an ideal place for this to happen, if we're being completely honest; unflappable Neil looks the tiniest bit flapped. Somehow, I know not how, he gets it working and drives me grimly back to the station, managing to deftly navigate the route without ever fully coming to a stop and thus avoiding total breakdown. The lesson is brought to an abrupt end, and I'm convinced the car is busted for good and that I'll never, ever get to take a driving test.

It's hot the day I take my first-ever driving test. And when I say hot, I mean 'hottest day of the year'-type hot. It is not the kind of day you want to be stuck in a sweltering tin can, forced to wear a mask while your face is pouring with sweat.

The AA managed to fix Neil's car without much of an issue. (Something to do with some kind of fluid? I wasn't really listening; I'm never going to be a person who knows a lot about cars, and I've just got to accept that about myself.) Neil even had my trusty steed cleaned for the big day, like a proud dad. It felt like an auspicious start.

Well, driving around in 37°C heat for three hours immediately before the test with no water – I forgot to bring any because, as we've already established, I am not a proper person – might have seemed like a good idea in theory, but in practice it had its flaws. By the end of it I was so hot, cross and dehydrated I was doing some pretty crazy s***: switching into fourth gear when I meant second; following a bus on a right-hand turn at a junction even though the lights had already changed and forcing oncoming traffic to stop and wait for me; almost bursting into tears when having to change lanes on the dual carriageway.

The closer we got to the test, the worse my driving got. 'I'll just be pleased if I don't kill someone,' I quip as we pull up at the test centre, only half joking. A nice man comes out to do my test, introducing himself as Wes. He is instantly very reassuring – not the uptight faceless clipboard guy who lives to crush people's dreams that I had imagined – even asking me what I do for a living. *He wants to put me at ease! He wants me to pass!*, I think triumphantly. Well, let's give him what he came for, baby. I pull off one of the smoothest starts I've ever accomplished, mirror-mirror-signalling as if my life depends on it. We pull up to some traffic lights. I am told to turn left. The lights go green. A man is ambling across the road I am supposed to be turning into, so I stop until he has finished crossing. I start to turn. *Another* man, unbeknown to me, has started ambling across the road I am turning out of. Clearly, this should have been beknown to me. Wes slams on the brakes, enquiring in a strained voice, 'Didn't you see him?' OBVIOUSLY NOT, WES!

He tells me to take the next left, then left again, and we pull over outside the test centre. And that's it: my first-ever driving test lasts approximately ninety seconds. After six months of waiting; after more than thirty hours of lessons. In the era of Covid, instead of letting you finish, they make you stop as soon as you have failed so that you spend less time with a potentially contagious person in the car.

I am a full-grown woman, and yet I find myself crying while Wes, immune to girls' tears (well, you have to be in his profession), discreetly lets himself out of the car. All that preparation, waiting, build-up, money, adrenaline – all over before you've even gone anywhere. I'm sure there's an excellent word for that feeling in German; I'll settle for 'deflated'. Neil rails against the unfairness of life but we both know I messed up.

'Book another test, maybe we just had to get one out of the way,' he says with his typical positive attitude. But the cheeky universe is back to its old tricks – no new driving tests are being booked because of Covid. Back to waiting. Back to the drawing board. Back to the longest intensive driving course in human history.

A final word on this – eighteen months after my first lesson, I am no closer to booking another test. Pent-up demand along with various lockdowns has scuppered my every attempt. As far as I can tell, at the time of writing, there is not a single slot available in the entirety of the UK. It's been so long, in fact, that trusty Neil isn't even a driving instructor anymore. That's right – he had an entire *career change* in the time I've been waiting for just one more shot at the big time.

There was a point at which I was angry about all this, but I have now reached a place of deepest zen. Maybe I will be able to drive at some point; maybe I won't. In all honesty, the part of me that is becoming increasingly desperate to champion sustainable travel is kind of OK with it. I've always been happiest when not in the driver's seat. Perhaps it's the perfect incentive, then, to get to grips with becoming the ideal passenger – the kind you'd feel comfortable picking up at the side of the road ...

Sun's out, thumb's out – it's time to get hitching.

The hitchhiker's guide to the galaxy (well, the A40)

'Might I just offer a brief critique of your thumb technique?'

It's not a question I've ever been asked before, but I nod meekly.

'It's a bit ... reticent.'

We both look down at my hand. If it's possible for a digit to look embarrassed, my thumb looks embarrassed. It's exuding an air of 'who, me?'

I try to bolster it a bit; raise my hand a bit higher, make the angle a bit jauntier. It's not a vast improvement, but my companion nods reassuringly.

In my thumb's defence, it's never carried this level of responsibility before. Normally when pointed skywards, it's to indicate someone's done a good job or that all is well with the world. It's all fun and sunshine, a cheesy gesture of 'A-OK'. Today, my entire journey rests heavily on its diminutive shoulders (or should that be knuckles?).

Yes, this is baby's first hitchhike. How I got to my mid-thirties without ever having hitched a lift is easy enough to explain – almost no one I know has ever hitchhiked. Well, almost none of the women I know. My generation was raised under the influence of myriad urban legends and horror stories involving axe-wielding nutjobs.

When I told people I would be spending my morning thumbing from London to Oxford – a distance of some 88km, providing very little scope to perform a murder undetected – the identikit response was: 'That sounds dangerous! Are you sure?'

Where do these stories come from? They seem to spring straight up from the soil of storytelling itself and weave themselves perniciously around our collective consciousness, distorting the entire narrative like a weed choking a flower. But at least part of the perception can be attributed to intentional propaganda. In the US, some states started passing laws to prevent

147

hitchhiking in the 1960s and '70s; alongside this, law enforcement agencies used scare tactics, according to a *Vox* article on the lost art of hitching.[6] A 1973 FBI poster warned drivers of the dangers of giving a lift to a hitchhiker, declaring they might turn out to be a 'sex maniac' or a 'vicious murderer'.

Elsewhere, 'police officers at Rutgers University handed out cards to hitchhiking women that read, "If I were a rapist, you'd be in trouble",' Ginger Strand, author of *Killer on the Road: Violence and the American Interstate*, wrote in a 2012 *New York Times* piece.[7]

And then, of course, horror movies like *Texas Chainsaw Massacre* and *The Hitcher* that make use of the ever-popular 'hitchhiker being a murderer/murdered' trope probably haven't done much to clean up the practice's reputation.

None of this was connected to a real statistical increased likelihood of either hitchers or drivers encountering violence, by the way – according to Strand, there's never been strong evidence to suggest this. In a 1974 study by the California Highway Patrol on incidents of violence on the state's roads, the conclusion was that 'the results ... do not show that hitchhikers are over represented'.[8]

I was able to reassure worried friends and family members that I would not be alone, having roped in my colleague Simon Calder – *The Independent*'s illustrious travel correspondent and a hitching veteran with decades of experience under his belt – to act as my mentor. I never would have considered hitchhiking as a green travel option without his timely – and quite accurate – assertion that it's 'the most sustainable form of motorised transport'. The idea being that the vehicle will be making the journey regardless – as an extra passenger, other than the minuscule amount of extra fuel being burned due to your additional weight, you aren't contributing any further emissions through your travels. Your carbon footprint stays close to zero.

Rather than safety concerns, it was my complete lack of knowledge of car travel that prompted me to enlist Simon as my guide. I'm not exaggerating when I say that I have no idea where any of the roads go. Whenever people talk about their car journeys, rattling off meaningless collections of letters and numbers – the A30, the M4, the B2116 – they may as well be talking in enigma-level code. My brain switches off and my eyes glaze over and I just nod and smile, as if I know exactly what they're talking about. But the names mean nothing to me; they are as intangible as a dream wreathed in smoke. This is a consequence of not being able to drive, yes, but also of finding the minutiae of someone's car journey – which they will often share in painstaking detail, for no reason I've ever been able to discern – excruciatingly boring.

The upshot is that, when I decide I will hitchhike part of the way to visit a friend in Hereford, I draw a total blank when it comes to the logistics. Should I just ... walk out of my front door and stand on the street? Which side of the road would I even stand on? I mention my plans (or lack thereof) to Simon, and, like the unbelievably good Samaritan he is, he swoops in to save the day.

'Why don't I come with you?' he says kindly, as if dealing with a simpleton. Which, let's be real, he is.

We meet at Hanger Lane tube station in the darkest recesses of north-west London at 8 a.m. on a Saturday, with the city still bathed in the magic of mist and sunrise. It's a stop I've never alighted at before, probably for the exact same reason we're starting off here today – it's best known for the Hanger Lane gyratory system (which has the dubious honour of being voted Britain's scariest road junction in a 2007 survey by the Highway Insurance Company).[9] It's right on the A40 – which, as people who aren't me may already know, is the road you want if you're going to Oxford. We set up shop at the side of the road and Simon gives me my first lesson in hitching, schooling me in the psychology behind attracting a lift. 'You're trying to meet the eyes of the driver,' he says. 'You only have a moment to make a connection with them – so try to catch their eye and look friendly and nice. Smile at them!'

We both stand there for fifteen minutes, him looking confident and happy with a boldly elevated thumb, me radiating British awkwardness with a smile that is more apologetic grimace than inviting beam. Lesson number two is about the practicalities, as Simon decides we must move further down the road.

'It's too busy here,' he clarifies, as cars come whizzing past at speed with no real time to slow down, let alone stop. There preferably needs to be a sedate enough flow of traffic that a driver has time to see you and make the split-second decision to pick you up, along with somewhere they can pull in safely should they decide to help you out. We move up to a busy junction and I'm instructed to construct a quick sign. I pull out my pre-packed rectangle of cardboard, writing 'OXFORD' on it, pause, and then add a '(PLEASE!)' underneath (the brackets designed to project an ingratiating sense of deference and humility).

I feel happier with a prop in my hand than I did with my lack-lustre thumb, and focus all my energy on grinning like a loon at every driver who passes. This is a much better spot – we are opposite some lights, enabling drivers coming in our direction to see us and weigh us up, an essential component in the process, according to Simon. There's also a driveway behind us where a kind-hearted soul could potentially pull in.

One of the things that has always put me off hitching – other than the general murder-y associations – is the worry that, perhaps, no one will stop. What if you're just standing there waiting ... forever? I'm used to having so much control over my life but, in this endeavour, you are completely reliant on the unknown.

After another ten minutes, I ask Simon what the longest time he's ever had to wait for a lift when hitching is.

'Hmm ... I think seven hours,' he says matter-of-factly. 'But that was in the middle of nowhere, with no cars,' he quickly adds, seeing the anxiety writ large across my face. For him, part of the joy of this way of travel lies in the uncertainty – the reliance on the kindness of strangers, the meeting of people you'd never have come across otherwise. He hands me a worn book called the *Hitch-Hikers Manual: Britain* – a book I only discover later that he, in fact, authored – originally published in 1979. I'm not sure how accurate the road information is more than forty years on (the description of the M25 as the 'new' orbital motorway around the capital certainly dates it), but the principles remain unchanged.

'There are two things which set hitchhiking apart from any other mechanised transport. Most important is that it is free, but it also enables you – in fact compels you – to meet and converse with complete strangers,' reads the intro:

> In this ever more paranoid world there are still many good people who will stop their cars and give complete strangers free transport and their company ... If your faith in human nature ever needs restoring, just head out on to the open road on a sunny day.

Chuh, I think. *Maybe that was true in the free-loving '70s. But this is 2021, mate.*

Perhaps my 'faith in human nature' isn't sufficient, but I simply cannot believe that someone will stop. Why on earth would they? What's in it for them? It is this lack of belief, more than anything, that led to my lukewarm thumbing technique; it is this that means my smile has an undercurrent of incredulity.

But whaddaya know – fifteen minutes after we move locations, a car indicates and pulls in ('keep looking behind you to see if anyone's stopped' is another of the practical lessons from the Calder school of hitching). Surely there must be some mistake? But no, it is legitimate. Even more implausibly, the timing of our lift perfectly matches the predictions outlined in the decades-old hitching manual. It asserts that one man and one woman hitching will get picked up in 'thirty minutes' – the exact amount of time we've been on the roadside.

'I'm going past Oxford,' says our new-found saviour, a young man with an open, friendly face, and we jump aboard. He seems absolutely nothing like an axe murderer, and I feel the rush of gratitude and adrenaline that comes with losing your hitch-hiking virginity.

Whatever happened to the art of hitchhiking though, aside from the aforementioned scare tactics? For people like Simon, the answer is 'nothing' – he started at the age of 13 and hasn't stopped since. Elsewhere, it's a more complicated story. My parents' generation were voracious hitchers – it's how all my uncles and aunts went travelling around the UK, Europe and beyond. I vividly remember being told a family story about Uncle Stephen deciding he wanted to get to France, packing a bag and simply standing at the end of his quiet residential street in Torquay, Devon, until someone picked him up (this took somewhere in the region of twenty-four hours). From the 1950s through to the 1980s, it was a completely legitimate and common way to get around, both at home and abroad.

Simon puts the demise of hitching down, in part, to public transport becoming cheaper. 'Back then, trains were extortionately expensive,' he says, as we settle into our new friend Jared's car (you could argue that they still are now, of course – the difference being that it *is* possible to access very affordable fares when booking well in advance). 'Hitchhiking was the only affordable way of getting around.' Cars themselves becoming cheaper and more common-place was also a leading factor, according to David Smith, a British academic who wrote a 2001 paper entitled 'The Neglected Art of Hitch-Hiking: Risk, Trust and Sustainability'.[10] 'Probably the most important thing is the huge growth we've seen in car ownership,' he says. 'People who don't have cars and are trying to hitchhike might be perceived as weirder, more deviant, or more dangerous.'

These factors undoubtedly played a major part in the decline of hitchhiking, but I can't help but think that a spiralling lack of trust in strangers in general must have also contributed. Although 24-year-old Jared is challenging that assumption. With nothing to do until we get to Oxford except chat, we all get to know each other a little better. We discover Jared's a design manager for a construction company, and Simon deftly demonstrates another of the key tenets of hitchhiking – namely, be a charming and curious passenger. (There's even a chapter dedicated to this in the book, which includes the immortal words: 'The only thing you have to offer is your dazzling wit and sparkling conversation ... Many people on long journeys pick you up not from altruism but just for company. Don't let them down.') He asks question after question of our driver with genuine interest, and we learn that Jared coordinates big residential building projects – more than 500 flats in Stevenage is the latest job – recently moved to London with his partner and is heading home to Wantage for the weekend to see his parents and play golf. He couldn't be a lovelier host and, after explaining that I'm writing a book about sustainable travel, I discover that Jared has quite a bit to say on the subject of climate change. Before you know it, he's recommending I read Bill Gates' book *How to Avoid a Climate Disaster* and outlining his company's plans to include electric car-charging points for every parking space in all their upcoming developments.

Why did he decide to pick us up? 'I was hitching myself not long ago with my girlfriend in Scotland,' he says – perhaps indicating that a person's propensity to pick up a hitcher directly correlates to whether or not they've ever hitchhiked themselves.

After we've lamented the state of the world but agreed on the need for hope if we're to keep fighting the good fight, Simon more than pays off our debt for the lift by regaling us with some of his best hitchhiking anecdotes. They often open with sentences like, 'I was hitchhiking across the Jordanian border in the back of an army van when [insert story here]' and are reliably, gloriously bonkers. He has hitched all over the world, and the experience sounds an overwhelmingly positive one – although there have been some, ahem, sticky moments:

> I was in Greece this summer, and a nice-seeming man called Nikos pulled up. We'd been driving for a few minutes when he put his hand on my knee and asked if I wanted sex. I politely declined and told him I was married.

After what sounded like a *very* awkward few minutes, tenacious Nikos asked, 'Why not? Your wife's not here', at which point Simon made a swift exit. 'You'd have to be pretty desperate to pick up a middle-aged Englishman in hopes of *that*,' he says ruefully.

We have a very jolly time indeed, and it is with a tinge of regret that I see we're almost on the outskirts of Oxford. We shower Jared with a flurry of 'thank yous' as we jump out at a red light – being prepared for a swift exit being yet another fundamental tool in the hitcher's arsenal – and shuffle along a grass verge to catch a bus into town. I feel strangely elated; I can see how Simon has become addicted to this feeling over the years. He explains, as we take a seat on the top deck:

> It is a unique experience, because it's one of the only situations in which you spend time with a stranger where you've both chosen to be there. Unlike the doctor's waiting room, you've intentionally decided to accompany one another on the road.

I nod enthusiastically, the newly converted zealot to this strange religion. It occurs to me that hitching may be one of the exceptionally few circumstances in modern life that falls outside the iron-hard grip of capitalism. No money is changing hands. There is nothing in it for the driver other than some company and the benevolent glow that comes from offering a small kindness to a stranger. Although the benefits go both ways, according to

Simon: 'You often act as a free therapist,' he says. 'A woman in the States who was just going to take me down the road ended up driving me five hours out of her way because she just needed to download emotionally.' (I can't help but feel she might have got the better end of the bargain.)

It's a beautiful thing when you think about it: a pure exchange of resource and need. We got to Oxford for free; Jared got an interesting conversation and an amusing story to share with his parents when he arrived home. I feel giddy, not because I saved a few quid, but because I had a moment of unexpected human connection in an increasingly disconnected and fragmented world. Not to sound like a total freewheeling hippy, but my life was enriched just that little bit by sticking my thumb out on the Hanger Lane gyratory system (a sentence that has quite possibly never been uttered before).

Maybe it's time to shake off the prejudices of the past and rediscover this, the greenest form of motorised transport. As Simon says in his veteran hitchhiking tome: 'If you're prepared to invest the energy required for a successful hitching trip, there's no better way to travel.'

7

But ... What about Tourism?
The Dark Side of Going Cold Turkey

If you were about to give up hope of ever going on holiday again, please do keep reading.

We may have established by now that air travel is not great for the planet and that offsetting isn't the magic cure-all we think it is – but what we haven't looked at are the less positive consequences of curbing our sky-high habit. The tourism industry worldwide contributed a staggering $8.8 trillion to the economy in 2018, accounting for 319 million jobs worldwide.[1]

People often talk about the impact that reining in excesses and proper taxation would have on the aviation industry itself: the loss of jobs for airport staff, airline workers, pilots and cabin crew. What we talk about less is the other side of the equation – the destinations that at this point are almost completely economically dependent on tourism. Globalisation means that everything we do or don't do has much further-reaching implications than we can ever realise; there's no escaping the fact that if we all stopped flying, some of the poorest communities in the world would undoubtedly become poorer.

The pandemic has perhaps provided the perfect test case. Not only did airlines and travel companies go bust, not only were an estimated 400,000 airline workers fired, furloughed or told they could lose their jobs due to coronavirus, but countries that relied on tourism money found themselves struggling to survive.[2] Hawaii saw one in every six jobs vanish by August 2020 as a result of tourism grinding to a halt, according to a report by the International Monetary Fund (IMF).[3] According to the United Nations World Tourism Organization (UNWTO):

> The global pandemic, the first of its scale in a new era of inter-connectedness, has put 100 million jobs at risk, many in micro, small, and medium-sized enterprises that employ a high share of women, who represent 54 per cent of the tourism workforce. Tourism-dependent countries will likely feel the negative impacts of the crisis for much longer than other economies. Contact-intensive services key to the tourism and travel sectors are disproportionately affected by the pandemic and will continue to struggle until people feel safe to travel en masse again.

The report highlighted the fact that often the hardest-hit destinations – the ones that are most heavily reliant on tourists to stay afloat – are less wealthy nations for whom travellers have for years provided a much-needed economic boost. The IMF reported:

> The crisis has crystallized the importance of tourism as a development pathway for many countries to decrease poverty and improve their economies. In sub-Saharan Africa, the development of tourism has been a key driver in closing the gap between poor and rich countries, with tourism-dependent countries averaging real per capita GDP growth of 2.4 per cent between 1990 and 2019 – significantly faster than non-tourism-dependent countries in the region.

One 2020 study highlighted the important role of tourism in the development of emerging economies.[4] Taking Pakistan as an example, it found that just a 1 per cent increase in tourism enhanced a country's GDP by 0.051 per cent, foreign direct investment by 2.647 per cent, energy development by 0.134 per cent and agriculture development by 0.26 per cent – plus reduced poverty by 0.51 per cent in the long run. 'Hence, policy-makers should be informed that through public interventions, tourism can advance development by the design and implementation of integrated policies in developing economies,' wrote the study's authors.[5]

Developing countries also now rely on tourism for foreign-exchange reserves – which nations accumulate to ensure that a central government agency has backup funds if their national currency rapidly devalues or becomes altogether insolvent. For the world's forty poorest countries, tourism is the second-most important source of foreign exchange after oil.[6]

Smaller, tourism-dependent countries – often island nations such as the Seychelles and Mauritius and those in the Caribbean – have very few, if any, alternative industries to prop them up in terms of jobs and revenue. People and planet are both equally important when we talk about sustainability; if something is beneficial to the environment while exploiting or having a heavily negative impact on local communities, it's not really fitting the bill. It means that the issue of long-haul travel is a less straightforward one than it might first appear.

The irony is that, pre-pandemic, we were talking about the opposite problem. 'Overtourism' was the watchword, so much so that it was shortlisted for the *Oxford English Dictionary*'s 2018 word of the year (pipped to the post by 'toxic', FYI). Every other story I reported on at that time seemed to be about the phenomenon: locals were protesting in Barcelona as Airbnbs pushed up the cost of accommodation, pricing out people who had rented and lived there their entire lives; Venice and Dubrovnik were forced to confront the blight of giant cruise ships offloading thousands of passengers at a time; Machu Picchu had to introduce ticketed timeslots; and Amsterdam cracked down on tours of the Red Light District, 'beer bikes' and non-locals frequenting the Dutch capital's famed coffee shops (the ones that sell a lot more than just caffeinated beverages), following countless incidents of bad behaviour from inebriated, cannabis-addled visitors.

In perhaps the perfect epitome of life imitating art, 2018 saw the beach made famous by Danny Boyle's *The Beach* – a film about an exquisite, undiscovered piece of paradise being ruined by humans in all our awfulness – have to close because of the havoc caused by too many tourists. Thailand's Maya Bay on the island of Ko Phi Phi Leh had to shut itself off indefinitely due to the damage excessive numbers of visitors were doing to the local ecosystem, including its delicate coral reefs.

We had reached a point at which the world's most popular and feted destinations were increasingly crumbling under the strain of too much tourism – victims of their own roaring success. The pandemic saw life switch to the other extreme, stripping places bare of essential visitors for months on end. Sure, there were positives – lockdowns and lack of visitors led to temporarily improved environmental conditions and water quality at some popular beach locations, according to one study,[7] while locals got to rediscover their own stomping grounds without having to compete with out-of-towners – but on the flipside was the human cost. Bars, restaurants, hotels and attractions were left barren in the wake of the harshest travel restrictions seen since the Second World War, with their proprietors struggling in vain to eke out a living as a result.

Force for good

Lack of tourists, too, has much wider implications than just the harm it does to the hospitality sector directly. Intrepid is a travel company that has long partnered with charities in its destinations, including Education For All (EFA) in Morocco. Its big focus is to provide girls in rural communities in the country with access to education. But with much of the charity's funding coming from tourist donations, the pandemic saw cash reserves plunge by 50 per cent. 'In 2019, EFA had a 100% pass rate at Baccalaureate [the French equivalent of a high-school diploma], while in 2020 this rate went down to 70%,' says Intrepid's managing director EMEA, Zina Bencheikh. 'And this rate could have been much lower if the charity didn't launch a specific fundraiser to raise money to buy IT equipment for some of the girls who could pursue their studies from home during lockdown.'

Meanwhile, in east Africa, there were worrying stories of game reserves being rife with poachers because the lack of tourists meant a consequent lack of funds to pay anti-poaching ranger units, Tom Barber, founder of Original Travel, tells me. 'Likewise, some of the most pristine reef systems in the Coral Triangle in Indonesia were being trashed by illegal drag fishing when normally there would be dive boats there to report and frighten off illegal fishing boats,' he adds.

Zina, who is from Morocco herself, has seen the tangible benefits of inbound travel first-hand:

Tourism has the power to truly change a destination, to reduce gender inequality, to reduce economic inequality, to increase education. It's not an easy thing to do well, but when it is it has an amazing potential to help the social-economic development of destinations, to empower locals and to decrease all kinds of inequality.

She argues that we need to take a more holistic view when we're talking about the travel industry and climate change. Some of the communities Intrepid operates trips to in Peru and Myanmar accessed education for the first time ever as a direct result of foreigners travelling there. Zina continues:

> The impact is so powerful. We need to think of all the different elements that have an impact on global warming; people in these places who earn money from tourists can then afford to pay to educate their kids for the first time. And education is a key element in the fight against global warming.

Travel also plays a key role in educating the tourist, too. Think about it: how can you persuade someone they should care about the havoc that climate change is wreaking on the planet if they don't care about the planet in the first place? 'It's hard to want to conserve nature if you don't interact with it,' says Sam Bruce, co-founder of adventure-travel company Much Better Adventures:

> You can see the changes as well when you travel – I always find it really interesting listening to our guides telling us how their environment has changed over the last few years. You get to hear about the real-world impact of climate change, of capitalism, of constant growth, that you don't see in your own postcode day-to-day. Travel provides an essential perspective on the impact we're all having.

That kind of cultural exchange can have an even broader effect than helping us appreciate nature, argues Tom Power, CEO of travel company Pura Aventura, a certified B Corp (an exacting sustainability certification that demands businesses balance purpose and profit). He goes so far as to attribute enduring peace in Europe (at least until Russia's shocking and unprovoked attack on Ukraine in February 2022) in large part to tourism:

> This world is a far, far poorer place without travel, economically and culturally. In Europe, we were at war every decade. But

people got used to visiting other countries and staying there. Travel is what I think has basically turned the idea of European war from an inevitability to a laughable impossibility.

Aside from that, the economic value of a tourist's visit can help bolster the protection around precious environments, cultures and lifestyles, says Tom, 'because suddenly, because of tourists that will pay to see it, that tree's worth more standing than chopped down'.

Like many of the tourism professionals I speak to, Much Better Adventures' Sam cites Covid as the perfect example of why tourism is so desperately needed as the ultimate wealth distributor. Ordinarily, his company reaches communities in remote places with its trips – places whose key pillars of income were demolished overnight. 'Tourism employs 10 per cent of the population globally and contributes 10 per cent of GDP,' he says. Without that income, the cost, both human and environmental, was devastating. 'We witnessed communities whose tourism industries were still in their infancy, such as in Colombia, struck down – it was like chopping off a flower that was just starting to flourish before it had a chance to grow.'

Not only were local guides and their families left with almost no income, but a huge number of environmental conservation projects funded by tourists – whose sole job it was to look after the most beautiful, vulnerable pockets of the natural world – were left in a perilous financial position.

Ben Lynam, head of strategic communications for The Travel Foundation, which works with governments and businesses worldwide to help foster tourism models that are beneficial for destinations, from both an environmental and a community perspective, agrees that the boost tourism brings is hard to replicate:

If you took tourism away from some of these places, and especially at pace, it would clearly have lots of devastating knock-on effects. Where destinations have no option but long-haul, we need to be pragmatic rather than pulling away a lifeline. I don't think stopping tourism is going to be a helpful thing; it can be brilliant for places if done well. What other industry values nature, biodiversity and culture in the same way that tourism can?

He points out that it's often one of the few options a destination has, and one that is seen as a fairly low-investment industry to build and grow:

It's a good way of bringing in foreign exchange; it helps to boost other industries within a destination and support other local economies (for instance retail, food and agriculture). And it's often got an SME (small and medium-sized enterprises) component that's good, both for encouraging entrepreneurialism and for money going back into communities.

But he's very aware of the flipside of the tourism coin. 'You do have to look at what the impact is versus the benefits that you gain. There are lots of costs involved too – you want to make sure they're outweighed by the benefits.'

Where does the money go?

Tourism could be described as the single greatest experiment in wealth redistribution in human history, argues Pura Aventura's Tom; it can represent an extraordinary transfer of wealth from the better off to the less well off, broadly speaking moving money from the Global North to the South. But it certainly isn't a perfect system.

'You'd be a fool to think that it was always equitable,' he says. 'There are vast resorts in Cancun, Mexico, for example, that are essentially Spanish-owned tax havens – so it's silly to think all tourism magically redistributes wealth.'

This idea of the money from tourism not staying within a community or country even has a name: economic leakage. The phenomenon is hard to track and it's even harder to get data on. 'Some of the money might go straight to shareholders of large multinationals,' says The Travel Foundation's Ben:

> Equally, money spent in a destination might quickly leave again, for example via imports – on islands this is happening to meet tourist demands. I've seen one bit of research based on the Caribbean that suggested up to 80 per cent of spend can leave.

It was exactly this 'leakage' that inspired Sam to start his travel company, Much Better Adventures, in the first place. He saw a stat in a 2008 UN report that said as little as 5 per cent – £5 in every £100 – of tourism spend could end up staying in a country. 'That really pissed us off and inspired our whole model,' he says. 'We make sure £80 in every £100 spent on our trips stays in the local economy.' He argues passionately that the beneficiaries of tourism should be the people who live in that destination; 'otherwise I don't see how that's sustainable at all, you see resentment brewing locally.'

The University of Bournemouth's Professor John Fletcher, an economist known for his work on the economic impact of tourism, argues that much of the potential economic good is effectively neutered by the fact that the money spent often never reaches communities in the Global South:

> The vast majority of tourism takes place between industrialised countries rather than from North to South economies. I don't think tourism has done a great deal to bridge the gap between the North and South divide. If tourism was developed

properly in poorer countries, then it could be of enormous economic benefit, where the profits and the higher wages remain in situ. If the local economies built the hotels, owned the transport systems and tourists bought local food and beverages – but in practice, there are too many instances where tourists are flown in on airlines owned by foreign businesses, stay in hotels that are built and operated by multinational companies and where the food and beverages are imported. Under such systems it is also not unusual to find that the higher paid jobs are occupied by staff brought in by those companies and the local employment tends to be left with the lower paid jobs.

So, too, the way a person is travelling can negate the economic benefit they might otherwise have had as a visitor. James Higham, a tourism professor at the University of Otago in New Zealand and co-editor of the *Journal of Sustainable Tourism*, gives cruising as an example:

In New Zealand, cruise passengers account for 9 per cent of total visitors but only 3 per cent of total spend. It's because their expenditure is locked up by the cruise companies – who want customers to spend as much money as possible when they're onboard, not when they're off the ship. In fact, they spend almost nothing in destination.

Worse still are suggestions that even the experiences that should be putting money into local hands are sometimes stolen by unscrupulous companies. Sam reports:

I've heard stories about cruise liners hiring a local guide for the first excursion, learning the route, and then using a staff member from the ship to lead the tour instead. So from then on the local guide loses that business. I find that despicable.

It's incredibly difficult to navigate all this as an ethically minded tourist wanting to ensure your money does some good. Lack of transparency means even your most basic assumptions might turn out to be wrong. Pura Aventura's Tom gives the following example:

> It's perfectly possible that you might choose a boutique hotel with six rooms and manned by local staff over the massive Hilton down the road, in the belief that you're better benefiting the local economy. But the truth is, the owner of that boutique hotel might be a millionaire businessman who takes all the money out of the business each year and squirrels it away in a tax haven or spends it all on elaborate trips to the Maldives; his local staff might be paid a pittance and have no holiday allowance. Meanwhile, the Hilton could be a franchise, operated by a local boy-done-good who pulled himself up by his bootstraps and now treats all his staff fairly and pays them a great wage.

He adds that we shouldn't waste time beating ourselves up too much: 'We always have to bear in mind that we're working with our best endeavours, rather than holding ourselves to some impossible standard of perfection.'

The distribution of tourist spend is something that many of the more sustainable and environmentally conscious travel businesses are being transparent about. But until this practice becomes more mainstream, it's up to us as consumers to be a bit more diligent and do some research. 'It's a case of looking down the supply chain and seeing where that money is going,' says Sam. 'With the current lack of transparency, it's up to the consumer to look into that – and sometimes you do have to dig, but it's worth doing.'

Destinations themselves often say they are keen for foreign investment, and this isn't necessarily a bad thing, in and of itself, because it's what's needed to introduce tourism in the first place. Ben states:

> It's about looking at the life cycle of a destination – about when it's helpful to have international brands and foreign investment, and when you should localise. That's what we advocate for. It's not that we're against big brands even – some of them might be particularly mindful about how they're sourcing, both in terms of materials and staff, and prioritising locals so they have a beneficial impact on the local economy.

We're not forensic accountants – we're not always going to get it right. But, broadly speaking, many of our instincts are likely to serve us well. Using a local guide, eating at what is clearly a locally owned, independent restaurant or café, seeking out locally owned shops rather than global chains – these things can all help ensure our spend is staying in location.

Or, easier still, you can always book through one of the companies mentioned in this chapter – all of them are doing the work of proactively ploughing money back into the communities they visit.

The invisible burden

Aside from the complex dance of money flowing in and out, destinations face other less obvious costs from tourism – something Ben refers to as the 'invisible burden'. A lot of these costs go unaccounted for: the use of land and space to suit visitors instead of residents; the extra wear and tear and strain put on public amenities and facilities by a steady stream of extra bodies who do not have to live with the consequences. The impact of this is borne by locals, yes, but often the actual monetary cost as well in the form of taxpayer money to maintain services – for example roads and public transport infrastructure. Ben states:

If no one bears these costs, that means you end up with a degraded destination. We're advocating for destinations ensuring that their communities really get what they want out of tourism at the right cost – not just any cost. Any economic benefit needs to be weighed against the potential negative costs on the environment and community.

We even saw this in the UK. During the pandemic, residents of Cornwall became less and less tolerant of Brits from other parts of the country flooding their beaches and local amenities every weekend, bringing rising Covid rates with them.[8] Anyone not directly employed in the hospitality industry ends up bearing the negative brunt of an influx of visitors – prices go up, beaches are rammed, they can't get a table at their local pub, etc. – with no obvious personal benefit.

Professor John Fletcher saw this resentment first-hand when undertaking economic research for the islands in the South Pacific:

> There was certainly a tension in many of the islands between the general local population and those that would benefit directly from tourism activity. Many islands have little in the way of resources other than their environment and culture – these are the very things that attract the tourists. The tour operators and airlines need volume to be able to make it pay, and so when tourism starts it is difficult to keep it at relatively low levels. It tends to snowball, particularly if the destination is attractive.

Traditionally, the problem has occurred, in part, because destinations focused on visitor numbers above all else. They wanted bums on seats, regardless of whether it might be to the detriment of the people who lived there and the place itself.

According to Ben, destinations need to shift the question to what they want to get out of tourism:

You need to reset what you're measuring. There has to be a public and private shared vision for a destination that's not just about what visitors want, but about where the destination wants to be in five to ten years' time, and looks at how tourism helps you get there. If you asked residents, especially those who maybe feel like they don't directly benefit, you'll get other answers – for example, better facilities. Once you know what you want out of your tourism industry, you can try to focus on that – it creates a new value that comes from tourism, not just this calculation of the number of arrivals and measuring visitor spend.

Although some destinations have already made the switch from volume to value as their primary determinant of tourism success – ranking 'quality' over quantity when it comes to visitors – even this is missing the point, argues Ben:

> When we talk about what a community would value from tourism, most people assume it's money. There's a tendency to think that we want high spenders. But, although they do spend more, high spenders bring a different balance of benefits and costs. The five-star hotel they stay in probably has a far higher carbon footprint than a cheaper alternative; they might buy more premium products that have been imported rather than spending money in a way that would drip through the community.

It may be better than the old 'pack 'em in at any cost' model, but it still fundamentally fails to address Ben's primary question: what do you want tourism to do? 'Destinations need to understand that and get the balance right to achieve what they're trying to achieve for the local community.'

What are destinations doing?

Despite the doom and gloom of the previous paragraphs, there are destinations that are making great efforts to grapple with these difficult questions to build a better kind of tourism industry – particularly in the wake of the pandemic.

Barcelona – which has had more than its fair share of over-tourism in the past – has set up a governance model bringing in numerous stakeholders, including community representatives, to be involved in decision-making. Greendestinations.org has a list of the 100 top destinations that are working hard to balance local needs with tourism to create something mutually beneficial.

Talking to Professor Higham about how New Zealand is reshaping its stance towards tourism as it builds back after coronavirus – having literally shut down its borders for going on eighteen months – is especially inspiring.

'The post-Covid rebuilding discussion in this country is fascinating,' he says. 'We're focusing on a so-called regenerative tourism paradigm, inspired by indigenous world views and Maori views around nature. We're reframing the whole thing to dovetail with the government's commitment to the four capitals.'

That's right – *four* capitals. Rather than the government just focusing on GDP – or economic capital – it is now equally invested in how activities contribute to social, cultural and environmental capitals. It's completely switching up New Zealand's tourism model:

Under this regenerative tourism paradigm, we're interested in decarbonising tourism, yes, but we're also looking at how tourist activities contribute to local communities, how they contribute culturally, how they contribute positively to the environment – and how they contribute economically.

He gives the example of a Maori project that takes visitors to see a breed of little blue penguin that had almost disappeared before the local intervention. Visitors pay NZ$35 for a guided visit to the colony, with pretty much every cent reinvested into helping protect the species. The project hires a scientist to monitor the penguins, engages local volunteers to help out and allows visitors to be part of the conservation project. It hits all of the four capitals: economic, in that tourists pay to visit; cultural, in that it allows the Maori people to educate locals and visitors about the principle of guardianship (the idea that we are responsible for protecting the environment); social, in that it engages local volunteers; and, of course, environmental, in that these adorable penguins have been brought back from the brink of extinction.

It's such a refreshing approach to tourism – and to how we assess whether businesses and enterprises are 'successful' in general. The idea that financial performance should be the only, or even primary, indicator of something's worth seems wholly outdated at this point in the climate emergency.

New Zealand is a useful case study to use too because of its status as an island nation plopped in a remote location – international tourists have very little choice but to hop on a plane to reach it. But those in government are even talking seriously about whether they really want the same volume of foreign visitors as they had pre-pandemic.

In the summer of 2021, the minister for tourism, Stuart Nash, released a new strategy for the phenomenally popular Milford Sound attraction (a fiord in the south-west of New Zealand's South Island): he closed the local airport, put a ban on cruise ships sailing in and introduced visitor caps. The previous formula – to attract as many visitors as possible – was not only unsustainable, it was undesirable for the visitors themselves. Most people felt rushed and crowded; there was often a bottleneck of bus tours. The minister declared that that system no longer complied with New Zealand's vision of regenerative tourism and that a new formula was needed. It presents a radical shift in the thinking behind what tourism should be – in this case, something that provides the visitor with a valuable experience while not overwhelming the precious piece of nature they've come to see. Professor Higham says:

> When Covid struck and we closed the border, Tourism NZ was told to refocus its energy on the domestic market. Domestic tourism has zero international aviation emissions – so the future of tourism in this country will, by necessity, have to focus on that market.

In comparison, the average international visitor flies 10,000km to reach New Zealand. And the emissions-to-visitor ratio rarely adds up; Europe provides about 18 per cent of total visitors, who produce around 50 per cent of the emissions from aviation. Meanwhile, much-nearer Australia provides half of visitors who only produce around 12 per cent of aviation emissions. It means the latter is a far more sustainable tourism market.

Does that mean they don't want us Europeans to ever visit again? Not necessarily – but, as Professor Higham describes, they do want us to visit differently:

> We're looking for tourists offering the lowest carbon impact, the highest length of stay, the highest visitor spend, the highest contribution to social and cultural capitals. When it comes to the environment, we want visitors who are committed to offsetting all unavoidable emissions. Currently aviation is unavoidable for international tourists – but we want visitors who are prepared to pay for that. We want tourists to come here with the regenerative paradigm in mind; we want them to think about it every step of the way, to spend more time here, to have a lighter footprint, to have contributed a net positive effect through their visit.

Even the country's airline is getting on board – Air New Zealand, which claims to be the least unsustainable airline in the world, is committed to offering a zero-carbon domestic network by 2030. In the carrier's latest report, British environmentalist and writer Sir Jonathon Porritt, who sits on Air New Zealand's Sustainability Advisory Panel, actually challenged people to fly less and be more mindful, reflecting Dutch airline KLM's 'Fly Responsibly' programme (which amazingly encourages people not to fly: 'In some cases, railway or other modes of transportation can be more sustainable than flying, especially for short distances such as within Europe. KLM is a supporter of sustainable alternative models of transport for short distances instead of short-haul flights.').[9]

What are travel companies doing?

There are many other reasons to stay positive. One of which is that if you book with a business that cares about this stuff – and a fair number of them do – they have already been engaging with the tangle of issues above and are doing their utmost to have a net-positive impact with the trips they run. As well as creating their own comprehensive sustainability strategies as businesses – measuring their carbon footprint, reducing as much as possible, offsetting what's left – they're committed to engaging with local stakeholders to ensure they put back more than they take.

Companies like Responsible Travel and Exodus have decided that the idea of being carbon neutral isn't enough – they've both committed to going a step further and offering 'nature positive' travel. The aim is to make sure every element of a trip does more good than harm, leaving the environments not just in the same state that we find them, but better off. Responsible Travel's goal is to be nature positive by 2030. The company is proactively sourcing accommodation and transport options that use renewable energy – and is encouraging holidaymakers to take fewer flights.

Exodus has an aim of being 'nature net positive' by 2024. 'For us, it means ensuring our adventures give far more to nature than they take,' says Kasia Morgan, the brand's head of sustainability. 'We are seeking first to understand the negative impact of our travel, and then to offset that with the three Rs: removing, reducing, restoring.'

Another trend gaining traction is 'philantourism' – a model that positions travel as a force for good, with itineraries that focus on using local guides, staying in homestays or properties that employ locals or are owned locally and enjoying experiences that support or contribute to conservation or community projects. 'It's a natural evolution of voluntourism, but less of a commitment; you don't need to do anything after you arrive, other than enjoy the culture, buy local and put your spending money into the tourism economy,' says Tom Barber of Original Travel, which offers a portfolio of philantourism packages. 'We have no doubt that this trend will continue to grow once travel restrictions are lifted and people are able to help the worst-affected countries get back on their feet.'

And it doesn't need to be seen as some worthy, selfless decision either: 'The destinations we recommend in the Philantourism portfolio are amazing places that just happen to have been dependent on tourism and suffered some unfortunate circumstances such as a natural disaster, or a terrorist attack, which have dented tourist numbers,' says Tom.

Some companies, like Intrepid and Pura Aventura, are beginning to encourage customers to travel closer to home, offering incredible, one-of-a-kind itineraries to domestic or near/short-haul markets. Intrepid's teams in destination are all staffed top to bottom by local people, too, ensuring that only local suppliers are used and that money stays in the community. 'It means we can control who we contract and fully control our supply chain,' says

Zina. Recent initiatives the business is getting involved in include partnering with a programme called MEET, which selects places badly affected by overtourism in Europe and works with the local population to do capacity-building and create eco-tourism in lesser-known locations, training up locals as guides. These are often the experiences tourists rate the most highly, according to Zina – an example of something that benefits the destination while also benefiting the visitor.

Introducing changes that are good for the holidaymaker and the place they're visiting has also been a focus for Much Better Adventures. They've put a cap on group sizes, reducing the maximum number of people from eighteen to fourteen, or twelve for a more intimate experience. 'You can ruin the place you're there to enjoy so quickly if you're not careful,' says Sam.

Pura Aventura has limits in mind too, separating out travel parties so that destinations aren't overwhelmed, aiming to spread the economic benefit out without throwing off the balance of the local-to-visitor ratio. Tom says:

> It's a restricted growth model – a Small Giants model. I don't want to walk in rural Spain and speak to someone from Hove, I want unmediated interactions with the local people and landscapes. We sacrifice that if we're just on a conveyor belt with a bunch of people who look and sound like us. That's why we limit the number of people we take at a time – otherwise we bastardise the product, the very thing we claim to be championing.

The company also measures its holidays to get a clear picture of how many local partners are involved in delivering the trip – the idea is to make sure that around fourteen local people or small businesses are profiting directly from any one holiday.

It's enough to restore your faith in this whole travel business. It's certainly enough to make me want to go on holiday again.

But with responsible companies putting in so much effort, how can we guarantee we're playing our part as responsible tourists?

How can we do tourism well?

Go for longer

Everyone I speak to is agreed on this one: we need to break the trend for short breaks (at least if we're not travelling domestically). 'Go away less for longer' is one of the cornerstones that will see our travel habits become more sustainable. One reason is that if we adopt the principles of slow travel, we can take our time getting to a destination without flying.

But even if this is impossible and you have to get on a plane, you can at least make it count. Having one long break instead of three or four shorter ones will mean fewer aviation emissions, but it has other benefits too. Spending more time in a destination means, to put it bluntly, you will spend more money in that destination. More than that, you'll likely spread your money further – once you've done the big-hitting attractions that tend to suck in a lot of visitor spend, you'll gain confidence, get exploring, go further afield, visit places that don't tend to attract so many people (and their shiny tourist pounds).

'Don't go away twice a year for two weeks, go away once for four weeks,' says Pura Aventura's Tom. The company has stopped selling any packages fewer than five nights for short haul; the long-haul minimum trip length is two weeks. One benefit of the pandemic is that people seem to be embracing the longer break, in large part because of the new opportunities for remote working. 'The average length of our trips has gone up by 50 per cent,' says Tom.

If you're in a position to speak to your workplace and embrace your inner digital nomad, consider whether you can plan a lengthier holiday, scheduling in days when you'll be working amid days when you'll be exploring.

Respect local customs

Part of being a 'good' tourist is accepting and embracing the fact that you are somewhere new with its own cultural norms and customs. Intrepid's Zina explains:

> Sometimes it starts with your behaviour when you're in a destination. It's about respecting these communities, looking at how you dress, how you communicate. And choosing what activities you participate in: don't visit orphanages and take pictures of the children; don't take part in any activity associated with animal cruelty or child labour.

So, as cute as that snap of you riding an elephant or posing with a tiger might look on your Tinder profile, probably best to swipe left.

Pick your destination with care

The world is shrinking ... or at least that's how it feels. Of the 195 countries across the globe, the top twenty most-visited account for almost two-thirds of tourist visits. Put simply, 'overtourism' means too many of us in too few destinations. The result? 'We are destroying the very places we love the most: enraging locals, damaging historical monuments and fighting for photo ops,' says Original Travel's Tom. 'It's time to trade in Instagram hotspots for offbeat havens and rediscover our curiosity for travel beyond the guidebook or the Facebook feed.'

To that end, the company is promoting 'undertourism' – visiting destinations away from the tourist trail. Choosing somewhere lesser known for your holiday (such as swapping Santorini for the Cycladic islands in Greece or exchanging Peru's Inca Trail for its Lares Trail) can have wide-ranging positive impacts, from being more beneficial to the local economy to ensuring you're not contributing to the damage suffered by destinations already groaning under the pressure of too much footfall.

Visit popular places in the right way

Does that mean you can never visit Venice? No, according to the experts. But it's all about how – and, crucially, when – you visit.

Intrepid's Zina recommends visiting in 'shoulder season' (the period between high and low season) or off-season instead of peak season – 'think Italy in November or March rather than focusing on June to September' – a recommendation backed up by Original Travel's Tom. 'Visit out of high season, when the tourist trade will be more grateful of your investment and you are not contributing to a throng of people,' he advises.

Overtourism isn't the simple problem we think it is, according to The Travel Foundation's Ben – we need to unpack the concept more. 'Speak to many of these destinations, and they'll say overtourism is an issue in these particular streets or at this particular attraction, or on these particular dates. So a more sophisticated understanding is needed to negotiate the question of overtourism.'

One of the tactics destinations are using is to try to encourage people to see different types of attractions, and to attract a different type of traveller – for example, in Amsterdam, they want visitors who aren't coming for the Red Light District, but who are there to appreciate culture further afield (something I'll be taking on board in the next chapter).

Seeking out undiscovered bits of a city means you won't be contributing to the strain – but, equally important, you'll probably have a better experience because of it.

Make long haul a treat

We need to reframe travel as the luxury that it is. It is one of life's true privileges, not a right – it shouldn't be something cheap and disposable to be mindlessly consumed and taken for granted.

'It might be better to see it as a real treat to go on a long-haul trip,' says Ben. 'Maybe you allow yourself one short-haul trip a year instead, and long-haul becomes even more occasional.'

Pura Aventura's Tom agrees that we need to change our perception of travel as something we do heedlessly:

> I like to think that people wouldn't feel the need to jump on a plane to go away for a weekend anymore. If you're getting on a plane, just think about it – do you need to? How long are you going for? How many times have you been on a plane this year? If we rethink it and give ourselves an allowance in our head – one short-haul flight a year and one long-haul flight every other year, perhaps – what would you do with that, where would you go?

The bottom line

The cost versus the gain that comes from tourism is an intensely complex equation, and one that doesn't come with easy answers. Clearly, stripping away all tourism in order to stop long-haul flights would cause a huge amount of damage. But the notion of being able to mindlessly fly wherever and whenever we want and using the 'tourist economy' as our justification also doesn't stack up.

If we follow some of the previous advice – really being mindful about where and when we go, what we do when we get there and how our money is spent – our holidays have the potential to do some real good in this complicated world. It's up to us to step up to the challenge; and, when we do, we might just find we have a much better time because of it.

8

I Love to Ride My Bicycle
From Commuter to Explorer in Amsterdam

Having touched on some of the issues that come with tourism – when there's both too much of it and too little – I'm determined to put some of my new knowledge about how to travel more responsibly to the test. Where better to do it than Amsterdam: both the undisputed poster child of overtourism's dark side, and the undisputed king of cycle culture, where the greenest way to get around is also the easiest?

Until the pandemic hit, Amsterdam was *the* cautionary tale – the scary bedtime story held up to frighten the bejesus out of other European cities about the dangers of attracting 'too many' tourists. In 2019, it had a record-breaking 9 million visitors,[1] more than a third of whom came from the UK, US and Germany alone (the single-biggest international market was Brits, totalling 1.43 million).[2] The number of guests who stayed overnight had risen 9 per cent year-on-year. To put this in context, there are only around 1.16 million residents in the Amsterdam Metropolitan

Area (and more like 820,000 in Amsterdam proper). Just imagine living there – every weekend your hometown buckles under an influx of tourists that almost matches the number of residents. You feel outnumbered in your own city; you feel surrounded and outcast.

The City of Amsterdam thought things had gone far enough too. In 2017, it boldly revealed that not a single euro was being spent on advertising or marketing. 'Cities are dying from tourism,' said Frans van der Avert, Amsterdam Marketing's chief executive at the time. 'No one will be living in the historic centres anymore. A lot of smaller historic cities in Europe are getting destroyed by visitors.'

He went so far as to declare that Amsterdam didn't 'want to have more people'. He highlighted visitors 'with no respect for the character of the city', and pointed the finger squarely at travellers on low-cost airlines, funnily enough, claiming that the ones who flew with Ryanair were 'the loudest'.

The city had reached the point where the job was no longer to attract visitors, but to manage them, pointing them in the direction of different, lesser-known spots. 'We want to increase the quality of visitors – we want people who are interested in the city, not who want it as a backdrop for a party,' said van der Avert.

Amsterdam's problem was that a fair percentage of those millions of annual visitors who descended were very much the 'wrong' kind: stag parties. Big groups whose main aim was to get drunk, stoned and ogle sex workers in the Red Light District. Essentially, people who would never leave the city's medieval centre, particularly the seedier few streets within striking distance of the central station, lined with fast-food joints and weed-touting coffee shops.

Fast-forward to 2021, and the opposite problem to the Dutch capital's previous overtourism woes had occurred. Amsterdam's statistical analysis service, the OIS, said in April 2021 that, at best, it expected 45 per cent fewer visitors to turn up that year.

In the worst-case scenario, visitor numbers could drop by more than two-thirds.[3]

In response, the City of Amsterdam asked amsterdam&partners, a not-for-profit in the public-private sector 'dedicated to making Amsterdam an even better place to live, work and visit', to issue a recommendation on the future of the visitor economy. The advice was drawn up in collaboration with more than a hundred stakeholders, with the focus being on how a sustainable visitor economy could be created as the city built back after the pandemic.

'We aim to create a visitor economy that adds value and does not cause disturbance or disruption by 2025,' the report reads, detailing 'seven pillars' to help create a more balanced approach that values the needs of those who live and work in the city on a par with those who visit.[4] They include getting the community involved, redesigning public spaces, rewarding good business practices, making the city centre liveable and 'managing the night' – this last achieved partly through 'tackling disturbance and disruption in a targeted manner'.

Some people have the impression that the city no longer wants tourists, but that was never the case. What they want is a more curious kind of traveller: one who'll try new things and visit new places, spreading their money far and wide on cultural experiences, museums, galleries, restaurants and bars. And that's exactly what I intend to do.

When I head off to Amsterdam, it is after a week I can only describe as a bag of shite. My deputy editor was ill for half the week (not in any way her fault, but always a recipe for extra stress); the bathroom ceiling in my shared flat had sprung a leak, which swiftly escalated into the entire ceiling collapsing, causing a small flood; and the house purchase I'd spent months waiting for so I could finally live my best life by the seaside had fallen through with barely an explanation. It is in a state of high anxiety and bitterness, therefore, that I set off for London Liverpool Street station after work, from where I'll catch the train to Harwich International.

I'd never travelled to the Netherlands this way, taking the Stena ferry service to the Hook of Holland, but the ease of the entire process goes some way to soothing my barbed-wire nerves. I finish the workday as normal; by 7.30 p.m. I'm on the train; by 8.45 p.m. I'm at Harwich; and by 9 p.m. I'm in my cabin on board the good ship *Stena Hollandica*. Honestly, the whole thing is a masterclass in how to provide smooth-as-a-Galaxy Caramel, end-to-end travel. Harwich International station is inside the ferry port, for goodness' sake! Getting through security, even with the added pandemic paperwork, takes all of ten minutes. And then I'm on board, in a modern little wood-panelled cabin that feels exactly like a travelling hotel room. I vaguely consider getting out to 'explore' the ship, and then my eyes fall on the freshly made bed; my half-finished book; and – the clincher – my can of M&S raspberry mojito cocktail. I think not.

I experience the sleep of the dead, spurred on by the sexy growl of the ship's engine, and only awake when an unnecessarily upbeat jingle is played through the tannoy as a mandatory, ship-wide wake-up call at 6.30 a.m. And ... that's it. We're in the bloody Netherlands! It is a feat that consistently holds no small portion of magic for me, just as it does on a train – any form of transport, in fact, in which you fall asleep and wake up in a different country. I blearily order a coffee and croissant and head out on deck with the chain-smoking truckers as we chug our way into port, watching the sun rise and flush the sky blusher-pink.

Out the other side, and the process continues in its easy, breezy, traveller-friendly fashion: down the gangway, through passport control and round a corner for the metro to Schiedam Centrum.

From there, it's a handy seventy-minute fast train to Amsterdam.
By 10.30 a.m., I'm checked into my hotel, the *extremely* vibey
Kimpton DeWitt, which seems to have implemented some sort
of policy that requires all guests to meet a fairly high minimum
attractiveness threshold (I do not include myself in this; all I can
say is, thank goodness for face masks).

Much like the sleeper trains to Scotland and Cornwall, this
method of flight-free travel enables you to spend the entire
weekend somewhere new without missing a single hour of
work. I don't need to catch a train back into port until 6.30 p.m.
tomorrow evening; I'll arrive back at my desk in London by
9 a.m. on Monday. One of the things I often hear from people
of my generation is that they'd struggle to give up or cut down
on flying because of the city-break element – they're time-poor
but have disposable income they'd like to spend on weekends
away. Putting aside the fact that it might be preferable to rethink
this model in general – as we've seen, one of the key tenets of
the responsible travel movement is encouraging people to spend
more time in places, to engage with them more meaningfully
and contribute more economically – this trip shows me that you
don't have to give up international city breaks when you give
up flying. I am about to spend a rich, full weekend abroad, all
without taking a moment of annual leave.

It becomes clear to me after ten minutes of cycling along the
Amstel River that in my six or so previous trips to the Dutch
capital, I'd barely scratched the surface. In fact, a wave of toe-
curling embarrassment hits me that I had ever presumed to
think I 'knew' Amsterdam in any real capacity. What I meant
was that I 'sort of' knew the canal ring, or Grachtengordel – the
seventeenth-century district surrounding the Old Centre of
Amsterdam encircled by four major waterways. The gall of me!

As I cycle along the river that gave the beer its name, I realise that Amsterdam's overtourism problem disappears the second you get clear of this inner sanctum: the pathway is crowd-free, populated by cheerful locals. Within twenty minutes, the cyclists have thinned out even more. And within half an hour, I seem to have found myself slap-bang in the middle of the countryside, surrounded by fields, cows and epic Dutch mansions, in which I can only assume Amsterdam's wealthiest folk must dwell (I see more than one hedge maze, if that helps clarify the extent of the fanciness). Old men fish from the riverbanks; there seems to be some kind of genteel boat race happening. I stop every so often to take a picture – the requisite selfie with a seventeenth-century windmill at De Riekermolen, a photo of the Rembrandt Hoeve cheese farm, famed for its traditional Dutch Gouda – but mainly I just enjoy meandering along under the weak October sunshine.

When I reach a deep curve in the river, I notice there is an enticing-looking selection of riverside restaurants and decide there could not be a finer place to stop off for lunch. By chance I stumble into what turns out to be a superior purveyor of refined Indonesian fare – the Netherlands does a great line in this cuisine, complete with its own Indo-Dutch speciality, *rijsttafel* (translation: rice table, a resplendent selection of little dishes), thanks to an influx of Indonesian immigrants who flocked to the city after the Second World War. I mull over a *rijsttafel* for one, before sadly concluding that I can in no way handle that amount of food without a substantial nap afterwards. Instead, I fill up on rice crackers and creamy satay sauce, nasi goreng rice and a rich, warm jackfruit rendang curry. It's still too much food, of course, but there's no time for napping. I'm on a mission.

The cycle route I've picked up from the tourist board – one of a number of 'cycleseeing' tours, designed to get travellers into new parts of town – would have me head down the river one way, cross over, and then come back the other side. Instead, I decide to take the opportunity to explore another neighbourhood I've never been within striking distance of before – Zuidoost. This multi-cultural urban hub is a world away from the quaint canal-and-windmill paint-by-numbers Amsterdam I've always visited. It's like going to a different city – two for the price of one. I'm hit straight away by the wave of colour: buildings painted in rainbow slices that sing even through the gloom, as the day turns a more overcast shade of autumnal and a persistent drizzle sets in for the long haul.

I've never minded cycling in the rain. Instead, come shower or shine, I'm a big believer in the wrong gear being the only barrier to a jolly nice time on two wheels. And so it is that I pause the pedalling and swiftly don my waterproof trousers and rain mac (I'm already wearing my incredibly childish red wellingtons with bows on the front). Dressed like this, I could go for hours. And I do.

I head first to the Heesterveld Creative Community, where the buildings are daubed in diagonal stripes of orange, yellow, blue, green, pink, like one big colour wheel, and any spare walls are canvases for elaborate street-art pieces. Taking a brief pause from the enduring precipitation, I duck in for a coffee alongside a bevy of trendy types at Oma Ietje, housed in an old shipping container.

From there I head further east to the green expanse of Gaasperpark, which is dominated by a large, man-made lake. It is pindrop quiet as I cycle around empty paths through the trees, the canopy providing a brief shelter, and make a circuit of the water. The peace is perhaps the antithesis of the vision we so often have of pre-pandemic Amsterdam – streets spilling over with crowds, rowdy groups behaving badly, the city bursting at the seams.

In my search for the final stop on the Zuidoost tour, I end up seeing a lot more of the area, thanks to my own sub-par sense of direction. I'm seeking World of Food, a cool-sounding food hall that gathers together stalls of various international cuisines under one roof, reflecting the diversity of the neighbourhood's residents. I push off down a path, check my map, and realise I've gone the wrong way. Again. This happens regardless of the direction I head in, until I wonder if there's some sort of gremlin hidden deep in the recesses of my phone whose sole aim is to prevent me from eating something else delicious today.

But no matter; it turns out to be the ultimate way to appreciate the wonder of Amsterdam's cycling infrastructure. If you're the sort of person who would never countenance cycling in London or any other UK city because you don't feel safe, you're not alone. In 2020, the National Travel Attitudes Survey found that 66 per cent of Brits over the age of 18 agreed that 'it is too dangerous for me to cycle on the roads' (and this figure was even higher for women, at 71 per cent).[5] I am a regular cyclist in London and, despite having been hit by a car before (not my fault, I'd just like to make clear) and having had several, let's call them 'hairy', incidents, I always convince myself that there's nothing to fear. But getting lost in this outer district in Amsterdam – one dominated by busy roads and junctions – I finally experience what safe cycling *really* feels like. I am never, ever on those busy roads with all those cars. I am always off to one side, totally separate, wheels flying on a well-maintained path just for me that's as smooth as the baby's proverbial backside. There's a constant anxiety when cycling in the UK, for me, that I will lose my way (inevitable with the aforementioned lack of sense of direction) and end up somewhere terrifying. A busy junction. A four-lane roundabout. A dual carriageway. And then it will be like that scene in *Clueless* where they accidentally drive onto the freeway and everyone starts hyperventilating and screaming. Because there is rarely a defined separation of church and state, cars and bikes; we're supposed to rub along together like one, big, happy (read: dysfunctional and wildly dangerous) family.

There is a tendency to think that the fabulous cycling infrastructure in Amsterdam – and the Netherlands more generally – is in some way inevitable. To assume that they're all so bike-mad, it was always going to happen. In contrast to this assumption, Gerrit Faber of the Fietsersbond (Cyclists' Union) says that 'it's not what we have because of our genes. We built it – and other cities can, too.' Investment in the city's cycling infrastructure properly began in the 1970s in response to high death rates for cyclists (in 1971, more than 3,000 people, 450 of whom were children, were killed by cars). 'At that moment, people decided we don't want it and we built what we have today,' says Faber.

The result? Some 400km of bike paths, 881,000 bikes and an estimated half of all journeys in Amsterdam taking place on two wheels. Not bad.

It makes for a glorious environment to get lost in, where there is nothing to fear, other than arriving too late at World of Food to eat more things. Which is pretty scary to contemplate, truth be told. Eventually, after cycling down what feels like every street in the entire district, I stumble upon it, more due to the laws of entropy than by design. Inside an old car park converted into a multi-cultural food court, I find crowds sheltering from the rain while chowing down on Dominican sancocho (seven-meat stew), Indian thali and Caribbean johnnycake. I am still groaning from my ridiculously decadent lunch, and so I limit myself to buying a giant pastry from a Surinamese bakery, humbled by my own restraint.

By now time is ticking on – I feel pleasantly far from the thick of things, while being painfully aware that I have to find my way back into town with less than 5 per cent battery left on my phone. But this time, following my nose couldn't be easier; it somehow feels instinctive, which I suspect I can attribute more to the splendid cycle path infrastructure cutting a clear line back to the city centre than my miraculously improved inner satnav. The best part is that, once again, I'm alone on the roads. Perhaps because of the rain (yes, it's still going), I find myself going for long stretches without seeing a soul. I reach an underpass, a road running high overhead transporting the cars at one remove (of course), and I pause to try out a line from a favourite song. The echo is magnificent, and so I stay and bellow the whole thing into the void, before pushing off once more, a goofy smile plastered on my face for the rest of the journey.

I come to the Amstel River again, a trusty old friend by this point, and let it lead me all the way home, like a watery bread-crumb trail. But as I make my way further in towards the city's unerring centre of gravity, I find myself getting annoyed for the first time all day. There are so many damn people! Not only do I not have the streets to myself, but pedestrians are spilling over from the pavement and into the bike lane – *my* bike lane – and I have to stop and tut and ring my bell. It hits me like a freight train – the reason locals became so resentful of tourists (*coming over here, blocking our bike paths*) and why the city is so keen to create a different kind of tourism model. I'd never really noticed it before, but after a crowd-free day of purest joy, returning to the swarm suddenly seems utterly unendurable. I escape my rising disgust for humanity inside the warm cocoon of my hotel, where a dinner of smoked butter and asparagus alongside a frosty cucumber margarita marginally smooths down my ruffled feathers.

Another day, another district. While Saturday's explorations took me a good 10km out of the medieval centre, Sunday's adventuring isn't transporting me far at all – a mere ten minutes is all it takes – but the thinning-crowds effect is similarly striking. Amsterdam-Noord is, despite the name, pretty darn central – within spitting distance of Amsterdam Centraal station, in fact – but it's separated from its tourist-laden counterpart by the IJ waterway. This has always been enough to keep it at arm's length from the rest of the city and, until fairly recently, it was seen by many as the poor relation. Whether a long hangover from when it was used as a gallows field, where the corpses of convicts were hung after executions up until 1795, or because it was the victim of Amsterdam's heaviest bombardment during the Second World War due to its industrial focus and numerous factories, it garnered something of a rough-and-ready rep. But a surge of cultural regeneration has helped change that over the last decade, spurred on by the opening of the Eye Filmmuseum in 2012 and the tourist board who, let me tell you, are *clamouring* for visitors to hop aboard one of the frequent free ferries that make the crossing in under five minutes. But, even with such inbuilt convenience, it's an uphill struggle to get visitors to leave that blasted canal ring. I'd roll my eyes at the collective unimaginativeness of tourists were it not for the fact that I, too, had never once thought to head across the river.

Rolling my bike off the boat, I eschew Noord's big tourist attractions – as well as the Eye, the A'DAM Tower, which gives a 360° view of the city from 100m, plays a major part in enticing people over the water – in favour of pootling around on largely empty streets. I make my way to Vliegenbos, a century-old forest of elms and ashes, and am slack-jawed in wonder to find myself, fifteen minutes after leaving my hotel for the day, riding through a canopy of lush trees, the only sound the putt-putt-putt of raindrops on leaves. Attempting to follow another 'cyclesee map', I head out along Nieuwendammerdijk to eyeball the quaint cobbled streets and wooden gabled houses painted in pastel shades – a far cry from Noord's formerly gritty, industrial image.

As you may already have gleaned from previous chapters, I plan entire days when travelling around opportunities to eat and drink, and so I've already sussed out my hot-chocolate stop – De Ceuvel, a workspace for creative, sustainable and socially minded entrepreneurs housed in a former boatyard, which also happens to have a banging café. There are all manner of delightful workshops set in old houseboats, plants for sale and, most satisfying of all, a fluffball of a pale-grey cat who makes the rounds, strutting, purring and wrapping himself around ankles with the unerring confidence of one who finds nothing but unadulterated adoration at every turn.

Not far from here is one of the area's hippest draws, NDSM. This former shipyard is now the cool post-industrial setting for a gargantuan flea market (one of Europe's biggest), events spaces, festivals, restaurants, bars and the recently opened STRAAT, the museum of street art, based in a former ship-building warehouse. Here, we ask the graffiti equivalent of the ancient 'does a tree falling in the woods make a sound if there's no one to hear it?' question: can street art really be street art when it's not, well, on the street? Why yes, yes it can! The industrial setting and 8,000m2 space matches perfectly with the 150+ large-scale artworks, allowing them room to breathe. There is so much colour, so much raw talent on display, that I find myself losing hours amid their splendour. I've done the Rijksmuseum and the Van Gogh Museum and the Hermitage, just like everyone else, but I'm not sure I've ever enjoyed myself quite so freely as I do wandering between giant abstract canvases and portraits, some cartoonish, some blisteringly realistic. (I particularly admire the sheer chutzpah of the artist whose temporary installation, housed in a separate room, seems to have been designed purely to flog copies of his own book. A stack of several hundred of them have been piled high, graffitied with a giant version of his tag along their spines, and accompanied by the display caption: 'The artist invites you to interact with this installation by purchasing a book from it. The piece will then slowly disappear, just like in the streets. Please pay for your unique book in the giftshop, €30.' Entrepreneurialism at its finest, that.)

From there it's the merest skip to Pllek, a restaurant in a shipping container that claims to be 'the largest green restaurant in Amsterdam'. There's a big focus on local produce, with fish from the North Sea, vegetables grown and harvested in the city and suppliers who 'contribute to a slightly better world with a minimal food footprint'. On these grounds alone it would seem rude *not* to order a generous portion of sourdough loaded with aubergine, goat feta, dukkah and pomegranate, and so I grudgingly oblige. Not all heroes wear capes.

There's a handy ferry stop up this end of Noord too, so I hop on board and enjoy the wind in my hair on our ten-minute sailing back to Centraal station. It's finally time for me to visit the attraction my inner child has been dreaming about all weekend.

I know Willy Wonka's chocolate factory isn't a real place, but, if it was, it would arguably be the Tony's Chocolonely store in Amsterdam (albeit on a smaller scale). Tucked away down some stairs on a side street off the central Damrak road lies a hidden cavern of chocolate. There is an entire wall of bars with wrappers in every colour of the rainbow, and levers you can pull to release samples and try different ones. There are limited-edition flavours never before seen, experimental combinations of fillings and chocolate types. There are various multipacks and miniature versions to load up on as gifts. And then there is the pièce de résistance – machines that allow you to create your own personalised bar, selecting your chocolate and up to three fillings before designing your very own wrapper (I go for milk chocolate with pretzel, caramel and cinnamon sugar, in case you're wondering).

Aside from picking your preferred wrapper colour, you also get to write a tagline on either end of the bar. I um and ah but, as I am still deep in the journey of writing this book, I bashfully type out 'Zero Altitude' at one end and 'Flight-free 4eva' at the other, a bit like when I graffitied the name of the boy I fancied in secondary school, and tell myself I won't eat it until I've filed my entire first draft. Like a vastly less glamorous version of laying down a celebratory bottle of wine, you might say.

I get so overexcited that I end up spending more than £20 on chocolate and gushing about how wonderful the shop is to the nonplussed staff behind the counter, stuffing the company's annual report into my bag for good measure as I go. Why am I telling you so much about my regression into kidulthood in a Dutch chocolate emporium? Because Tony's is a modern-day success story of a company that started with sustainability and social justice at its core and flourished on a phenomenal scale. Founded by Dutch journalist Teun van de Keuken, the brand was brought into being to address the modern-day slavery that still exists within the cocoa-farming industry and global chocolate trade. The aim is to end child labour in the industry worldwide, and Tony's pays farmers 25 per cent more than the standard price they receive for their cocoa on top of paying a Fairtrade premium. Plus the beans and cocoa butter are fully traceable throughout the entire supply chain, going all the way back to farmers the company actually knows. It is one of those tales that helps bring back a little bit of my faith in the world; the only reason the company has thrived is because people cared enough to pay more for their chocolate in return for knowing the workers weren't being exploited. And that is a very heartening thing indeed.

At this juncture, with just ninety minutes left until I need to head for the station for the return journey to the Hook of Holland, the only real question is: should I get stoned by myself in the city best known for its chilled-out drug laws? Emboldened by all the weekend's new experiences, I decide that, yes, that's exactly what a real maverick would do, and wheel myself off to Dampkring, one of the city's highest-rated coffee shops. The air is thick and heavy with smoke, the music loud, and there is a long and slow-moving queue for the counter. There is nowhere readily available to sit, and a large group of guys wearing matching Amsterdam beanies seem to be taking up every available space, all looking vaguely sick and fatigued. I spend five minutes waiting in line before I have a moment of purest clarity. What in God's name am I doing here? Wasting my precious final hour indoors in the midst of this fug, surrounded by men whose acquaintance I would go to great lengths to avoid under normal circumstances?

I make a swift exit and, as a reward, finally allow myself the indulgence of cycling around the canals, the prettiest canals in the whole world to my mind (apols, Venice). As if on cue, it finally stops raining and the sun comes out, washing the gabled buildings with hazy, yellow, autumnal light against a scuffed pewter sky that promises more rain later. But not yet. That magical glow turns everything into an Old Masters painting come to life, and I feel overwhelmed by my love of this oft-blighted city as I hurtle along, stopping on every single bridge for a photo like the basic bitch tourist I am deep in my heart. But even here, in peak quaint-Amsterdam territory, I am struck by the dearth of people – the overtourism problem truly does seem starkly confined to those few streets right in the centre. How strange, I think, to come to such a beautiful place and never get further than its least attractive bits. Humans, eh? Still, it's nice to be able to cycle freely again without transforming into a grumpy old woman, raging and spitting at the 'youth' blocking her path.

As I bid farewell to my bike and make my way back to the ferry port via Schiedam, I reflect on how much I've been able to see and do in such a short space of time. And all of it new and fresh; none of it feeling like it contributed to the overburdening of the city. I genuinely feel good about the places I've spent my money. I genuinely feel like my visit might have had a net-positive impact, were it possible to measure it. What's more, challenging myself to get out of the familiar bits was, y'know, exciting! I felt adventurous, and exhilarated, and pioneering (and yes, I do know how ridiculous that must sound to people who are *actually* all those things – we're hardly talking off-the-beaten-track territory here). But the point is this: rethinking where you go and what you see doesn't just benefit the destination in some worthy, holier-than-thou, what-a-martyr-I-am sense. Just as Pura Aventura's Tom Power had pointed out to me already, it directly benefits you, the traveller, too.

When I post bits from my trip on social media, someone shares a tweet and calls me 'cool, imaginative travel editor Helen Coffey'. I don't think anyone has ever used the word 'cool' to describe me in my entire life. It turns out that, if nothing else, getting far from the madding crowd could just improve your street cred.

Carbon comparison
190kg of CO_2e for a return flight London Gatwick–Amsterdam Schiphol[6]

11.4kg of CO_2e for a return train Liverpool Street–Harwich;[7]
66.3kg of CO_2e for a return ferry Harwich–Hook of Holland[8]
= 77.7kg of CO_2e

Carbon emissions saved: 112.3kg of CO_2e

9

Get on Your Soapbox
Infrastructure Changes
to Save the World

As I settled in for the congenial ferry ride from the Hook of
Holland back to Harwich, I couldn't stop thinking about just how
indescribably great Amsterdam's cycle network was – all 400km
of it. How did such a thing of wonder come to be? Ensconced in a
booth on Stena's onboard restaurant, I paused in my inhalation
of a generous slab of veggie lasagne to look up more stats on this
sublime cyclists' paradise. According to the tourist board, it only
exists as a result of a 'hard-won combination of urban planning,
government spending and people power'.[1] So why hadn't the
same thing been done in the UK? And not just with regards to
cycling culture – why did our overarching infrastructure seem to
hold us back in terms of building a truly comprehensive transport network of buses, trains, trams and, yes, fabulous bike lanes?
And alongside that, running in perfect tandem, why were there
still government policies – decisions made by the most powerful
public servants in the land – that overwhelmingly benefited the
aviation industry, continuing to incentivise flying to the point
where Edinburgh–London flights are five times cheaper than
getting the train?[2]

It was time to find out what needed to change closer to home – and how we as travellers could add our voice to the conversation and campaign for better.

This will come as no surprise to anyone who regularly uses the rail network of Britain, but it has some ... shall we say ... deficiencies. It is a strange beast, shaped by the privatisation and deregulation of the 1990s. When Conservative Prime Minister John Major took a sledgehammer to the nationalised railways under the Railways Act 1993, selling different bits to the highest bidder – like a macabre auction of body parts – travellers were promised that competition would lead to cheaper fares and a more efficient system. Instead, we were left with an unruly, oft-unjoined-up system of train franchises run by different businesses. There is frequently little cohesion on timetables or price.

As with so many well-intentioned plans in life, the system that sprung up in place of a publicly owned overarching transport network has proved a fairly disastrous experiment – as was proven in 2020 and 2021, when the government was forced to step in and take back control of the Northern, LNER and Southeastern franchises.

While the franchise system did bring with it innovation in the form of a complex, dynamic pricing system, resulting in incredibly cheap fares if you had the foresight to book weeks ahead of time – in 2019, BBC Reality Check found that the UK had the second-cheapest rail travel in Europe if tickets were booked one month in advance – it also saw Britain's train tickets become the most expensive in Europe when bought on the day.[3]

Not only did all this lead to the death of spontaneous, non-essential domestic train travel, it also left travellers bewildered by the pricing system, ever in flux, different depending on when you booked and which operator you booked with.

'I hate dynamic pricing – I find it incredibly stressful,' Ellie Harris, founder of Bring Back British Rail, tells me. 'I live in Glasgow and work in Dundee – and the only way to do that commute affordably is to book months in advance.' She set up her campaign group back in 2009 in response to her own frustrations as a commuter using a rail network that she believed was in no way fit for purpose:

> I was travelling long distances across England and Scotland for work and experienced so many problems: delays, a lack of cooperation between different private train companies, expensive tickets. I thought it was ridiculous that no one was talking about putting railways back into public ownership. It was common sense-driven rather than ideological – if you want a cohesive, efficient network, it makes sense to bring it under one body, and to ensure it serves customers rather than being a means of creating profits for private companies.

The idea has gained real traction over the past decade; alongside the 100,000 members who have joined the Bring Back British Rail Facebook page to add their voice to the clamour, renationalising the railways was a cornerstone of the Labour Party's 2015 manifesto, and consistently polls as being a popular idea with voters.[4] Meanwhile, as previously mentioned, some franchises are already being stripped from private rail operators and brought 'in-house', under the remit of the Department for Transport instead. In many ways, what Ellie has been calling for has already come to pass.

'Franchising is dead – if it wasn't before, it is now after Southeastern,' says Norman Baker, adviser to the chief executive of the Campaign for Better Transport, set up in 2000 to lobby for sustainable transport for all communities for social, environmental and economic reasons:

The railway is effectively renationalised anyway. It was renationalised under the coalition government; the Department
for Transport effectively controls everything. In that context,
I'm not quite sure what 'renationalisation' means. And when
Great British Railways comes along, it will be even more under
government control.

This is the next big step forward: Great British Railways (GBR), a
planned state-owned public body that will oversee rail transport
in Britain from 2023, replacing Network Rail and essentially
kicking the now-defunct franchising system to the curb.

Grant Shapps, the transport secretary, announced in 2021 that
rail would be driven by the 'guiding mind' principle – a reform
that sees one organisation oversee and coordinate everything, set
service standards and create a cohesive, coherent network. But
even this doesn't go far enough, according to Ellie.

'It's not just about railways,' she says. 'We need a fully integrated public transport network that takes in trains, buses, cycle
hire, active travel – across all different modes.' Good examples are
Switzerland and the Zürich region. Even if you live in a tiny village,
you are guaranteed in law certain service standards – a bus every
hour, seven days a week. 'They put that in law in the 1980s at
the same time that we were destroying our bus network through
deregulation,' says Ellie. Not only are buses guaranteed, but they
also take you to the nearest train station, where you'll have a brief,
perfectly timed interchange to catch the train to Zürich.

Munich, too, has a public transport slogan that we can only
dream of here in Blighty: 'one network, one timetable, one ticket'.
In most German cities, including Hamburg and Berlin, public
transport is run by one transport association that integrates all the
various modes – S-Bahn, U-Bahn, trams, buses – into one network.

'It's not just about planning bus routes, it's about how it all fits
together,' says Ellie. 'Buses filling the gaps to get people to the
nearest train stations as quickly as possible.'

It sounds like a beautiful utopia. But why does all this matter in relation to aviation? Well, because flights are just one part of the transport picture – it all fits together. If you had a fully functioning, efficient, joined-up and, crucially, *affordable* network, we'd be able to decarbonise the transport sector as a whole – which contributed the biggest proportion of the UK's overall carbon emissions in 2020 – much more quickly and easily.[5] We'd likely see a rise in domestic tourism as people could better access different parts of the country for less money. People would be more easily convinced to leave their cars at home. And, most importantly, you'd see a dramatic decline in people flying within the UK. At present, domestic flights are often significantly cheaper than the alternatives – which is a big problem at a juncture when we're supposed to be reducing emissions across the board. This price gap looks set to get worse, too; the UK government saw the 2021 Budget as the perfect opportunity to announce it was cutting air passenger duty (APD), the only tax on aviation, on domestic flights from 2023, further disincentivising the use of public transport.

Ahead of the 2021 United Nations Climate Change Conference (known as COP26), which was hosted in Glasgow in November that year, Dann Mitchell, a professor of climate science at Bristol University, summed up the issue in this tweet:

> Booking my travel for COP26 – £330 (16hrs) for a return on the train. £46 (2hrs) for a return on the airplane. Really not an ideal situation given the main COP agenda is how we reach Net Zero. I'll be sure to mention this to every UK politician I bump into there.

Ellie adds:

> It's from an environmental perspective more than anything that we need to price transport fairly, taking into account the carbon impact. It seems an absolute no-brainer that that's got

to happen. During the pandemic, while governments were offering bail-outs to the aviation sector, in other countries they had conditions attached to that, requiring airlines to make certain emissions reduction commitments. But there was nothing like that in the UK.

France is the most prominent example: Air France, the national carrier, received €7 billion of taxpayers' money but with 'climate conditions' attached, including slashing its domestic flights.

Meanwhile, in the UK, rail services were being cut, at odds with the 'build back better' stance that should have been governing decisions, Ellie argues. She's convinced fares will go up as a result.

Norman agrees that 'the price is wrong' for the UK's public transport: 'If you look at the last ten years, bus prices went up 77 per cent in real terms, rail went up 36 per cent, and motoring just 9 per cent,' he says. 'We think there needs to be a better relationship between the carbon emitted and the price of transport.'

So what would be a fair price for transport? Better Transport launched a campaign in 2021 calling for a complete overhaul of the fares system to make rail travel more affordable, more attractive and easier. It included a fares freeze for 2022; extended pay-as-you-go travel options outside London, in cities like Manchester and Birmingham; fairer single-ticket pricing (so that a single isn't basically the same price as a return, always a kick in the teeth); and the end of the peak/off-peak cliff edge that sees trains run half-empty at 9 a.m. and jam-packed fifteen minutes later as travellers avoid the rush-hour price spike.

Meanwhile, Ellie says that train fares need to be 'slashed in half at least, if not more. It needs to be significantly cheaper than flying. And all local transport needs to be free, too.'

By this she means local bus, train and tram networks – a measure that has already been adopted in more than a hundred towns and cities worldwide, including the Estonian capital of

Tallinn and the entirety of Luxembourg. It's bold moves like this that will actually convince travellers to get out of their cars and transition to greener ways of getting around.

Norman Baker says:

> You can't fault the government's ambitions – they're very radical. They've learned to say the right things. But what you *can* fault is the failure to implement them. If we're serious about climate change, we need to act NOW. And if you're serious about that, the government needs to be getting people onto public transport. Electric vehicles are all well and good, but getting people to switch to public transport is the quickest way to decarbonise.

How did things go so wrong?

Britain has seen a steady and relentless decline in its public transport network since the middle of the twentieth century. First, local tram networks were destroyed everywhere except Blackpool; then came the infamous 1963 Beeching Report, which recommended that great swathes of the rail network – 2,363 stations and some 5,000 miles (around 8000km) of railway lines – should simply be scrapped as not enough people were using them, destroying the previous holistic connectivity enjoyed by rural communities; then came the deregulation of the UK's bus network in 1985; and, finally, the wholesale privatisation of our trains in the 1990s.

What's so devastating about all of this is that not only did it *not* benefit the traveller in terms of service, it also wasn't a successful cash cow either. In 1989, the cost of British Rail was low for the taxpayer because it was run incredibly efficiently, according to Bring Back British Rail. It costs three times as much to subsidise the network now that it's privatised 'because it's so inefficient', their report claims.

Meanwhile, the former UN special rapporteur Philip Alston released a report about the UK's bus network in the summer of 2021, in which he called it a '35-year masterclass in how not to run a bus service'.[6] According to Ellie, campaigners in other countries routinely use the UK as the cautionary tale when arguing against the deregulation of their own networks: 'Campaigners always point to Britain and say, "look at the mess".' Ouch.

Alongside all of this, Britons were being encouraged at every turn to travel by car. 'We've had decades of car-orientated planning and development, decades of cultural discourse positioning private cars as the "future" and a symbol of status and representative of independence – and the same thing could be said of flying,' says Jools Townsend, chief executive of the Community Rail Network. Set up in the 1990s as the rail network was being changed beyond all recognition through privatisation, it's a grassroots movement driven and run by local communities, encouraging people to engage with their local stations and railways and to get more out of them. 'I think car use in particular has become so ingrained and embedded in people's way of thinking and lifestyles that, for a lot of people, public transport use has become a whole other world,' she says. 'Lots of children we work with have never even been on a train.'

It didn't have to be this way; at the same time as we were building thousands of kilometres of motorways in the 1970s and '80s, France and Japan were building high-speed rail networks. Three decades on, we're *still* talking about HS2 here in the UK.

It's not too late to change things but it does require a radical overhaul. 'We didn't realise back then how important the public transport network would be in meeting climate targets,' says Ellie. 'Transport is the biggest cause of emissions in the UK – it needs our urgent attention, and we can't reduce our carbon output without taking control of the network and making it work.'

And there are positive signs. As well as the Great British Railways development – the biggest shake-up in decades – Grant

Shapps vowed to undo some of the worst of the Beeching cuts legacy. In February 2021, he tweeted:

> On This Day in 1965: Beeching published his 2nd report on the state of the railways. Beeching's reports led to the closure of 2,128 stations. Fifty-six years later, this government has committed to reversing Beeching's axe to re-connect towns and villages across the country by rail.

Part of the government's £500 million Restoring Your Railway Programme, the first 'Beeching' reversal was put into practice when the restored Dartmoor line between Okehampton and Exeter was reopened in November 2021 after languishing for fifty years.[7] An investment of £34 million has also been pledged to rapidly progress plans to reopen the Northumberland line, which closed to passengers in 1964, while £100,000 of funding has been set aside for a feasibility study on reinstating the Fleetwood–Poulton line.[8]

An easy ride for aviation

I've said it before and I'll say it again: aviation currently gets a ridiculously easy ride, both in the UK and elsewhere.

It doesn't pay any tax on kerosene (aviation fuel); it doesn't pay any VAT on tickets; and the one tax it does pay in the UK, APD, was frozen for domestic flights for two tax years in March 2021, and will be cut to zero from April 2023. If you've ever pondered how it's possible to buy a ticket from London to Budapest for less than two coffees from Starbucks, this is why. It means airlines – particularly budget carriers – are able to offer insanely cheap fares in order to fill seats. Ryanair and other low-cost carriers' business models are based on filling as many seats as possible on every flight (known as a high load factor), selling tickets as cheaply as necessary in order to achieve this.

No other mode of transport gets this kind of tax break, by the way. Trains, buses, cars – all pay tax on their fuel. It's an outdated hangover from the Chicago Convention 1947, the piece of legislation that first established the set of rules that still governs international air travel today. It's since been updated eight times, the last revision being in 2006, but much of it has remained the same, including Article 24:

> Aircraft flying to, from or across, the territory of a state shall be admitted temporarily free of duty. Fuel, oil, spare parts, regular equipment and aircraft stores retained on board are also exempted from customs duty, inspection fees or similar charges.

Hence the tax break. Professor James Higham, a leading academic in the field of sustainable tourism from New Zealand's University of Otago, says:

> It's absolutely outrageous – disgusting even – that we are still subsidising the least sustainable form of transport. We think around 90 per cent of humanity has never set foot on a plane; the vast majority of humans have never flown. So how can it be fair that aviation is still being subsidised?

It's why campaigners' major focus is on taxing aviation fairly, rather than introducing mandatory cuts or quotas for flights – they argue that if the industry was properly taxed, the price of flying would go up to better reflect its carbon impact, and people would naturally fly less as a consequence.

Identifying the way in which aviation policies contribute to the broader picture of how we choose to get around, Better Transport launched a campaign in October 2021 calling for several measures to reduce domestic flights and encourage rail travel for journeys within the UK instead.

They argued that domestic flights where the journey can be completed by train in five hours or less should be banned; that cheaper rail fares should be introduced to compete with domestic air travel; that there should be mandatory emissions labelling on plane tickets; and that a frequent-flyer levy for anyone taking more than three international flights a year should be instated. Other demands included the shelving of airport expansion until 'net zero' flights are possible and the continuance of APD, which airlines have called on the government to shelve.

'Cheap domestic flights might seem a good deal when you buy them, but they are a climate disaster, generating seven times more harmful greenhouse emissions than the equivalent train journey,' said Campaign for Better Transport Chief Executive Paul Tuohy in 2021:

> Making the train cheaper will boost passenger numbers and help reduce emissions from aviation, but any cut to APD – coupled with a rise in rail fares in January – will send the wrong message about how the government wants people to travel and mean more people choosing to fly. The government has led the way with bold climate ambitions, now it needs to take similarly bold actions to make those ambitions a reality.

The suggestions outlined are closely mirrored by other campaigns operating in this space, although sometimes the methodology behind figuring out who should foot the bill for aviation's climate impact varies. It's a complex issue, says Cait Hewitt, policy director for the Aviation Environment Federation (AEF), a UK-based organisation campaigning for aviation's impacts on people and the environment to be brought within sustainable limits:

> There's no one magic answer. Above all else, it's about ending the special treatment aviation has had over the years. That comes both from Labour and the Conservatives – there are bits

in the Tory ideology that lend themselves to not wanting to tell people what to do, that people should be free to fly; they're loath to even intervene in local airport planning decisions. And on the Left, there's really strong pressure from the unions that unless aviation grows, people will lose their jobs – plus there's also the idea that we need to increase access to flying for people on lower incomes. There's a standard of living expectation attached, so it's difficult for Labour to come up with a clear narrative on aviation and the climate.

This is what has led to the industry benefiting from so many tax breaks and falling through the net on all kinds of climate policies over the years. AEF advocates similar policy changes to Better Transport: ending airport expansion, taxing kerosene, and refocusing tourism policy around domestic travel and near international destinations that can be reached sustainably. Cait adds:

> We think there's a case for APD to stay, not as an environmental levy but to ensure that aviation makes a basic contribution to society – because there's currently no VAT on flights – as well as introducing additional climate levies alongside it.

Setting an actual emissions trajectory, too, to net zero would be hugely helpful in terms of focusing on near-term action and policy and holding the industry to account:

> The UK government just looks at 2050; and a lot of its projections are all very techno-optimistic. Whereas Transport Scotland commissioned a report[9] about decarbonising all of Scotland's transport that found it's much more useful to look at 2030.

If you zone in on the 2030 timeframe instead, transport emissions need to be cut in half by then – which just isn't possible without meaningful reduction in aviation emissions. AEF also supports the idea of some sort of frequent-flyer levy – 'polluters should pay' – with the money funding decarbonising other areas of the transport sector.

Climate charity Possible has focused much of its attention on the need for a frequent-flyer levy with its Free Ride campaign – but, crucially, one that doesn't unfairly squeeze those on lower incomes. Alethea Warrington, the charity's campaigns manager who leads on aviation work, says:

Free Ride started as a way to demand flight reduction in a progressive way – because the link between how many flights people take in a year and their incomes is inherently connected. The stat that says 15 per cent of people [in the UK] take 70 per cent of flights each year gave scope to reduce flights and emissions without penalising those who only take one flight a year. If you try to manage aviation demand just with flat rate taxes – on kerosene, for example – that would have a regressive impact and would mean that those who fly least would be impacted most.

Policies need to be seen as fair and as targeting people who are causing most of the problem: i.e., wealthy travellers with more disposable income.

In its report 'A Frequent Flyer Levy: Sharing Aviation's Carbon Budget in a Net Zero World', Possible advocates for an incremental tax on flying, starting at zero for the first flight, but increasing for every subsequent flight taken within a year.[10] It's modelled using the Climate Change Committee's (CCC) fairly generous calculation that, to meet the net-zero 2050 goal and stay in line with the 2015 Paris Climate Agreement, aviation demand in 2050 cannot exceed a 25 per cent increase over 2018 levels. (Even with this limit in place, aviation would constitute the largest source of UK emissions in 2050 and consume 36 per cent of the available carbon budget – arguably not a fantastic state of affairs.)

Under the report's proposals, modelling suggests that the 20 per cent of the UK population with the highest income would reduce their flights significantly (by around 30 per cent) with the levy in place compared to a world of unconstrained growth. At the same time, the lowest-income 20 per cent, who currently fly five times less frequently than the richest 20 per cent, would be able to take just as many flights as they would if there was unconstrained growth. By comparison, when Possible looked at what would happen if APD increased instead, the opposite was true: as all tickets increase in price, it would be the lowest-income segment of the population who would reduce their flights the most (minus 19 per cent), while the top quintile would reduce their flights the least (minus 13 per cent). In terms of direct-tax impact, on average, the lowest-income 20 per cent of the population would cough up just £7.75 a year if frequent-flyer payments were introduced, while a far higher share of the tax burden would fall on the country's richest people, with the highest-income 20 per cent paying on average £165.85 per year. It's a compelling argument.

Another example of why a frequent-flyer levy would beat fixed-rate taxes can be found in Australia. It previously implemented a carbon tax for aviation – which had precisely no effect on the number of domestic flight miles taken between 2012 and 2014, according to a paper by Professor Higham. 'The market was so competitive, airlines effectively swallowed the tax and didn't pass it onto the consumer.' Within two years of being introduced, the tax was shelved.

It shouldn't stop other measures being taken in tandem with imposing a levy though, clarifies Alethea:

Someone filling up their car with petrol is taxed but someone taking a flight isn't. The EU has proposed starting to tax kerosene – we wouldn't be an outlier if we introduced that. And plane tickets are currently exempt from base VAT; those tax exemptions should be addressed too.

The EU announced it would be looking to end jet fuel's tax exemption, and instead drive airlines to use cleaner, low-carbon fuels, as part of its Fit for 55 plan. It's a good step forward, but to get around the pesky Chicago Convention the reforms will only apply to fuel used on private and commercial flights within Europe, exempting 60 per cent of fuel sales, according to the European Federation for Transport and Environment.

As to what the money from taxation could be used for, there are various ideas, including investing in low-carbon transport alternatives and supporting people working in the aviation sector to retrain and change industries. (There's even a separate campaign group, Safe Landing, made up of aviation industry workers who are calling for a 'just transition' for those with jobs in the sector.)

Although the UK government has been making an awful lot of noise about their commitment to hitting carbon emissions targets, it can feel like an uphill struggle at times when it comes to flying. Speaking ahead of a key UN climate conference in 2021, Rachel Maclean – the minister in charge of government policy on the future of transport and decarbonisation – said flying was one of the things that 'make life worth living' and that the government would not place any restrictions on it and had no plans to try to reduce demand for flights. Yes, you read that correctly – the minister *in charge of transport decarbonisation* is basically a cheerleader for unconstrained aviation growth. She went one step further and argued that people needed to *continue* to fly for airlines to decarbonise:

These are commercial decisions that are led by the industry. I think the broader point that I've made is that actually we need the aviation sector to be successful, so that it can invest in those technologies that we know will drive towards technological solutions.

Whether it's SAF [sustainable aviation fuel], or whether it's electric or hydrogen aviation aircraft: these are technologically feasible solutions, they do exist, we've got these planes that fly already, supported by government investments, clearly they are at very early stages but if the sector lacks confidence in its future, it will not be backed by its shareholders, it will not place those big bets.

Scientists and campaigners responded with incredulity. 'It's like advocating donuts as the confidence boost you need to make yourself go to the gym,' said Dr Doug Parr, chief scientist for Greenpeace UK, at the time:

All of the technological silver bullets which the government are relying on have severe limitations due to their cost, availability or weight, which means we can't have any confidence that they can do more than decarbonise a very small part of our flying. This is why the Committee on Climate Change, and the Airports Commission, insisted that demand constraint was essential for aviation to meet our carbon targets.

AEF's Cait agrees: 'The government is in denial about the reality of the situation. Airlines have had years to do something about their emissions before the pandemic, and they never have – the idea that they'll change if we keep flying is ludicrous.'

Alethea from Possible says that while the government talks a good game, it's still 'running in the opposite direction' in terms of policies:

If you look at the Department for Transport, they're very resistant to even moderate changes asked for by the CCC. They're saying they don't want to inhibit demand – they're still not accepting that we will need any limit on growth. That's because of the techno-fixes: things that don't exist yet, or are problematic for various reasons [we'll look at this in chapter 11].

The irony is that the government is out of step with public opinion on this one. People in the UK are generally supportive of curbing flights via raising the price, particularly through a frequent-flyer tax. In October 2021, 89 per cent of people said they supported these measures in order to tackle the climate crisis, according to the biggest analysis of policy preferences ever published.

More than 21,000 Britons were surveyed on which policies they preferred in order to meet the UK government's carbon emissions targets for 2030 in a poll by WWF and thinktank Demos – flight levies were one of the top-five options.[11] A frequent-flyer levy could be more than just a climate winner; it could be a vote winner too. Future governments, take note.

The case for a cycling utopia

As you may have already gleaned from reports of my Amsterdam travels, boy, do I love to ride my bicycle. Even in London, which saw an increase in deaths and serious injuries for cyclists during the pandemic (six cyclists were killed in 2020, up from five in 2019, while the number suffering serious injury increased from 773 to 862), I absolutely love travelling on two wheels.[12] I am deeply infatuated with my own bike – I mean, she's objectively a real looker, all pale blue-green frame and purple wheel arches – and often try to evangelise others. I preach on the wonders of the wind in one's hair (OK, helmet); the joy of feeling the sun on your face instead of being crammed inside the airless Underground; and the very attractive cash incentive that comes with not having to pay out an extortionate amount for transport on a daily basis. But even with my well-honed sales pitch, the majority of the time I'm met by fearful eyes and the words, 'No, thank you. I don't want to die.'

It's one of the biggest factors holding back potential cycling converts, and is the natural consequence of an infrastructure that has historically put cars and drivers first, according to Roger Geffen, policy director for Cycling UK, a charitable membership organisation supporting cyclists and promoting bicycle use:

> Historically, the UK has been relatively backward. We're still a long way behind Europe's leading nations: Belgium, Sweden, Switzerland, Denmark and the Netherlands. Some of it goes right back to the 1930s, when the County Surveyors' Society was deeply impressed by the German autobahns of the Nazi era. Cycle tracks were being provided, not to benefit cyclists, but to get cyclists out of the way of motor vehicles. That's what creates the distinction between countries that have really good infrastructure and what we've got. It's taken a long time to convey to road engineers the difference between the kind of cycle tracks we want and the ones we've previously been provided with; they've pleased nobody.

One of the biggest problems is junctions, where the majority of accidents happen – a whopping 74 per cent.[13] Roger says:

> You need good solutions at junctions. The Dutch have much better solutions. It's not just different road design, but different traffic rules. There's an assumption that any vehicle will give way to any cyclist or walker heading straight ahead at a junction – that's something that the UK is currently considering. It means that the highway code would be backed up by road design, and vice versa.

Prior to 2022, there were a mind-boggling fourteen different rules in the Highway Code meant to deter drivers from overtaking, cutting in and running into pedestrians and cyclists crossing side-road junctions – but there was no clear, overarching rule on giving way. It's one of the reasons cycle lanes disappear at junctions, even though this is where cyclists need the most protection. Most

European countries, meanwhile, have something that's referred to as a 'universal priority rule', where whoever is turning into a junction has to give priority to anyone going straight ahead.

Finally, after campaigning by organisations like Cycling UK, wholesale changes to the Highway Code were introduced on 29 January 2022. One of four key updates, designed to make roads safer and reduce deaths, is a new 'hierarchy of road users'. Those in charge of vehicles that can cause the greatest harm in the event of a collision (motor vehicles) have the greatest responsibility to take care and reduce the danger they pose to others. At the top of the hierarchy are those most at risk in a collision (pedestrians – particularly children, the elderly and people with disabilities) followed by the next most at risk cohort (cyclists and horse riders).

Drivers are also advised to leave a bigger space when overtaking cyclists. But the big change – the one that Roger was most hopeful about when I spoke to him in 2021 – is one overriding rule for junctions. If you're turning at a junction, you have to give way to people going straight ahead. It means a driver turning left has to give way to anyone walking or cycling on the left, and not cut across them. Simple.

'That will make it much more possible for British road engineers to design junctions that prioritise cyclist safety,' says Roger. It is indeed a game-changer – but it's not the only thing that needs to be implemented. 'The crucial thing is to normalise the principle that there will be protected cycle facilities alongside any road that carries high-speed or busy traffic,' he argues. He sets it out thus: on any fast or very busy road there should be protected cycle paths. So on 30mph urban streets, plastic bollards are adequate – but alongside 60 or 70mph roads you'd have a verge or hedge to protect cyclists from high gusts of wind.

Safety would undoubtedly go a long way to convincing more people to try out the bike life, but social and cultural barriers still prevail. Roger says of cycling infrastructure:

The whole thing is not as simple as 'build it and they will come'. You get so far with that – you attract the more affluent, health-conscious demographic. But the people who could most benefit for health and other reasons are often the least likely to take it up because they think it's not for them.

Women are less likely to try cycling than men; older people less likely than younger; black and minority ethnic groups less likely than their white peers; those with disabilities less likely than those who are able-bodied. Thankfully, there are a whole heap of initiatives that attempt to engage with these various demographics and convince them that hopping on a bike *is* for people like them. 'You need to give people the opportunity to try it,' says Roger, 'preferably in a group of people similar to themselves – you make it an enjoyable group activity, and that can be very good at maximising health and social inclusion.' Cycling UK runs numerous projects like this and the results 'can be lifechanging' – particularly for those with mental health conditions.

In a strange twist of fate, the pandemic spurred on the adoption of cycling for many Brits who'd never tried it before – and, in turn, was a catalyst for pushing improving biking infra-structure up the political agenda. With public transport reserved for essential journeys and only one hour of exercise permitted each day during lockdowns, people for whom travelling on two wheels had previously been anathema thought, hey, why not give it a whirl? It offered freedom and, crucially, transport that was socially distanced, out in the open air. The lack of cars helped cyclists feel safe, able to take back roads formerly dominated by drivers. Families started cycling on quiet streets; we saw pop-up bike lanes appearing around cities. Roger adds:

That momentum really happened in response to Covid. But a lot of the discussion about the Covid crisis also became

connected to helping tackle the climate crisis. There's been
such a growth in recognition of the severity of the climate
emergency in the last eighteen months – and that will be a far
more lasting factor I suspect.

'Momentum' seems to be the key word across the board for
the potential coming changes to aviation, public transport and
cycling infrastructure. Speaking to experts working in these
fields, it really does feel like we've reached an exciting tipping
point where a disruption to the transport status quo is not just
desirable, but inevitable. But there's no room for complacency
– now's the point at which we need to keep the pressure on to
ensure these issues remain at the very top of the agenda.

What can we do?

Plenty, as it turns out. From changing your own behaviour to
joining local grassroots campaigns, here are the experts' best
tips for becoming part of the growing movement demanding a
low-carbon transport system that's fit for purpose.

Use public transport more
Keeping the 'use it or lose it' mantra in our minds, it's important
that we make an effort to jump on a train or bus where we can if
we want public transport to become a political priority. I know
it's tough, but if we are in a position where we can conceivably
leave the car at home or pay a bit (OK, perhaps a lot) more to
travel by rail instead of air to reach domestic locations that are
further afield, we should do it.

'It is important to use the public transport system we have, no
matter how bad it is,' says Bring Back British Rail's Ellie. 'I dream
of the day when public transport is a joy to use. But we need to
keep fighting in the meantime.'

The Campaign for Better Transport's Norman Baker agrees:

> People need to literally vote with their feet – walk, cycle, take
> the train or the bus. And keep raising these questions – why
> is it more expensive to take the train than to fly? The more it's
> raised, the more pressure the government will face to change it.

Fly less
Of course I'd say that, eh? But your own behaviour is a powerful
thing – not always because of the difference you make with your
individual actions, but because of the impact those decisions
have on influencing the other people in your life and wider
social network.

'It's quite powerful for people to stop flying,' says AEF's Cait.
'Individual action can have a ripple effect that starts a public
conversation, and obviously we saw that around the flight
shame movement. It was about individual change, not about
judging others.'

She cites a study by PhD Researcher in Environmental
Leadership Steve Westlake that looked at the impact it has when
one person tells friends and family they're giving up flying for
climate reasons.[14] In a survey he conducted in 2018, he found
that half of the respondents who knew someone who had given
up flying because of climate change said they flew less because of
their example. Cait adds:

> It has quite a significant effect, in terms of other people scaling
> back their own flying. Our focus has always been policy – but
> any government is only ever going to do what they think
> the public expects of them to some degree. I can say from
> experience, you can tell the government and civil service
> as much as you want that their policies don't add up, but if
> they're not feeling that pressure from the public, they will not
> be interested.

Contrary to popular belief, the tipping point for an idea to gain
traction is much lower than people think – scientists have found
that when just 10 per cent of the population holds an unshakable
belief, their belief will be adopted by the majority of society.[15]
Making the decision to stop flying or cut back, therefore – and,
of course, telling other people that we're doing it and why –
can have a much more wide-reaching impact than we might
have realised.

Get political
With any of these ideas being put forward – more affordable
public transport, fairer taxation on aviation and an end to airport
expansion, better cycle paths and road rules that prioritise cyclist
safety – you can add your voice to the call for improvements
by writing to your local MP. It's something that has fallen out
of fashion for younger people (I don't claim to be particularly
youthful, but I also can't remember the last time I wrote a letter
that wasn't a Christmas thank you note to my gran), but it's
also one of the most effective tools when it comes to demanding change as a civilian. Your MP is there to represent you, their
constituent – but it's up to you to let them know which issues
matter most.

Join a group or volunteer
There are plenty of ways we can become part of the movement
while getting more involved in our local communities, a 'two
birds, one stone' approach whose benefits are further reaching
than just improving the transport system.

Community Rail is an umbrella organisation underneath
which sit seventy-four community rail partnerships around
Britain, and well over 1,000 'station friends' groups. It's very
much grassroots work, led by 10,000 volunteers around the
country who are committed to making their local train stations
nicer places to be.

'We don't tell our members what to do, we encourage them to be led by specific local needs,' says Chief Executive Jules Townsend. 'Our team are very happy to speak to people and advise them and share best practice, though.' There are community gardening groups, events for locals, special 'bucket and spade' trains taking families to the seaside on cheap fares. A big focus during the pandemic was around community wellbeing, with the station being a focal point around which local residents could gather. See what's going on at your local station: communityrail.org.uk.

Cycling UK also has various national and local campaigns to get involved with. 'There are all sorts of roles available,' says Roger. 'Some people want to focus on national lobbying and advocacy, some want to improve their local neighbourhoods. There's something for everyone.'

Sign up to a campaign group

All the campaigns mentioned in this chapter have ways you can engage with them, typically by signing up as a member. The more members they have, the more lobbying power they have. You can sign up to the Bring Back British Rail campaign at bringbackbritishrail.org; you can support Better Transport's campaign at bettertransport.org.uk; you can become an AEF member and support its work calling for policy change at aef.org.uk; you can find out more and donate to Possible's Free Ride campaign demanding a frequent-flyer levy at afreeride. org; and you can join Cycling UK as a member and help to lobby for change at a local level through its cycling advocacy network at cyclinguk.org.

10

Walk the Walk
A Real-Life Pilgrim's Progress

The concept of pilgrimage may be an ancient one, but traditional pilgrimage routes are enjoying something of a renaissance in these modern times – for the spiritual and non-spiritual alike. From the BBC show *Pilgrimage*, which invites seven celebrities, spanning everyone from the religious to total atheists, to take on a different pilgrimage each series, to a 2021 *National Geographic* article that declared pilgrimage to be the next post-pandemic trend, it seems the idea of swapping a hectic and heavily digital day-to-day for the stripped-back simplicity of walking is becoming increasingly popular.[1] According to the Cathedral of Santiago de Compostela's Pilgrims Reception Office, 347,578 hikers received their Compostela certificate in 2019, a year-on-year increase of 6 per cent. Meanwhile, travel company Responsible Travel reported that 'pilgrimage bookings have risen markedly' in recent years. 'Lockdown has shown us that community is important,' said Tim Williamson, the company's director of marketing and content. 'People want space but miss human connection. Pilgrimages tick many of these boxes.'

Disconnecting from the everyday stresses of life while embracing peace and solitude and reconnecting with the beauty of nature – and, of course, yourself – is something that holds a broad appeal that appears to transcend the Christian tradition these days; the Cathedral of Santiago de Compostela team found that only 40 per cent of all pilgrims claimed religion was their sole motivation.

Now, it was my turn to get to grips with the lowest-carbon form of transport in existence. I'd talked the talk; now I was determined to, quite literally, walk the walk.

I don't get off to the most spiritual start with my Camino de Santiago pilgrimage, unless you call drinking too many red wines in the Plaza Nueva and teaching a Dutch cyclist how to kiss properly 'spiritual'.

After a staggeringly beautiful day arriving at Santander by ferry, walking along the promenade as the sun rose and plunging my feet into honey-coloured sand, I caught the narrow-gauge railway to Bilbao. Now that, my friend, is a fabulous train ride. It trundles through the most idyllic countryside imaginable, slicing through forests and green hillsides, with views of stately mountains, silvery lakes and tinkling streams at every turn. Arriving at the de facto capital of the Basque region already completely won over by the rugged beauty of northern Spain, I wandered along the Estuary of Bilbao, gazing up at handsome buildings, scarlet-leaved trees and the mountainscapes that encircle the city, in something of a lovesick stupor.

Sometimes I wonder if this tendency I have to fall head over heels for every new place I visit is a blessing or a curse as a travel writer – but I can't help it. I am simply incapable of objectivity when it comes to destinations. They are all equally likely to leave me floored by a rush of chemicals more often associated with teenage crushes.

After dumping bags and spraying an extra spritz of deodorant, I was ready to grab some of the region's famed *pintxos* (the Basque answer to tapas) before getting an early night in preparation for the next day, when I would start my Camino journey. This iconic walk, which has several variations all winding their way towards the Cathedral of Santiago de Compostela in Galicia, where the remains of Saint James the Great are buried, first dates back to the eighth century. Pilgrims from all over the world have undertaken it for more than 1,000 years, and, in 1492, it was declared one of the three great pilgrimages, along with Jerusalem and Rome. It is therefore with an air of some gravitas that I wish to embark upon my journey, which will see me walk a section of Spain's Camino del Norte route, covering more than 120km in five days. Plenty of people make the journey without any spiritual intentions whatsoever, just to experience one of Europe's finest trails – but, as I am a Christian, the religious element has always appealed as well. Just me and the open road, with nothing to distract from communing with the Divine.

But the best-laid plans and all that. I'm sitting quietly at a table, eating insanely good *pintxos* comprised of toasted bread and some sort of fish – with zero Spanish, I haven't the foggiest what it is I'm eating and have happily embraced the mystery – when a man strolls in, orders in Spanish much more proficient than mine, and immediately asks if I'm English. Slightly offended that this is *quite* so obvious, I soon get over the indignity after he buys me another rioja and tells me about his own flight-free journey – he's cycled through France from his home in the Netherlands and will follow the coast westward, down through Portugal, all the way to southern Spain. Several wines later I learn that his name is Tom and he's single, and several wines after *that* I'm telling him that, at thirty-nine years of age, he should really have learned to use less tongue when snogging. It's like a far, far less sexy bargain-basement version of *Eat, Pray, Love*.

It is with a heavy heart and heavier head that I wrench myself out of bed the next morning, determined to see the Frank Gehry-designed Guggenheim Museum before I begin my pilgrimage in earnest. The building is a thing of wonder and I actually gasp when clouds of mist from hidden smoke machines start billowing in, giving its shining curves an ethereal quality. Sadly, the beloved giant flowery dog out front has been shorn for the season – she's all sharp edges covered by unlovely scaffolding. Fighting the urge to either be sick or curl up in a ball on the museum steps, I know exactly how she feels.

But I'm here to walk, and a level-three hangover is not going to get in the way. With an air of some ceremony, I stand before the Cathedral of Santiago in Bilbao, the starting point, and close my eyes, waiting to feel something. And indeed I do – nauseous and dizzy. I quickly open my eyes again and take a deep breath in, noting the tang of urine in the air. *Fine.* I'll just have to accept that my Damascene moment will have to wait. It is with a sense of anti-climax that I start following the route described in my notes, provided to me by the company I booked through. I have done one thing right, at least – tired and busy, I threw some money at the problem and used a company called Follow the Camino, who promptly booked all my hotels, sent me the route information and organised transport to take my bag from place to place. All I'm carrying are the essentials – water, snacks, spare socks and waterproofs (and tissues – after that first big walk in Inverness, so long ago now, I'll never again fail to be prepared for an al fresco wee).

It turns out this section of the Camino matches my mood. I will later discover from another pilgrim I meet on the road that it is rated a measly one star for 'landscapes/beauty' on a website known as the Camino bible, gronze.com. Running from the centre of Bilbao, it leads out through the never-ending suburbs, surrounded by a landscape that could be kindly described as 'industrial'. Already tired before I began, I find myself frustrated at the slow speed, at the unpicturesque surroundings, at my walking notes that don't seem to match up with what I'm doing. Despite the fact it's mid-October, the air is warm and I'm soon uncomfortably hot. That's the kind of bad mood I'm in – I can't even appreciate the fact it's a glorious day. My goal is Portugalete, a town at the mouth of the Bilbao Estuary around 20km away, a walk that will likely take five hours.

After the first ninety minutes, things take a turn for the better. While I'm still trudging the suburban streets of the greater Bilbao metropolitan area, the way starts to become better marked, with bright yellow arrows, shells and official signs ushering me on every 100m or so. My eye starts to become more accustomed to seeking them out, and each flash of sunflower is like a tiny cheer-leader shouting, 'This way! Yeah, that's right! You can do it!'

By the time I reach the outskirts of Portugalete, my feet are on fire but my mood is buoyant. I check in to my hotel, which happens to be a perfectly chosen four-star with trendy decor and a position right on the waterfront, smack bang next to the town's UNESCO World Heritage-listed attraction of a transporter bridge. It shuttles people back and forth across the Nervión River in a cabin reminiscent of a ski-resort cable car. Although of a sunnier disposition, my body is just about fit for the bin, so I take a seat at the nearest open restaurant I can find and point dumbly to things on the menu, wolfing down toast with caramelised onions, goat's cheese and honey; fries with garlic aioli; and an entire platter of pleasingly salty pimento peppers. By 8.30 p.m., I am sound asleep.

The next day brings with it a new Helen Coffey. This iteration has not drunk too much red wine and had her mouth assaulted by a Dutchman – she is fighting fit and ready for a 27km stroll to Castro Urdiales. After the previous afternoon's struggles, things can only get better. They start well enough, with a five-part breakfast that includes pastries, fruit, yoghurt, fried eggs and smoked salmon and avocado on toast. *Walker's fuel*, I think to myself sagely as I resolutely clear every speck of food.

The morning has dawned bright again, and I feel a happy tingle as I consider the sheer good fortune of getting such pleasant weather in autumn. Slogging through constant rain while wrapped up head to toe in waterproofs, though 'character-building' I'm sure, would have made for quite a different experience. I strike out, expecting a similar level of confusion and agro, and perhaps a similar level of humdrum surroundings. But the path is clear and sure under my feet, the way clearly marked at every turn.

I have found my stride when a man passes me, ruddy cheeked and golden haired, with the look of a well-seasoned walker about him. He makes a remark in Spanish, which I, as the terrible gringo I am, don't understand. 'English?' he asks – again, why is it SO obvious? – and we get chatting. He's a Welsh folk singer who decided to take some time off work and walk the entirety of the Camino del Norte, combining his passion for hiking, love of excellent food and desire to improve his Spanish. His initial comment had been in relation to my impressively small bag, and I have to shamefacedly confess that my *real* one – the one with all my clothes, laptop and toiletries – is being transferred by cab as we speak, like I'm some kind of soft-handed noblewoman. My new acquaintance, Gwilym, is doing things properly – carrying his own hefty rucksack the whole way and staying in hostels each night, booked the same day. When that fails, he has a tent with him to camp. We've soon swapped life stories and bitched about my favourite gripe, the insanity of the lack of train infrastructure in Wales – 'the road down to the Valleys is gridlocked every morning and evening' – as well as exchanged important cultural recommendations (apparently I must look up videos of people singing to cows on YouTube because they love it). After a highly enjoyable ninety minutes we say our goodbyes, as I suspect his absolute belter of a pace might just kill me if I continue it any longer.

This is one of the great joys of the Camino, or in fact any famous pilgrimage trail. You meet travellers along the road; you share stories and tips; you skip the small talk and get straight to the interesting stuff as your feet beat the well-trodden path that so many before you have walked. And then you wave them off, with no expectation that you will ever see them again. You hold each new interaction lightly, enjoying it while it lasts before letting it go without awkwardness. In many ways it's the greatest of levellers; you all have to walk the same distance, no matter who you are. I'm reminded of Chaucer's *The Canterbury Tales*, in which a group of pilgrims share their (often bawdy) stories to pass the time as they go. They represent people from all classes and walks of life, but there on the road they compete as equals to tell the most compelling tale.

The origins of the concept of pilgrimage are hard to determine. It's a feature of many world religions, but in the Christian tradition, at least, the idea of travelling to places considered particularly holy first gained momentum in the fourth century. The twelfth century is considered to have really been the golden age of Christian pilgrimage, but it's remained a devotional practice throughout the centuries, while being embraced more widely in modern times by those without a particular faith.

The English term 'pilgrim' stems from the Latin word *peregrinus*, meaning a foreigner, stranger, someone on a journey or a temporary resident. Before we came to know it as the spiritual journey on foot it conjures up today, in the earliest roots of Christianity the term applied to all believers – because all Christians identified as being temporary residents on this earth who were journeying through life, while their true home was in heaven. There's something powerfully poetic in this idea for me: that we're all ephemeral residents on this planet; that we can claim no real ownership over any of it. All the more important, then, that we see ourselves as caretakers, treading lightly as we travel through a world that will pass from us to the generations to come.

While our reasons for pilgrimage may be different, my encounter with Gwilym has imbued the first part of the day's hike with extra oomph and I realise his long legs – and compelling conversation – have propelled me over a third of the way, all through rolling green countryside, in far less time than anticipated. I feel buoyed up for the next section – which is more beautiful still, snaking across a wide sandy beach before heading onto a coastal path that wraps around the rockface with views down to the peaceful, shimmering blue waters of the Bay of Biscay below.

My feet are starting to feel just a little less enthused now, although they get an extra skip to them every time a passer-by wishes me 'Buen Camino!', a frequent occurrence. This is another wonderful gift of the pilgrimage – if you're walking in the right direction, carrying a rucksack and wearing a pair of hiking boots, locals know exactly what you're up to. And it's traditional to wish you well on your journey: a small but hugely motivating kindness when you've spent four hours on your feet.

It is a humbling thing, walking. If the concept of 'slow travel' comes up a lot in the flight-free movement, this is surely the slowest form of travel there is, trusting in your own feet to transport you somewhere. You must resist the temptation to try to speed things up; you must let go of your frustrations that this new gait is totally at odds with the usual busy franticness of life. It requires, above all things, patience. The Dutch cyclist imparted one good piece of advice, both for life and for pilgrimaging: 'Go at your own pace.' You have to find the natural rhythm that your body wants to follow; fight it and you're done for.

For me, walking is, in and of itself, an act of supreme faith. Logically I know that if I put one foot after another, I *will* reach my destination. The outcome is assured – it's only a matter of time. But it's one thing knowing and quite another believing. The progress is so slow, it reminds me of watching the hour hand of a clock; you know it must be moving, because eventually it will be pointing at a whole other number, but you can't ever really see it happening. So it is with walking. The time feels endless and elastic, drawn out like a wad of bubblegum. Distance becomes a different beast entirely. As I continue at my steady, rocking pace, my mind flits back to my previous train ride from Santander. It is known as the slow train, because it chugs along gently through the countryside, often on a single track, taking three hours to reach Bilbao. That same journey back will take me five days on foot. It's a sobering thought.

But if there is something of the impossible in the notion that walking will get you somewhere far away, there is equally something miraculous in it. I reach the commune of Ontón and see that only a couple more hours' hiking stand between me and the day's destination. With the sun beaming down, a snack bar demolished and a pair of new socks on my feet, that seems no distance at all.

We've left the quaint seaside territory behind on this next leg, though. Official signs try to take you off on a detour, but all the guidance I've read, including Follow the Camino's notes, tells me this is a mug's game that adds 8km on to the journey. Instead, you're told to follow the N-634 for pretty much the rest of the way. It turns out to be a coastal road with no pavement – not built for pedestrians at all, in fact – with cars whizzing by at high speed every so often while you jump in a roadside ditch. It could not feel more at odds with the idea of the ancient pilgrims' way – treading the same path that my Christian forefathers did and so forth – and I make the juxtaposition even weirder by popping on my headphones to listen to an Ignatian spirituality meditation, which I struggle to hear over the blare of engines and car horns.

I find myself crying a lot these days at the beauty of the world, and so it is on the distinctly unlovely N-634. I cried in Santander as I walked along the seafront; I teared up on the train as we rumbled through archways of trees; I shed a tear meandering along the river in Bilbao; I welled up when I started to see signs for the Camino; and I wept on the coastal path from Pobeña earlier in the day, as I looked down at the rippling turquoise shallows. Now, I cry while walking alongside an ugly highway when my meditation prompts me to consider that God has already forgiven me for the things I've done wrong in my life (including, hopefully, all those flights). Perhaps it's that the writing of this book has brought the climate emergency sharply into focus, but I feel near constantly overwhelmed by gratitude that I am lucky enough to be seeing different bits of this mesmerising world of ours – and by my sadness that it has taken us so damn long to value the things in it whose worth is beyond measure.

One big advantage of this section of the walk is the lack of people. Part of the appeal of a pilgrimage was the idea of getting a little solo time, especially after a year of lockdowns and being trapped in a basement flat with housemates. Well, at the side of the N-634 I finally get my wish. Apart from the occasional truck and the brief accompanying anxiety that I might get mown down, I am utterly alone. As always in such situations – which are rare enough to be one of life's greatest delights – I sing at the top of my lungs.

During the final stretch, a long pedestrian street that morphs into a wide promenade along the seafront, I allow myself the treat of listening to music. I strut into the seaside resort town of Castro Urdiales in time to the beat with the zest, if not the body, of a woman who has not been walking for six and a half hours, beaming stupidly at everyone I see. My mode of transport is my own two legs, and I could not be happier.

Day three dawns bright and gorgeous. Shouldering my backpack and pausing to marvel at the sun rising in blazing orange over the harbour, I set off on my longest day of walking so far. The destination is Laredo, a town further along the coast. The forecast said the temperature would hit 28°C today – nice, sure, but a little spicy for a day-long hike. The first hour passes in a happy blur, with the sun filtering through leaves on a trail through forested glades. And then comes the most flat-out fabulous part of the entire thing: a rough, rock-strewn track suddenly opens out onto a blistering vista of the sea, so blue it almost hurts to look at. I can't help but laugh out loud at how ridiculously, staggeringly beautiful it is.

There is a point on this section of the walk where you can choose to do the official route, which adds a further 12km onto your journey (taking the total up to a not insignificant 37km) or do the much more popular shortcut. Most people opt for the latter, and it's what the notes from the holiday company recommend. But guess what that shortcut involves? Kilometres upon kilometres back on our old friend the N-634, ugly as sin and with no pedestrian provisions. You walk the entire way to Laredo along the side of a road dodging vehicles zipping by at 70kph. By the time I reach the juncture, I am feeling good – my legs sturdy, my feet firm, my heart stout. And the idea of taking the short road seems, well, a bit of a cop-out. I didn't come to the Camino to take the easy way, especially if that way happens to be deeply unattractive. Before I've fully thought it through, my feet have selected for me, following the official shell sign and waltzing up through a tree-lined path. And thus continues one of my longest-ever days of walking – and my descent into the mild madness of the solo pilgrim.

I have rarely felt more alone than I do in this endless stretch of path through the northern Spanish countryside. I do not see another human for the next four or so hours – not another walker, not a rural farmer. I do see cows though. Making my way up a steep gravel path, which I attack with gusto using a technique I like to call the 'invisible rope' (you 'pull' yourself up hand over hand as if there's a rope in front of you, surprisingly effective), I spot a field of them near the top. Remembering the wise words of my new friend Gwilym, I try singing to them – a rousing rendition of 'Que Será Será' that I think Doris Day would be proud of. I don't know what I was expecting – a cacophony of approving moos? – but they look their signature brand of extremely nonplussed. (Although one does look up at me briefly, and I like to think we've made a fleeting yet powerful musical connection.)

From that point on, things get weirder. If this kind of long-distance walking puts you in touch with your inmost being, mine is exceptionally vocal. Not only do I continue to sing, I talk aloud to myself in a range of accents; giggle into the wind at nothing; engage in loud yogic breathing; float my arms up and down like a dancer warming up for a show while giving myself stirring pep talks. I utter the phrase 'You got this, girl!' out loud more than once – words I have never said in my entire life.

The hours pass in distinctly unregimented fashion, sometimes gone in the flap of a butterfly's wings, sometimes slow and thick as molasses, when I have no choice but to wade through step by arduously gruelling step. My mood changes so quickly I feel on the edge of mania, one second thinking, 'I hate this I hate this I hate this', and the next laughing with purest euphoria at the achingly sumptuous view of rolling hills beneath me. I thought it would be a time for having deep, meaningful conversations with God; instead, I find that, at my lowest points, all that keeps me going is mumbling the words of the Our Father over and over under my breath like some crazed, religious zealot.

I see an official sign that says 'Laredo, 11km' and in a state of wildest delirium think to myself, 'Just another two hours! Excellent!' (the word 'just' working exceptionally hard here). But what a final stint. The official path once again turns seawards, winding its way along coastal clifftops. I look up and see four birds, too far away to make out what breed they are, gliding in majestic circles on an updraught just above a rocky outcrop. I laugh out loud again, and shout to the wind, 'Are you f***ing kidding?' – because it's just silly, really, how perfect it all is – and of course this is the point at which I see my first humans of the day. They politely pretend not to have heard my outburst as I crumple down beside them on a grass verge, looking out across to Laredo with its sweeping beach, now visible off to the west. They're two Dutch guys, also walking the Camino, and we trade stories of our travels so far. They took the long road today too – but it was worth it, we all agree – and one of them will be doing the entire pilgrimage trail, all the way to the Cathedral of Santiago de Compostela. His friend is just joining him for a few days and heading home when they reach Santander.

'I'm still waiting for my body to get used to walking every day,' says the first, Jeroen. 'It's been nine days and it hasn't happened yet ...' I tell him to think about how good it will feel when he finally gets to the cathedral in Galicia, and he smiles and shakes his head. 'The final destination isn't important,' he says firmly. 'I can't wish away the time – the point is to enjoy every day as much as I can. If I stop enjoying it, I stop walking. It's not about the end goal.'

Well, blimey. It's like running into the Dalai Lama in the middle of the wilderness.

I tell them how little time it's taken for me to go slightly crazy and start talking to myself, and Jeroen says that's the whole point of walking the Camino. What, to go mad? 'No, to really get to know yourself; and to learn to love yourself.' I much prefer this interpretation to the one that says I've got only the slimmest of grasps on reality, and so I pop it into my mental folder of pilgrimage wisdom.

Our unexpected meeting is exactly the pick-me-up I needed to plunge on for the final hour, and I do so with a literal spring in my step, hopping from rock to rock. I march into Laredo, chest out, pride holding my back ramrod straight. I have walked for eight hours, and I am still upright and alive, and if that's not a miracle, I don't know what is.

Laredo is a beach town, dominated by a long stretch of mustard sand and lapped by waves of tantalising blue. My Dutch cyclist from Bilbao has turned up here too – what can I say? Once you've been harangued about your kissing technique by an acerbic drunk English woman, you never go back – and we agree to meet for a dip. I just have time to remove my hiking boots, which feel like they've been surgically attached to my feet, and massage my toes back to life (undoubtedly the greatest physical pleasure I have ever experienced) before heading out again. As I sink my bare feet into soft sand and saunter languidly along the place where the sea meets the beach, letting cool water lick my ankles, I feel contentment deep in my bones. I wish I could bottle this feeling; I wish, more than anything, that like Jeroen and Gwilym I was doing the whole pilgrimage.

I can already sense a slow change deep within me – each day brings more punishing humility, yes, but more respect for what my body and mind are capable of. Buried beneath all my nonsense lies something that I am only just starting to make out: a steel cable of stoicism that can withstand much more than I give myself credit for.

After three days spent in near-perfect solitude, it is genuinely enjoyable to talk to a person again. Tom and I greet each other like old friends before running into the sea, where the chill of the water acts as a healing balm on my sunburned calves and swollen hooves. I float, weightless and carefree, under the late-afternoon sun. That evening we sample the nightlife of Laredo, where the top-rated place for dancing on TripAdvisor turns out to be a pub solely occupied by men over the age of 60. Still, life is what you make of it, and so we order round after round of 'dos cervezas!', so many that we decide we could probably do some dancing anyway. The old men watch grimly, quite possibly wishing us dead. I feel a surge of national pride – a rare experience for me – when Tom remarks that I 'can really hold my drink'. 'Of course,' I reply, 'I'm English!'

The fact that the only patriotism I feel is in relation to hailing from a country of functioning alcoholics is something to mull over another time – for now, I am queen of the beers. Keep 'em coming.

This feels less of a strength the next day as I scramble to pack my bag for my final section of the walk. My original ferry crossing has been cancelled – something about 'the sea' and 'the weather conditions' – and so I'm having to leave a day early. I still have time to tackle today's section, a breezy 14km that will see me wind up in the small town of Escalante, from where I can catch a bus to Santander. Aside from the mild hangover, there are two extra obstacles to contend with: as I will be going straight from there to the city, I will finally have to put on my big-girl pants and carry my own hefty bag; and, given the sporadic nature of rural buses and a later than ideal start, I have left myself less than three hours to complete the journey. I figure this is fine, provided I have absolutely zero stops and keep up a good pace. It will be tight, but possible.

Things begin incredibly badly, as I struggle to find my way out of Laredo and waste precious minutes comparing Google Maps, my written instructions and the gronze.com website. By the time I'm on the right road, I've frittered away a quarter of an hour – not a big deal in normal circumstances, but a real problem when working to a very fixed timeframe. Still, off I trot, the bag, though heavy, feeling curiously like it's giving me a cuddle via straps that comfortingly girdle my waist.

It's a rather delightful walk once you're off the main road, with paths winding through charming pastoral farmland and the quaintest of Spanish villages, complete with rough-hewn stone buildings and pretty, ancient churches. Of course, I have left myself no time whatsoever to stop and appreciate any of this. The sun beats hot and heavy again, and it is with a flicker of annoyance that I momentarily pause to suncream up. *I don't have time for this!*, I think while haphazardly slapping factor fifty onto strips of exposed flesh.

Keeping up a strong pace, I sense that I'm making good progress and wonder briefly if perhaps there might be time to grab a drink in Escalante. But when I double check projected timings on my phone, it is to discover that I should reach my destination in forty-five minutes. The bus comes in thirty-five minutes. There is no time to panic or cry out to the heavens; there is only time to accelerate. I charge onwards with a new energy that comes from somewhere deep within – quite possibly my inner well of skinflintedness, which has absolutely no intention of paying through the nose for a taxi – and am soon striding to the beat of a non-stop mantra of 'the pace was quick but the pace got quicker' in time to the squeaking of my rucksack's shoulder straps.

It's in something of a daze that I see I have fifteen minutes till the bus comes and twenty minutes left of walking. Walking clearly won't cut it, in that case. It's time to run. I start to jog, my legs squealing in protest at the sudden change in expectations. *You want us to RUN now, do you? Wasn't it enough that we were walking faster than a London commuter while carrying all your worldly possessions?*

I gently but firmly tell them to shut the f*** up and concentrate on the task at hand. The final couple of kilometres zoom by at double the speed and I arrive at the bus stop, dripping with sweat and panting, with two minutes to spare. I experience a burst of purest elation along with the sudden realisation that using your body as a mode of transport is bizarrely thrilling. I had control over my speed; like the equivalent of putting your foot down in the car when you're running late, I covered more ground when I had to. I don't know why, but this idea seems revelatory, maybe because we so often think of walking – and indeed running – as something purely recreational, and seldom as a serious means of getting from place to place.

The bus arrives three minutes late – pah, I needn't have jogged that last kilometre – and I sink into my seat in a state of blissed-out relief.

It's a rough ride on the ferry back to Portsmouth from Santander. Sleep is almost impossible to come by, even after the past few days' exertions and following a slap-up meal of tomato salad, grilled squid and crema Catalana in the Brittany Ferries restaurant. But come daylight, the relentless up and down provides a strangely soothing sensation akin to the stomach-flipping experience encountered on a rollercoaster. The dance of gunmetal waves is more fascinating to watch than placid seas; powerful blasts of white sea spray catch the sun and dazzle with blink-and-you-miss-them rainbows. (The unkindest part of me also finds something sadistically amusing in watching bemused fellow passengers try and fail to find their sea legs around the breakfast buffet.)

Along with the intense weather, a 'technical fault' with one of the engines delays our arrival to the UK further. We were due to dock at 7.15 p.m. on a Thursday; we wind up pulling into Portsmouth at 11.45 a.m. the following day. We foot passengers must wait longer still, scattered around the information desk until a shuttle bus deigns to pick us up. Again, I register how my days of walking have shifted something within. While other pedestrians carp and complain, approaching the harassed woman working the customer service beat every few minutes to demand an update, I placidly relax in my chair. Haranguing her won't speed up the process, just like getting frustrated didn't lessen the distance that needed to be traversed. It's not only me that has to go at my own pace; the rest of the world works according to its own timetable too. You can choose to fight it or accept it. The slow traveller I am evolving into is ever so gently being drawn towards the latter.

I feel I have been away forever and for no time at all. The whole experience has been one of constant contradictions, in fact: humbling yet empowering; black moods followed by wildest bouts of ecstasy; drinking and dancing counterbalanced by fervently mumbled prayers reminiscent of a fifteenth-century monk; the ugliness of the industrial Bilbao suburbs balanced out by some of the most remarkable natural landscapes I've ever had the privilege of seeing. And the only way to witness all of these things, the only way to really experience them, was on foot.

I'm reminded of the famous line uttered by Bilbo Baggins in *The Lord of the Rings*: 'It's a dangerous business, Frodo, going out of your door. You step into the road, and if you don't keep your feet, there is no knowing where you might be swept off to.'

I couldn't agree more.

Carbon comparison
280kg of CO2e for a return flight London Gatwick–Santander[2]

12.6kg of CO2e for a return train London Waterloo–Portsmouth;[3]
340.3kg of CO2e for a return ferry Portsmouth–Santander[4]
= 352.9kg of CO2e

*Carbon emissions saved: -72.9kg of CO2e**

---

* As you may have noticed, this journey was my only flight-free trip that appears to have had a larger carbon footprint than the equivalent journey by air. It is hard to verify whether this is truly the case, as Brittany Ferries does not currently have data on the carbon footprint per individual passenger for each of its ships. Consequently, a very general emissions calculator has been used to calculate the CO2e for this journey based on the distance travelled, with no accounting for freight. The company is set to cut emissions over the next few years as it adds two ferries powered by Liquefied Natural Gas (LNG) to its fleet in 2022 and 2023 – significantly cutting air quality emissions such as soot and sulphur – and two hybrid LNG–electric vessels in 2025.

11

Whatever Next?
Introducing the Sustainable Travel Tech of the Future

Despite the pleasure I've derived from my flight-free journeys so far, I can (grudgingly) acknowledge the fact that not all air travel can realistically be canned. Aside from the issues it would cause for tourism (as we saw in chapter 7), there are plenty of other considerations: families spread across the globe, conferences and business collaborations that can only really happen in person, freight that needs to be transported by aircraft.

And, if that's the case, surely we need to be focusing all our attention and energy on the future tech that has a shot of decarbonising aviation. Just how far away are we from zero-emissions or carbon-neutral flights?

The good news is that there are several avenues being pursued in this space, some of them with truly exciting potential. The bad news is that the real technological game changers are a long way off making it into the realm of widespread commercial flights. Take my hand, dear reader, as we jump down the rabbit hole and into the world of the aviation techno-fixes – the good, the less good and the just plain problematic ...

More efficient aircraft

This is the least sci-fi, most practical method for reducing flight emissions, and it's something that's already happening on a wide scale. Upgrading an airline's fleet by swapping old jets for aircraft models with more efficient engines, can have a significant impact – for example, exchanging four-engine aircraft for modern long-haul twin-engine aircraft can represent an increase in fuel efficiency of more than 20 per cent per passenger.[1]

Airlines globally have been cranking up their investment in modernising their fleets in recent years; Jet2 said it had put in a 'new order for up to 60 Airbus A321 NEO aircraft, which is in our view the most efficient and environmentally friendly aircraft in its class today' in its 2021 sustainability strategy, while easyJet said it would be 'transitioning its fleet to increasingly more modern, fuel-efficient aircraft, flying them in ways which maximise fuel efficiency, and optimising passenger loads as much as possible'.

Carbon dioxide emissions per passenger flight have fallen more than 50 per cent since 1990 due to improved engines and operations.[2] However, improved efficiency in current aircraft technology has in no way increased in line with emissions growth. Between 2013 and 2019, passenger transport-related CO_2 emissions increased by 33 per cent, according to a study by the International Council on Clean Transportation (ICCT).[3] Over the same period, the number of flight departures increased 22 per cent and revenue passenger kilometres (RPKs) increased 50 per cent. 'This means that passenger air traffic increased nearly four times faster than fuel efficiency improved,' reads the report.

Though more efficient planes replacing creaky old models will reduce carbon emissions in-flight, evidently there won't be any real benefit if there's no curb on growth of the number of flights overall.

'Modernizing fleets and improving operational efficiency are important; however, in the best case, annual industry growth counters the emissions that they save,' according to analysis by consultancy McKinsey.[4]

Sustainable aviation fuel

Sustainable aviation fuel (SAF) is the latest Great White Hope that the aviation industry is throwing all its energy behind.

In 2021, it was as if the sector had collectively committed to this as the new party line. IAG, the group that owns British Airways, Aer Lingus, Iberia and Vueling, was the first European airline group to commit to powering 10 per cent of its flights with SAF by 2030;[5] the same pledge was made by all airlines in the One World Alliance (which includes American Airlines, Cathay Pacific, Qantas and Qatar Airways) a few months later;[6] and US airlines announced they aimed to use 3 billion gallons of SAF a year by 2030 after the White House promised to issue funding and fiscal incentives for the use of biofuels.[7]

British Airways, the UK flag carrier, said ahead of the COP26 conference in November 2021 that it would source SAF to take delegates between London, Glasgow and Edinburgh during the event, as well as committing to investing £290 million into SAF development over the next twenty years.[8]

But what actually is SAF? And how does it compare, emissions-wise, to traditional aviation fuel?

What is SAF?
From an outside perspective, all of the above sounds very positive. Airlines are taking the initiative and vowing to change.

And SAF must be, well, sustainable, right? It's right there in the name, for crying out loud! *Au contraire, mon ami.* At this point, I think we're all well aware of the sometimes chasm-like gap between sustainability claims and sustainability reality.

Most SAF in practice is jet fuel that's produced from 'sustainable' feedstocks, such as waste cooking oil and other non-palm waste oils from animals or plants; solid waste from homes and businesses, such as packaging, paper, textiles and food scraps that would otherwise go to landfill or incineration; forestry waste, such as waste wood; and energy crops, including fast-growing plants and algae. It's very similar in its chemistry to traditional jet fuel – which is why airlines are going so big on this as the aviation panacea. For SAF to be used in aircraft, it must have 'drop-in' characteristics – automatically be compatible with existing aircraft technology, with a performance comparable to or exceeding existing fossil fuels during the combustion process – which, simply put, means airlines can use SAF in the aircraft they already have.[9] Aside from the more efficient aircraft solution outlined above, it's the cheapest, easiest method of adaptation to achieve lower emissions from flying without having to reduce the number of flights (which, as we know, they are exceptionally keen *not* to do).

Another fuel type that sits under the SAF umbrella, and which is potentially pretty exciting, is synthetic fuel, also known as e-fuels or synfuels. These are derived from hydrogen and captured carbon emissions and require water, renewable electricity (to produce hydrogen) and CO_2. These fuels are several times the cost of conventional kerosene at the moment, 'though we expect a significant cost reduction for green hydrogen (via reduced costs of renewable electricity and "electrolyzers") in the coming years', according to McKinsey. It envisages that, in the short-term, the CO_2 could be captured as waste gas from carbon-intensive industries, such as steel, chemicals and cement, with longer-term production methods using direct air capture

(DAC – remember this from our look at the offsetting options?) to extract the necessary CO_2 from the atmosphere.

However, 'While synfuels could become an answer to cutting emissions over the long run, it is unclear, at this point, which SAF sources will emerge as winners,' writes McKinsey. All of the above fuels are way more costly than kerosene; it's a chicken-and-egg scenario, where airlines don't have a viable business case for scaling up SAF, so the production volume is small, so there's no economy of scale to make it cheaper.

How much carbon does it save?

One key thing to note before we look at the numbers is that this kind of fuel must currently still be blended with traditional jet fuel – the non-SAF kind – in order to be compatible with existing planes. SAF can be blended at up to 50 per cent with traditional jet fuel – so when an airline says a flight is being powered by SAF, it could be that half of the fuel (or likely more) being used is still of the fossil variety.[10]

In general, the number that airlines and the oil industry all bandy around for SAF is 80 per cent. 'SAF gives an impressive reduction of up to 80% in carbon emissions over the lifecycle of the fuel compared to traditional jet fuel it replaces, depending on the sustainable feedstock used, production method and the supply chain to the airport,' says BP.[11]

There are a fair number of caveats in that statement. First and foremost, it would be more accurate to say that SAF has 'the potential' to save this; second (and second-most), the 'up to' bit is quite important – it certainly doesn't mean that all or even most SAFs will be hitting this figure. And then we get to perhaps the most telling part – all of the above is based on 'the lifecycle' of the fuel. The wording is important: note that it is not claiming that this results in 80 per cent fewer carbon emissions from a SAF-powered flight compared to a kerosene-fuelled one.

It's all a bit sneaky, because if you're not reading the fine print, you could easily be forgiven for thinking SAFs saved in-flight emissions. But the reality is that SAFs emit at least as much CO_2 as kerosene.[12] *At least as much*. Additionally, SAF-powered flights produce the same amount of harmful non-CO_2 emissions, which also have a significant warming effect.

The greenhouse gas savings all come in the production stage, when the fuel is manufactured (for example, with some biofuels, fast-growing plants are used, meaning carbon has been removed from the atmosphere in the process). With the right balance – particularly in the case of synfuels using DAC, if the same amount of carbon was being removed from the atmosphere in the creation of the fuel as was then emitted when it was burned at altitude – this could arguably lead to carbon-neutral flights. Nifty, huh?

But often this 'life cycle' approach to fuel emissions is not based on carbon removals, but rather makes assumptions about what would have happened to, for example, the waste used to make the SAF if it hadn't been turned into a fuel. The AEF says:

> As waste with a high proportion of 'biogenic' material in it can generate methane – a powerful greenhouse gas – if left to rot, a large benefit is assumed to arise if the waste is instead turned into aviation fuel even though this still generates at least as much CO_2 as fossil kerosene once burned.
>
> The claimed 'net' reduction therefore relates to avoided emissions rather than to any actual reduction. But to achieve net zero by 2050 across the economy, these methane emissions will need to be avoided *as well as* aviation emissions reaching net zero, not instead. [13]

What are the problems?
Even with the aforementioned considerations, SAFs should be preferable to traditional kerosene if they're less emissions-

intensive in their production (and, in some cases, remove carbon in the process). But there are a number of other stumbling blocks to watch out for.

One of them is scale. As we saw, airlines – and the industry in general – are making some big claims about the projected use of SAFs by 2030. The thing is, this isn't the first time they've laid down impressive-sounding pledges. 'Aviation biofuel scale-up has been promised by the industry for more than a decade but this has not materialised,' wrote Finlay Asher from Safe Landing, a group of workers within the aviation industry who raise awareness of the climate reality of aviation, in an article entitled 'The Trouble with SAF'.[14] 'Targets have been routinely missed by significant margins, and then ambition ratcheted-down across successive years. There was a target for 25% by 2020, but SAF use is currently at less than 0.01%.'

According to McKinsey's analysis, in a 1.5°C pathway (as defined by the Paris Agreement), SAF would have to account for 20 per cent of all jet fuel by 2030 – or, at a minimum, 10 per cent, 'in a scenario in which transportation lags in decarbonisation compared with other sectors' (looking pretty blooming likely at this stage).

And yet a 2021 paper from the ICCT, which estimated SAF feedstock availability to meet growing European Union demand, concluded:

> Without taking into account the political or economic barriers to SAF production, we estimate that there is a sufficient resource base to support approximately 3.4 million tonnes (Mt) of advanced SAF production annually, or 5.5% of projected EU jet fuel demand in 2030. The estimated production potential takes into account feedstock availability, sustainable harvesting limits, existing other uses of those materials, and SAF conversion yields.[15]

It's unclear, then, how myriad airlines expect to be able to meet even the underwhelming 10 per cent SAF target by that same year.

The scaling up of synfuels is even further away – 2030 is looking like the earliest point at which these could be successfully blended with kerosene. It will then clearly take a significant amount of time before production in any meaningful quantities can be achieved.

Another sticking point is resource. Various biofuels come from 'virgin crops', not from waste; land is used for 'energy' crops, including palm oil, rapeseed or soy. This can be 'hugely damaging', according to Finlay, as they're a leading driver of deforestation and are a nightmare when it comes to biodiversity. 'The overall effect is that using biofuel can be worse than using fossil fuel,' he argues.

Land use is a hot-button issue in this context too. To properly scale up the production of this particular type of SAF, land currently used for food production would need to be used to grow biofuel crops instead. Finlay says:

> Biofuel has been scaled up for road transport and it's had a devastating effect on land in places like Malaysia, Indonesia and some countries in South America, leading not only to a decline in biodiversity but also humanitarian effects such as water shortages, rising food prices, and land conflicts.

Synfuels might on the surface look more promising but present their own resource issues. Creating liquid hydrocarbons is an energy-intensive process. The idea is to use renewable energy to power this – but we only have a limited amount of renewable energy available. 'We should be prioritising the use of renewable energy in powering our homes and our road transport before we start to power aviation,' writes Finlay. When we look at any energy use, there is a hierarchy of need – with transport, particularly aviation, coming near the bottom of the list. A 2020 independent study projected that it would take three to four times the current global renewable energy generation to produce enough synthetic e-fuels for aviation based on current consumption trends.[16]

In the UK, at least, it looks as if the government is addressing some of the above issues. In a set of proposals published in July 2021, there was a commitment not to allow SAFs from food or feed crops, and not to divert renewable energy from other applications into making e-fuels.[17] The proposals also focused on fuels capable of delivering high carbon savings that generally avoided direct or indirect land use or wider environmental impacts.

Only a small range of fuels was identified as meeting these criteria: waste-derived biofuels, renewable fuels of non-biological origin (RFNBOs), SAF from nuclear energy and recycled carbon fuels (RCFs). While on the one hand acknowledging and addressing these issues is to be commended, on the other it significantly curtails the scale to which you could realistically ramp up SAF use – rather than being the 'big solution' the aviation industry has been presenting it as.

'In fact these fuels may be a rather small and/or expensive solution, and there's a big danger in creating the illusion of climate action while in fact continuing very largely with business as usual,' says the AEF.[18]

So, should we just dismiss SAFs? Not necessarily – they could certainly have a place in the future of a lower-carbon aviation industry. But at present there doesn't seem to be a clear pathway of how this would be scaled up to what's needed to make a significant impact without further detriment to the planet; and, crucially, it won't put a stop to the emissions produced by flights themselves. Even the name 'sustainable aviation fuels' is probably misleading at this stage, suggesting that passengers will be stepping aboard some magic, zero-carbon aircraft.

Safe Landing's Finlay summed it up thus: 'There might be a place for SAF, but it must go hand in hand with an overall reduction in fuel consumption. As ever, the most reliable way to reduce emissions from aviation is to fly less.'

Hydrogen-powered and electric planes

There are two technologies currently in development that are capable of offering real, bona fide, zero-carbon flights: liquid hydrogen and electricity.

The former, H2 propulsion, eliminates CO2 emissions in-flight and can be produced carbon-free. Estimates show that H2 combustion could reduce climate impact in-flight by 50–75 per cent and fuel-cell propulsion by 75–90 per cent, compared to around 30–60 per cent for synfuels.[19] Hydrogen also means a significant reduction in the other non-carbon emissions associated with aviation that contribute to global warming (nitrogen oxides and water vapour, for example). The only waste product it produces is clean water, and it packs in three times more energy per unit of mass than conventional jet fuel, plus more than a hundred times that of lithium-ion batteries.[20] Ooh la la!

According to a 2020 study by Clean Sky 2 and Fuel Cells and Hydrogen 2 Joint Undertakings, 'hydrogen propulsion has the potential to be a major part of the future propulsion technology mix'.

'The 2020s will be the "Decade of Hydrogen",' said Ron van Manen, head of strategic development at Clean Sky Joint Undertaking:

There is no viable path to a zero carbon or climate neutral aviation system that does not involve hydrogen: whether in

liquid form as a true 'zero carbon' energy source, or as a key
building block in the liquid fuels of the future.

A fair amount of investment is going into the development of this
technology. In 2020, a partnership between California-based
start-up ZeroAvia and various other enterprises, backed by the
UK government, saw the successful maiden flight of a hydrogen-
powered, six-seater Piper M-Class from Cranfield airfield.

ZeroAvia's Founder and Chief Executive Val Miftakhov said the
company expects to offer commercial flights by as early as 2023;
flights of 500 nautical miles (926km) in aircraft with up to eighty
seats by 2026; and 100-seater single-aisle jets by 2030.[21]

Airbus, the world's largest aircraft manufacturer, announced
in September 2020 that hydrogen-fuelled propulsion systems
would be a key element of its ZeroE project, which will see it
produce a new generation of zero-emissions aircraft. Hydrogen
'is one of the most promising technology vectors to allow
mobility to continue fulfilling the basic human need for mobility
in better harmony with our environment', Grazia Vitaldini, chief
technology officer at Airbus, said.

The French planemaker has presented three aircraft designs,
all of which will be hybrids, combining gas-turbine engines that
burn liquid hydrogen with electricity generated via hydrogen
fuel cells.

The other possibility garnering attention is that of electric
planes. These are powered by one or more electric motors that
drive propellers, with the electricity usually sourced from batteries or solar cells.

Developments have come thick and fast over the last few years.
In 2017, Slovenian aircraft manufacturer Pipistrel developed
one of the first all-electric planes, which was certified for use in
flying schools. In 2019, Harbour Air completed the world's first
successful all-electric commercial aircraft flight; its ePlane, a six-
passenger DHC-2 de Havilland Beaver, flew for half an hour over

the Canadian Fraser River. This was swiftly followed up in 2020 by AeroTEC and magniX, who created the biggest commercial plane to take off and fly powered solely by electricity. The nine-seater modified Cessna Caravan 208B, dubbed the eCaravan, flew for thirty minutes after taking off from Grant County International Airport in Washington state. The flight, though brief, was incredibly cost-effective: around £4.80 as opposed to the £240–320 it would have cost using engine fuel.

Airbus, meanwhile, has made progress with this over the last decade. In 2010 it developed the world's first all-electric, four-engine aerobatic aircraft, CriCri; it followed this up with an all-electric, twin-propeller aircraft, the E-Fan, which successfully crossed the English Channel in 2015. It has since been working on electric vertical take-off and landing (eVTOL) projects, and in 2021 launched its inaugural 'electric airplane race', the world's first all-electric aircraft race.

Designing for Uber Air, American planemaker Boeing has created an electric passenger air vehicle capable of being fully autonomous, with a range of up to 80km. The idea is that it will provide a flying taxi service, potentially rolled out to customers within the next few years.

One of the big goals on the table is to develop a 180-seater electric plane that could cover 500km (roughly the distance between London and Cologne in western Germany). EasyJet has partnered with start-up Wright Electric to design a prototype with the aim of achieving this and being able to operate commercial electric flights from 2030. These would likely be used initially only on very short-haul hops, such as London to Paris.

The drawbacks
If all of the above sounds like a blessed utopia of zero-carbon flying, I'm afraid I've got some bad news (when don't I?). There's a reason – in fact several – that no one is talking seriously about

these two techno-fixes being the saving grace for the future of aviation.

For starters, both have significant built-in limitations with regards to capacity and distance. Assuming all necessary technological and infrastructure developments happen over the next five to ten years (a significant barrier in itself that we'll look at in a moment), H2 propulsion 'is best suited for commuter, regional, shortrange, and medium-range aircraft', according to the Joint Undertakings report. As it stands, it's very difficult to see how hydrogen could possibly be used for long-haul flights.

This is due in part to the volume of liquid hydrogen needed to power flights. Hydrogen has higher energy by mass than jet fuel, but lower energy by volume – so you need four times the volume of hydrogen compared to that of kerosene.[22] For a journey of the same distance, you would therefore need a fuel tank four times the size in your lovely H2-powered aircraft – not so lovely when you consider that's taking up valuable space that can no longer be used for cargo or passengers, and is adding significant weight into the bargain.

With electric planes, the issue is very much weight-based. Batteries' lower energy density compared to fuels means aircraft would need to carry more than 50kg of battery weight to replace 1kg of kerosene (based on current technology).[23] Oh boy. And because battery weight doesn't decrease as the plane flies – unlike fuel, which burns off, making the aircraft lighter and more efficient as it travels – extra energy is required to carry the extra burden. This affects longer flights in particular. Plus, current batteries are a more awkward and cumbersome shape to be accommodated in comparison to liquid fuel, which can be stored in the aircraft wing.[24]

Dr Duncan Walker, an applied aerodynamics expert at Loughborough University, calculated that the world's largest passenger plane, the Airbus A380, could fly just 1,000km powered by batteries compared to its usual range of 15,000km.[25] 'To keep its current range, the plane would need batteries weighing 30 times more than its current fuel intake, meaning it would never get off the ground,' he said.

'The use of fully electric aircraft carrying more than 100 passengers appears unlikely within the next 30 years or longer,' according to McKinsey's analysis.

Aside from that, when we consider hydrogen propulsion, we must return to our infrastructure problem. Unlike the SAF 'solution', the hydrogen techno-fix requires an entirely new, very expensive set-up, in addition to new aircraft.

Although 'smaller aircraft powered with hydrogen could become feasible in the next decade', according to McKinsey, 'for aircraft with more than approximately 100 passengers, significant aircraft-technology development would be required, and infrastructure constraints would need to be overcome.'

Airports would need new parallel refuelling infrastructures, including fuel trucks able to store liquid hydrogen; refuelling times would grow for longer-range aircraft, which would in turn impact on airport gate and aircraft utilisation.

'Creating a hydrogen infrastructure will be critical: no infrastructure means no ZEROe aircraft,' said Glenn Llewellyn, VP of zero-emission aircraft for Airbus. 'We will need efforts from energy providers, airports and the entire aviation industry in order to make it possible to refuel our ZEROe aircraft at airports in the future.'

Although the Joint Undertakings report champions the use of hydrogen, it acknowledges that 'as a disruptive innovation it will require significant research and development, investments, and accompanying regulation to ensure safe, economic H2 aircraft and infrastructure mastering climate impact'.

Cost will be a significant barrier too. Hydrogen fuel is around four times the price of kerosene at present. As improvements are made, that gap will get smaller – but it's still likely to remain around double the price for the next few decades.[26] This alone will put airlines off pursuing it in any meaningful capacity, unless they're forced to do so by some kind of legislation.

You see the problem? For this to be developed and rolled out with any kind of urgency, at any kind of scale, it needs a huge, coordinated effort from all the key stakeholders in the industry. It would take a monumental amount of investment in airports around the world, in addition to the development of all the necessary tech (which would then need extensive testing, as with everything in the air-travel sector, to ensure safety isn't compromised).

'Our belief is that it will take a while for all the technology and elements of hydrogen propulsion to be worked out before we can get to ... commercial use,' Sean Newsum, director of environmental strategy at Boeing Commercial, told the *Financial Times*.[27]

It's why these solutions, though clearly the most likely to achieve truly 'zero-carbon' flights, are only seen as playing a marginal role in reducing the aviation industry's carbon emissions in the next thirty years.

The bottom line

If it isn't obvious by now, all the techno-solutions that have thus far been identified come with their own challenges and pitfalls.

The 'cleanest' fixes are also the ones with the biggest hurdles – financially and technologically – and they're also the ones likely to take the most amount of time to implement due to infrastructure constraints.

The less clean ones – namely SAFs – are easier to put into practice but come with their own sizeable issues in terms of scalability, cost and question marks about whether they are really better for the planet depending on how they're sourced and produced.

More and more weight and money is being thrown behind R&D for all of this stuff – but even the most optimistic projections don't see a massive overhaul of the current system happening anytime soon. All of it is difficult and expensive; using untaxed kerosene is easy and cheap. There's therefore still very little incentive for the industry to aggressively pursue even the more problematic alternatives that are available.

I think it's clear that, at some point, the ingenious human race will achieve carbon-neutral flying – it's only a matter of time. But time is the thing we no longer have when it comes to making the reductions necessary to meet that 1.5°C climate target. This tech will not conclusively solve the problem of aviation emissions in the next ten, twenty or thirty years. And with 2050 as the big, booming deadline, that's simply not good enough.

As far as I can see, there is no way around it: reduction will be necessary. We need to fly less, no matter what noise the industry makes about SAF, synfuels, H2 propulsion, electric planes or whatever else. Technology is an incredible tool in our arsenal – but it isn't, and never has been, a magic wand.

12

The Big One
Just How Far Can I Get at Zero Altitude?

It was finally time to take my most ambitious trip – a culmination of everything I'd learned along the way during my flight-free project. The plan was always to conclude my journey – or at least, this particular chapter of it – by reaching another continent. It's all well and good to wax lyrical about the beauty of the UK, the wonders of western Europe, the pleasures of exploring by train, bike and foot. But I wanted to go further; to prove to myself, if no one else, that I could stretch the same principles of slow travel to somewhere not on the metaphorical doorstep. (And my deep-dive into the future of carbon-neutral aviation had shown me that, while there were exciting tech developments afoot, it would be a long wait before I could possibly hope to fly anything approaching even medium haul 'sustainably'.)

Originally, this was to be North America by cargo ship: an epic three-week trip, much of which would be at sea, taking in Nova Scotia, New York and Baltimore before making the return across the Atlantic to Liverpool. Eight days or more each way, without internet, without phone signal, with nothing but the barest of facilities on board to keep one entertained (a luxury cruise it is not). Well, Covid put paid to that, along with so many other things; the US closed its borders to UK travellers for almost twenty months during the height of the pandemic.

Back to the drawing board, then, but the new-continent idea still appealed, as did riding the waves and setting sail for new lands. Minimising border crossings was also a key considera-tion at a time when pandemic restrictions turned each one into a Kafkaesque exercise in mind-melting bureaucracy involving forms, apps, tests and reams of paperwork.

Africa would be something, I thought. Somehow, in my previous whirlwind of far-flung air travel, I'd never set foot there. In some ways, the pandemic simplified matters – so much of the continent was, fairly or not, on the UK's 'red list' when I was in planning mode, dictating that returning travellers would have to stump up thousands of pounds to spend ten days in a designated 'quarantine hotel'. Not really my style. But Morocco had escaped this fate; Morocco with its plethora of ferry services connecting it to mainland Europe.

The sea border with Spain was closed – 'temporarily' but also indefinitely – meaning the swift hop between Tangier and Tarifa was off limits. This left Italy and France on the table, with the latter offering a forty-hour or so sailing between Marseille and Tangier. Straightforward enough: it would only involve crossing two borders, and two trains to reach the port. In 'normal' times, it would have been an exciting prospect. In abnormal times, I had so little faith that I could pull it off I kept delaying booking my hotel accommodation even after I had spent an eye-watering sum on the return ferry. Three days to go; I still hadn't booked. Two days; it probably wouldn't happen. One day; OK, maybe it wouldn't hurt to reserve *something* ...

Considering I was only going to be passing through one extra country to reach my final destination, the details on precisely what would be needed to gain entry seemed wilfully obscure. If I were flying directly from the UK I could simply present a negative PCR test. As I was travelling via France, I would also need to present my fully vaccinated status to avoid quarantine in Morocco, yet the Foreign Office advice stated that the country didn't 'officially recognise' the UK's proof of vaccination. The experience made me realise just what a pampered, sheltered little traveller I've always been – safe in the knowledge that I am welcome in nearly all countries, rarely required to obtain a visa, and able to flash a smile to border police as I sashay by with the unearned confidence of a Caucasian woman from a wealthy nation. This was a different ball game: I rang the embassy, wrote to the British consul in Morocco, had several conversations with the ferry company, La Meridionale, all conducted in my woeful schoolgirl French, to ascertain whether they'd even let me in the country. When I told people about my upcoming trip, it was with a heavy note of scepticism designed to dampen any excitement. 'I just don't really believe it's going to happen,' I said, shaking my head with a rueful chuckle like some world-weary cynic who's seen too much of this cruel life to feel hope anymore.

But happen it did. I turned up at St Pancras station, which by now felt something of a spiritual home after months of terrestrial-only travel, armed with a folder of carefully ordered travel documents and the conviction I'd be back home again with my tail tucked between my legs within forty-eight hours. But breezing through passport control and taking a seat in the departures lounge, I finally felt it – the emotion I'd mourned without ever quite realising I was missing it. That rumbling growl of pleasure in the pit of the stomach that switches on, a key turned in the ignition, at the start of a solo adventure; that soul-deep joy of contemplating the unknown adventures that lie ahead, just out of sight.

'*À piedtons? Pas de voiture?*' The man looked me up and down. I nodded enthusiastically.

'*Oui! Je cherche le bateau pour Maroc!*' I trilled.

He looked me up and down again.

As much as his stern, made-of-stone face would allow – a face that spoke of having seen it all, and then some – he appeared ... surprised. He held up a finger and sauntered off to make a call.

Turning up as a foot passenger for a ferry in Marseille is not the simple, carefree pastime one might imagine – a fact I learned upon arriving at its expansive port. You are like some enchanted yet cursed thing, a unicorn wandered in from a mythical glade, commanding a heady mixture of awe and fear in all who cross your path.

I had spent the most enchanting evening and morning in this, one of my favourite French cities, with its gruff, unpolished charm. Arriving at St Charles station, from whose lofty position you are treated to stellar views of France's second city, I was still dazzled by the swiftness of the train journey. Even without the previous direct Eurostar service (cut when the pandemic decimated demand), it's impressive: at 12.29 p.m., I'd been in London; six and a half hours later, after a quick change in Paris, I was in Marseille.

I lugged my bags over to the Intercontinental, the city's premier grande dame hotel, and set out for dinner. Despite it being a Monday night, I was turned away again and again without a reservation, which, though galling, was gratifying in so much as it indicated an upturn in the city's fortunes after Covid had left it emptied out. On the fourth try I managed to bag a table by the evocative old port, where I waited an inordinate amount of time for moules frites under the twinkling fairy lights of the outdoor terrace.

The next morning, I took an obligatory selfie at the Port Vieux Pavilion, the famed harbourside mirrored canopy; I stuffed myself with a lunch of grilled sardines and *panisses* (chickpea fries) under the shade of a striped parasol on a pedestrian square.

And then, to the practicalities. If you haven't already picked up on this, I'm a bit of a tight wad. I often joke about my colleague Simon Calder's miserly approach to spending money (why book an expensive flight when you can hitchhike across three countries to catch a cheaper one?), but it turns out I'm cut from a very similar cloth. With no wish to pay the exorbitant prices for food and drink on board the ferry, I made a detour to Lidl, buying enough crisps, biscuits, bread, cheese, wine and chocolate to last a week rather than a day and a half. (The great news is, you can take all this and more – so much more! – on the boat with zero weight limits or restrictions on liquids. Take *that*, aviation.)

This is how I turned up at the pedestrian access point at Marseille port, a tram ride away from the city centre: laden down with a suitcase, rucksack, bum-bag and oversized shopping bag, a baguette cheekily peaking over the top. I don't know what I'd expected; something that even slightly resembled the airport experience, perhaps? And maybe it was ever thus pre-pandemic. But not now. At the gate, I showed my ticket and passport and was told to '*Suivez la ligne verte*' – a green line painted on the ground – and off I trundled, five minutes later coming to a building that declared itself the pedestrian point of departure for Tanger et Corsica. *Parfait!* But a serious-looking metal grate was pulled in front of the locked door; a peer in the windows confirmed a very obviously empty departures hall. I wandered around, looking my default setting of vague and hapless, when I came across the aforementioned man in high vis – the international symbol for someone who knows what's what.

After a swift call, he intimated that the boat was at the next dock along, or whatever the correct terminology is, and enquired as to how I would get there. '*Je peux marcher?*' He raised an eyebrow and shook his head wearily at the ignorance of youth, or perhaps landlubbers. Gruffly telling me we needed to hot-tail it there so I could check in *toute suite*, he jabbed a thumb at his van while I murmured '*merci, merci beaucoup, vous êtes très gentil*' on repeat like an idiot. Pedal to the floor, he whipped me down a long stretch of road, and I realised why my offer of walking was met with such disdain. Ports are BIG. Like, really, really big. It took a good ten minutes to drive a distance that would surely have taken me upwards of an hour on foot, broiling under the afternoon sun. We pulled up sharply and he deposited me with a curt nod, leaving me a strange mixture of grateful and, to be perfectly honest, a little aroused by his take-charge, no-nonsense attitude.

After all the urgency, I flung my various documents at the lady behind the portacabin desk. I identified, despite the shaky start, a rush of what can only be described as pride at my ability to smoothly present each in quick succession thanks to my trav-min folder. They popped up like fairy minions called to Titania's aid in *A Midsummer Night's Dream*. Passport? *Ready!* Proof of negative Covid test? *And I! Forme sanitaire* for entering Morocco? *And I!* Proof of vaccination? *And I!* If this woman was in any way impressed, she didn't let it show, but no matter; I'd impressed myself.

Everything was in order – *mais bien sûr* – and I finally relaxed as I was told to wait. Time passed. Half an hour, forty-five minutes, an hour. Official-looking people came and went, barking orders into walkie-talkies, but no other travellers joined me. I started to get the sneaking suspicion that I was the only foot passenger on this ferry; and then I started to get the sneaking suspicion that they had forgotten about the crazy English woman with the many, many bags. Cars kept trundling slowly through gates, and it occurred to me for the first time that the only reason most would make the forty-hour pilgrimage by sea is because they have to take a vehicle – they're transporting goods or returning home after a long stay in France with family. Otherwise, why on earth *wouldn't* you fly? By this point in the book we all know why

– but I hadn't quite pieced together beforehand that I would be something of an anomaly.

Eventually, just as I started to feel a bit panicky – and like there might be a very real chance I'd have to run after the boat waving my ticket and screeching '*Attendez!*' – an official-looking man directed me to my second van of the day. I was a 'foot passenger' in name only; to board the vessel, I'd have to rely on four wheels like everyone else. We sat and waited in the painfully slow-moving line of cars; with time to kill we got chatting, in so far as that's possible with a lack of shared language. Why was I going by ferry, he queried, looking at me with the same expression I came to recognise in most people's eyes when I relayed the finer details of my journey – like I had just escaped from the asylum. I did my best to explain in garbled French: that I had given up flying, that I was doing it because of climate change, that I was writing a book about flight-free travel – '*voyager sans voler*' – and he perked up considerably, telling me he hated planes, and airports, and everything that went along with them.

The whole process was lengthier and more complicated than getting on an aircraft, of course – I had to present my passport a total of *four times*, read 'em and weep, before boarding – but when we finally drove up on deck I was dispatched with a grin and a promise that my new friend-slash-chauffeur would be there to help me disembark when I returned the following week. It felt, in all honesty, like a real achievement to have made it this far – and I hadn't even set off yet.

We set sail under a sunset so spectacular it made my eyes swim with tears. Clouds flitted, chameleon-like, from candyfloss to baby pink, brightening to flaming, dayglo neon the colour of a school highlighter before, just as quickly, darkening to bleeding raspberry.

Passengers and crew gathered side by side at the ship's prow and a reverent hush fell – no one talked or laughed as we went forth to meet the coming night. The atmosphere was that of a vigil, a midnight mass, with the sky in flames above our heads. It struck me that there was nothing cold or clinical about this kind of travel: nothing of the anonymous airport lounge, the identikit safety talk, the fasten-your-seatbelt sign. As I stood, gazing upon the gently undulating water and reflected strobe flashes of lighthouses in the distance, I caught a glimpse of a plane overhead. I thought about how easy it would have been had I been on it – tickets purchased at the touch of a button, seamless check-in, the sheer speed at which I would have been hurled from A to B, touching down before my body had quite made sense of the journey. And I found that no part of me desired to be on that metal bird. Not just because of the emissions it was carelessly spewing into the atmosphere – emissions I now knew we have no real way of undoing as yet – but because it was transport without adventure, without the unknown, without the true sensation of travelling at all.

I didn't regret my decision later that night, either, as I curled up in the lower bunk of my cabin. Sleeping on a ship is not like sleeping on a train, let me assure you. There is no rattling track, no train announcements on repeat, and no screech of wheel on rail or rapid shaking of cabin to keep you awake. There is only the soft rolling of waves, like a mother lovingly rocking you to sleep in a cradle; there is only a deep, rumbling vibration, like a panther purring as it lies in the sun, to lull you into slumber.

The next day brought more exploration of my trusty vessel, the *Pelagos*. It was ... basic, if we're being polite. If we're being less polite, it was devoid of all but the scantest facilities, limited to a run-down 'lounge' and self-service restaurant only open at certain hours. Even my dreams of the deck being furnished with plentiful, quality seating turned out to be misguided. A handful of benches were haphazardly wedged in, half of them crossed by fluttering red and white tape indicating they were off-limits (which my fellow passengers studiously ignored and sat on regardless, much to their credit). And yet none of it really mattered.

The sea was the main event, plunging everyone on board into a zen-like, meditative state. The ceaseless, gentle movement; the navy waves accented with liquid mercury wherever the sun's rays struck. There was nothing to see but occasional ships. There was nothing to hear but the wind, billowing the T-shirts of straight-backed men who stood stoically at the prow, hands clasped behind their backs, as they gazed out at that vast blue expanse in respectful silence.

Thoughts ran slow and heavy, inspired by our unhurried, stately pace. I shuffled to my cabin and back; inhaled giant bags of crisps; read my book. Unlike the cramped confines of an aircraft, here one could stretch out, move from place to place, 'take a turn about the deck' to contemplate once more the 360° seascape: it was like being on the ultimate digital detox.

When night fell, I went and stood outside to feel the pang of fear that comes with seeing the sea minus the comfort of daylight to tame its raw power. The fact that the wind could whip me overboard to scream helplessly into the void suddenly felt much more immediate. The palette was all in greyscale, as if colour had been sucked out of the universe: the sky charcoal, the sea a deeper shade of sable. And, above it all, the stars in HD clarity, sharp pinpricks of white carelessly scattered across the night's sky. The pattern of constellations was clear to those who'd ever bothered to learn them (I, most definitely, had not) and I understood the phrase 'starstruck' as never before, prompted to contemplate my smallness amid the grandeur of the universe – thoughts, it must be said, more usually associated with bong hits in dorm rooms.

The next day, the ghosts of mountains haunted my eyes as I stood unofficial sentry, I-spy-with-my-little-eye-ing for land. Was it cloud, that shadow up ahead? Or was it the shoreline?

Then, unmistakably, there it was – a great mass, far off in the distance. Pale and faded as an old pair of jeans but growing ever more defined as we approached.

We all took to the deck again as we drew closer to Tangier, the boat flanked by Spain to one side and Morocco on the other. Unlike flying, when your destination looks small and inconsequential from above until all of a sudden you've touched down and you're *in* the landscape, the slow, steady arrival by sea makes for a humbling experience. It was I who felt insignificant – mountains loomed ahead and the full might of the working docks, with their larger-than-life cranes and shipping containers, swung into view.

The excitement was palpable as we approached – an excitement that, to me, was inextricably linked with the length of time it took to reach our destination. I had a brief pang as I thought about the original trip I'd planned to North America. Imagine the feeling of reaching Canada after eight days at sea! Imagine this sense of miraculous wonder magnified and multiplied tenfold! I waited till the last second to duck back inside the ship, gazing greedily at this new continent I'd never set foot on before. What would happen next, I was blissfully unsure of. How to even escape the machinations of Tangier's industry-laden port? But that was for future Helen to worry about. Present Helen could only sigh, and smile, and I-spy-with-her-little-eye, something beginning with ... 'T'.

'Hello miss, hello?'

'*Bonjour*, you can't hear me?'

'You very beautiful miss! You want Moroccan boyfriend?'

The calls followed me down the Tangier streets amid the clamour of countless other unfamiliar noises – the disturbing howl of cats that had learned to mimic the sound of human babies, constant shouts across the road in French and Arabic, whistles, hisses. I felt my Westernness, my otherness, shrieking out like a beacon. My skin, too white; my hair, too light. A stranger in a strange land.

I had been told before coming that being a solo female in Morocco would bring with it a certain level of unavoidable harassment. But while forewarned is forearmed, it was still a shock to the system after the calm reverie of the boat. There was so much else to take in – the pungent aroma of spices mingled with fresh mint, the technicolour brightness of climbing purple flowers on dazzling white buildings, the overbearing sun that forced me to slow my gait from high-speed commuter walk to lazy stride – that the unabashed stares and catcalling were overwhelming. I imagine it was less intense in better days, when the country was thronged with tourists and obvious foreigners – but the pandemic had left Morocco bereft of its usual 13 million annual visitors.[1] The country's official 'Vision 2020' tourism strategy had aimed to attract 20 million visitors by the end of 2020, an ambitious target that was completely laid to waste by coronavirus restrictions.

It's hard to hide your alien nature, too, when you're constantly lost. I steered down the wrong streets of Tangier's charming yet maze-like fifteenth-century medina again and again, hitting dead ends at every turn. But then, a blessed flash of turquoise! I was back on the main artery, looking through an arched doorway in the rampart walls, perfectly framing the sea – it always comes back to the sea in Tangier – and I walked underneath to stand and feel the breeze bringing me back to myself.

Tangier is perhaps the perfect example of Morocco's status as the gateway between Europe and Africa; the epitome of a city combining two continents in its genetic make-up. Spain is so close, after all, that you feel you could touch it. And Tangier's geographical location, jutting out jauntily into the Straits of Gibraltar – stretching towards the European mainland as if reaching out a beckoning hand – has always seen it hold a position of strategic importance. It was practically begging to be seized by every empire going, I learned inside the cool, quiet, intricately adorned halls of the Kasbah Museum, which brings together objects from the city's history under various occupations. The Romans, the Byzantine Empire, the Spanish, the Portuguese, the English – all left their mark. When the rest of Morocco became a French protectorate in 1912, Tangier was deemed so important it was given its own special status, overseen administratively by a commission made up of various European countries, including Britain, until Morocco finally gained independence in 1956.

To some extent, this rich and varied history is reflected in the population of the city itself: cosmopolitan in the truest sense of the world, a melting pot where different accents, nationalities, cultures and styles all rub along together. It was evidenced, too, when I took myself on a café crawl through some of Tangier's storied tea salons and coffee houses. I started at the iconic, stripped-back Café Hafa, founded in 1921 and located on tumbling steps built into the cliff face overlooking the sea. Plastic chairs are set up, backs to the wall, facing the water like viewing platforms; the waiters perform an elegant, non-stop dance dispensing glass after glass of sugar-laden mint tea, picking up leaf-filled empties as they go.

At the other end of the spectrum was the hipster-feeling café inside Tangier's beautifully restored art deco Cinéma Rif. Here, the cool kids hang out inside, chain-smoking and working on laptops surrounded by vintage movie posters.

Café Baba was different again. Up steep steps in the medina, and proudly advertising its affiliation with the Rolling Stones (who paid a visit many moons ago) with a faded framed poster on the wall, it has the kind of shabby authenticity that marks it as the antithesis of a tourist trap, despite the former famous clientele. The blue-green floor tiles were chipped, the assortment of leather chairs battered, but it was clearly the place to be – big groups of men had congregated, talking over each other, playing YouTube clips on phones. A chicly dishevelled woman smoked languidly in the corner while bashing away on her computer as if the keys had personally offended her, instantly earning her a spot as my new personal hero. I returned to *thé à la menthe*, bewildered once more at the way a searingly hot, sickeningly sweet drink can simultaneously cool you down and alleviate a sun-induced headache.

And finally there was an espresso at Café de Paris – all brown leather banquettes and polished wood – a mirror of the long-standing French influence on the city.

Once I'd shaken off my initial apprehension at being a woman alone somewhere new, I quickly felt what many generations of visitors before me had – that Tangier is a place where almost anyone could feel at home. Like its fellow port city brethren across the globe, here there is an unspoken, intangible welcome to outsiders who decide to set up shop. This was certainly true of the owners of my Tangier base, La Maison de Tanger, a beautiful boutique hotel oozing French colonial elegance. At the time of my visit it had recently been bought by a supremely cool collective, Hopeful Tragedy Records – a French-Canadian record label and band whose co-founder fell hard for the city during a visit after the death of his father.

Twenty-four hours was all it took to become more acclimatised to the hustle and the heat. As I walked through it all on my way to dinner, unhurried and serene, I realised there was no malice lurking beneath the frequent 'bonjours'. Overtures felt more like a reflex than anything else and, with practice, faded to a mild buzzing in my ear.

That night I ate like a duchess at a locals' joint where I was served five courses of expertly cooked seafood for the equivalent of £13. I was still reeling from the extraordinariness of it ninety minutes later as, stuffed as a stuck pig, I rose up on my trotters and made my way back to the hotel to sit in the sunken garden and consider my supreme good fortune. Thirty hours after arriving in Tangier, I felt I might just be in love.

I realised how naïve I'd been to consider Tangier's medina even vaguely 'mazelike' on my first full day in Fes. Ha! Tangier didn't know the *meaning* of the word 'maze'. It hadn't even a nodding acquaintance with the term 'labyrinthine'. The tangle of streets that make up Fes's epic, 540-acre medina LAUGH IN THE FACE of all other walled cities. It is thought to be the largest pedestrian zone in the world, made up of some 9,000 streets, lanes and alleys, many with no official names, let alone signs.

People who've lived their entire lives inside its maddening web can get lost. As a tourist, there's no point in doing anything other than accepting the fact you will never know where you are or where you're going and embracing a 'go with the flow' mantra. That, or get a guide.

I opted for the latter. 'It's "Fes", not "Fez",' Jamal clarified as we clambered from his car to the fourteenth-century Marinid Tombs, high above the city, to take in the view. 'With a "z", it's the hat; with an "s", it means pickaxe in Arabic – because legend has it that's what the founder, Idris I, used to mark out the parameters of the city.' Only from this elevation is it really possible to take in the sheer scale of the Fes el Bali medina, dating from the ninth century and a designated UNESCO World Heritage Site since 1981. It is huge, home to more than 100,000 people at one point; that number had since shrunk to around 60,000.

Fes is really three cities in one, with distinct sections: Fes el Bali, Fes Jdid (which includes the Jewish Mellah quarter) and the Nouvelle Ville or new town (this last furnished with a McDonald's, Starbucks and all manner of Western accoutrements one has absolutely no desire to see as a tourist). We took a drive through the Mellah, taking in the different architectural style to the Islamic one seen in the medina: 'Doesn't it look like New Orleans?' Jamal prompted, and I could just about see what he meant, with its buttermilk buildings, covered wooden balconies, green awnings and lamps slung across the wide streets.

Then it was time to take a deep-dive into the ancient walled city itself. 'People live the same way they have for hundreds of years here,' Jamal said as we strolled through narrow, hectic lanes, packed with noise and movement. Chickens clucked and settled their feathers; mules and donkeys gave gentle snuffles as they patiently waited in the shade. We ducked into a bakery where a terse man, fag in mouth, relentlessly shovelled loaves into a huge, wood-fired oven and removed them when cooked. These weren't for sale – local women made their bread at home and dropped it off to be baked for a few dirhams. (In a pleasantly sustainable twist, the heat from the bread oven is also used to warm the waters of the neighbouring hammam.) The most astounding thing to me, as someone who barely knows her neighbours to give a passing hello to, was that the baker knew every woman's bread by eye; none of it was labelled, nothing was written down. 'He knows it from looking at the dough,' said Jamal. 'The colour, the shape, the texture.'

We escaped the heat at a former madrassa, or Islamic school, covered in phenomenal mosaic work; we stopped for fava bean soup topped with olive oil, garlic and chilli pepper at a hole in the wall, followed by prickly pears from a street cart. And then it was time for me to receive more compliments in ninety minutes than I've had in the entire rest of my time on Earth.

'Your face shines bright with goodness,' the man in the rug shop pronounced, staring into my eyes with an intensity that thrilled and scared me in equal measure. 'Bright with goodness, like the skin of the moon.'

Now, I don't really care if a comment like that is true or not (although, hey, let's go ahead and assume it is). After eighteen months of lockdowns, a heart-rending break-up and some very lacklustre meet-ups via the dreaded dating apps, it was, I'm not ashamed to admit, *nice* to spend a day hearing assorted men gasp as I removed my sunglasses, accompanied by cries of 'Madame! Stop! Your eyes! They are TOO BEAUTIFUL!' Of course, these proclamations went hand in hand with trying to flog me a hand-woven bedspread, leather jacket and assorted cosmetics made of argan oil, and I was largely immune to the sales pitches – but I'll be damned if I didn't almost spend £300 on a rug after the 'skin of the moon' comparison. That one was pure poetry.

The medina is jammed full of specialised artisans, crafting bespoke wares using the same painstaking methods that have been used for centuries. But traditional arts like this are slowly dying out, and not just because younger generations can't concentrate on anything for more than five minutes (thanks, social media), but because of Chinese imports. Much of what gets sold in the souks now – here and elsewhere in Morocco – is not Moroccan at all, but imported from Asia. It's cheap, mass-produced crap, with none of the craftsmanship or expertise displayed in the real deal. 'But people don't care about quality, they care about price,' Jamal said sadly. The artisans simply can't compete on that score; not when a piece of hand-woven cloth might take five to ten days to complete. Not when one brass filigree lamp takes months of labour in the design and execution.

One area in which the government is trying to counteract this is the ceramics district, moved out of the medina to its own stand-alone location by UNESCO when they realised the smoke produced by the kilns probably wasn't all that great for human lungs. Here, they produce goods out of grey clay – vastly superior to the terracotta used elsewhere in Morocco, due to its mineral-dense make-up, I was repeatedly informed – which get shipped all over the world at a price subsidised by the government to encourage foreigners to buy.

I stepped into a treasure trove of pottery, a riot of colour splashed on everything from tea sets to custom-made fountains, and was again assaulted by a barrage of compliments. 'You have a soft voice, so gentle – I greatly admire your way of speaking,' the owner told me. Well, shucks. For once, I decided to loosen the cheapskate purse strings a little and buy something to remember my trip. I spotted a tagine in a combination I liked – bright blue the colour of the Moroccan sky with finely painted navy designs – just begging to be taken home and cooked in using the poor excuse for *ras-el-hanout* sold in my local Waitrose. I've never been remotely good at haggling, but we both gamely played our parts, me pretending to give it a go and the salesman pretending I was robbing him blind. Declaring me '*drifa*', which turned out to mean kind and charming, he threw in a Hand of Fatima tile – thought to bring good luck – and I left in a flurry of blushes, not really giving two hoots if I'd vastly overpaid.

My entry into Rabat was not the most elegant of arrivals. Only realising we'd stopped at Centre Ville station after my carriage companion alerted me, I hustled my bags off the train in such a hurry that I tripped over my suitcase, landing face first in the dust. I followed this up by stumbling the wrong way down the platform, a fact that was brought to my attention when the train driver honked his very, *very* loud train horn at me and yelled, '*L'autre direction, Madame!*' Every single person at the station turned to stare at me with polite interest. They carried on staring long after I'd murmured my thanks and amended my course, I can only assume to see what other amusingly stupid thing I might do next.

In my defence, Rabat Centre Ville station was something of a work in progress, with no signs and, in fact, no way to exit the platform other than lugging one's bags over the train tracks. It was much the same throughout the Moroccan capital. Everywhere I looked were cranes, diggers, men in hard hats and piles of rubble. The whole place was 'under construction, undergoing improvements, making renovations' – and not in a bad way. Rather, it gave the impression of being a city on the make; a town cresting the wave of a swelling surge of regeneration. The downside was that most of the city's big attractions were closed while work was being completed: the Mausoleum of Mohammed V, the Hassan Tower, the Chellah Necropolis and neighbouring Jewish cemetery. All were off limits.

I ascertained this first-hand as I headed out on what ended up being an extensive walking tour. There is a size and sprawl to Rabat, a grandeur and scale to its buildings that eclipsed the proportions I'd seen elsewhere. It is this, as much as anything, that marks it out as the country's administrative capital. Without really meaning to, I trekked kilometres upon kilometres on roads shaded by orderly lines of palm trees. But it certainly wasn't thankless: there's nothing like travelling on foot to get a deep-rooted sense of place, as my Spanish pilgrimage had already taught me.

If Fes was like going back in time, Rabat brought me screeching back into the twenty-first century. The second I stepped out of the station and into the Nouvelle Ville district, I felt it – a young and vibrant dynamism that was almost palpable. It had the most modern energy of any destination on my Moroccan tour – the city where I felt, without doubt, the most comfortable as a woman travelling *toute seule*. Maybe it's because there are so many young people, maybe it's because plenty of them have adopted a less conservative style of dress – I saw scores of women in miniskirts, heads uncovered – but I walked the streets with increasing confidence, left largely to my own devices. After the days in Fes, where my tourist status earned me an unending string of unsolicited greetings, it was like stepping from sweltering heat to delicious shade. I remembered how much I enjoy the anonymity of an urban escape – the sensation of seeing rather than being seen.

The arts were still open to me, and so I explored the Mohammed VI Museum of Contemporary Arts, a swish facility housing contemporary Moroccan artists in permanent collections alongside temporary exhibitions. It's as good a way as any to understand the country's fluctuating sense of identity: artists were influenced by European styles for much of the twentieth century; there followed a backlash and a resurgence of a more 'local' Moroccan aesthetic; and then the universality of art took over as contemporary creatives sought to find their own unique voice in an increasingly globalised world.

From there it was a swift walk to Villa des Arts, a set of beautifully restored art deco buildings from the 1920s housing contemporary art exhibitions, where my soul found rest in its peaceful gardens, filled with the sound of birdsong.

It may boast a more modern sensibility but this is still Morocco – and so there is, of course, a medina. After my experiences in Tangier and Fes, I was fully ready to get lost – but Rabat's version is a different beast entirely, comprised of wide, well-ordered streets with clear names, several major arteries and a grid-like layout that even Google Maps can navigate without throwing a tantrum. The style is different, too – most of the architecture dates from the seventeenth century, when Muslims from Spain's Andalusia region arrived. The west side has a more seedy, Western feel – shops flogging plastic tat, restaurants selling Tex-Mex – while eastwards things become more traditional, with holes-in-the-wall and stalls to buy loaves and pastries, fruit and veg, herbs and spices. It doesn't have quite the charm of the more ancient medinas, but it does offer the advantage of being able to stroll freely – to stop, look, listen, smell – without being accosted every few metres. I ambled through as afternoon melted to evening, taking in the blue and white buildings and admiring the traditional wooden doorways.

On my final morning I took advantage of Rabat's coastal position and made a beeline for the beach – not the nicest, with slightly gritty sand underfoot, but it'll be a cold day in hell before I'm near the sea and don't get in it. The waves here are fierce – it's not a place for a proper swim – so I joined the crowds of locals striding into the water to cool off, staying in the shallows but letting the swells hit me chest-high. Behind me lay the sand-coloured Oudaias Kasbah, dating from the twelfth century; further along the Oued Bou Regreg river lay the fluid, futuristic white curves of the Zaha Hadid-designed Grand Théâtre de Rabat, in its last stages of construction. The perfect reflection of a city rooted in history but looking ever forward.

That afternoon I was back on the train, the splendid high-speed Al-Boraq – the fastest railway line in all of Africa – that whizzed me between Rabat and Tangier in an hour and twenty minutes. Train travel in Morocco is, in this newbie's experience, just plain wonderful. Cheap, punctual, regular and well-connected – and it's undoubtedly the best way to see the country, allowing you to watch rugged countryside give way to cityscapes through the window.

From Tangier it was back to Tanger Med, the port, where I was once again treated to wide-eyed stares of disbelief as I turned up on just the legs God gave me with no car in sight. I'll tell you how unused to foot passengers they were – I had to wait for fifteen minutes while they tracked down the only guy qualified to man the passport control desk. He was deeply suspicious of me, and made no attempt to hide it, looking from my face to my passport picture – up and down, up and down – for a full minute, before asking incredulously: 'This is you?' *Even if it wasn't, I'm not likely to admit it, am I?*, I thought, somewhat deflated by the notion that I must have aged horribly since 2015 to prompt such misgivings.

Eventually I was ushered through, to sit in a hall the size of an aircraft hangar filled with hundreds of seats – every one of them empty. I'd blithely assumed I'd be able to board the boat on arrival, settle into my cabin, fully explore below decks. Not so. Instead, I spent a strange, enchanted four-hour stint alone in the giant departures hall, feeling like the last-known survivor of the apocalypse. Sustenance came courtesy of a wall of vending machines selling hefty slices of cake for less than 20p a pop; entertainment was derived from using the space to perform an elaborate interpretive dance, safe in the knowledge that there were zero witnesses. I was, quite literally, dancing like no one was watching.

Time slipped by shimmering and eel-like: one minute, I was bemoaning my long wait on Twitter; the next I was being given the nod to board the shuttle bus to reach the ferry. Once aboard, the difference in quality between this and my outbound passage was stark: it was *Titanic*-like by comparison. There was a handsome bar, restaurant, mirrored tables and velvet chairs upholstered in dusky pink and powder blue lined along floor-to-ceiling windows to show off the sea to her best advantage. Fairly standard on lengthy ferry crossings, but after the spartan conditions of the initial crossing, I felt myself ensconced in a heady world of luxury.

Forty hours felt like four amid such splendour, and before I knew it we were chugging our way into Marseille. From our unique vantage, I could appreciate the city's name displayed in giant letters on a hillside, much like the Hollywood sign (pure class, that). One more bout of feeling oh-so-special awaited – as the only foot passenger, I was fussed over by the dockside ferry workers, told I was a VIP and dubbed 'the queen of Meridionale', before being driven fifteen minutes out of their way so that I'd be within easy reach of the train station for my return journey to Paris. A final day of sightseeing awaited. A final day of eating and seeing and doing impossibly exciting new things. A final day of adventure.

There is a moment in Morocco – one of those perfect moments you know you'll remember for many years to come, maybe even a lifetime – that perhaps sums up better than anything my entire flight-free experience.

I am on the roof terrace of an elegant riad-turned-restaurant, drinking a frosty glass of vodka and pomegranate juice. The alcohol hits in just the right places and I feel loose-limbed and content as the sun ebbs away. The call to prayer erupts all around me, the sound alien and otherworldly, while the air is warm without being humid. I feel so wonderfully far from home and it assaults me all at once – the miracle that I am here, in this place.

It might sound strange given all my travels, but I am not, by nature, a very adventurous person. Honest. I'm timid in unfamiliar settings surrounded by strangers; I rarely take the lead in new situations; I'm not the sort of person who can conceive of going on a 'spontaneous' trip without planning every element down to the tiniest, most banal detail. And yet here I am – on a rooftop in Fes, feeling the bath-warm night come to life around me as the sky achieves an indescribably beautiful ombré of lemon morphing into midnight blue. I got here all by myself, over land and sea, despite the overwhelming amount of red tape that had to be deftly skirted to make it happen. As I think of it – as I think of all the terrestrial trips I've taken – a small but determined flicker of pride lights up my insides. I've learned that I can get out of my comfort zone by taking things a step at a time, one after another, until I wind up somewhere impossibly gorgeous and exotic, sipping cocktails in the soft evening light. It makes me feel as if anything were possible; as if I am strong, and powerful, and capable.

Flight-free travel is so much more than a climate commitment – so different from the exercise in joyless self-denial and martyrdom I originally thought it might be. Rather than limiting my opportunities, it has done the exact opposite: opening me up to a mind-bending new world of possibilities. More than that, in fact – opening me up to parts of myself I never knew existed. I am reminded once more of train guru Mark Smith's wise words early on in this project:

> Booking flights is easy – but a nightmare to do and it doesn't give you anything back when you actually do it. Booking trains is hard – it's a challenge. But when you actually do it and make the journey, it's wonderful. It's like everything else in life: if you put more effort in, you get a lot more out.

After eighteen flight-free months, months in which the pandemic made travel more difficult than it's ever been in my lifetime, I finally understand exactly what he meant. I have never had such poignant experiences; never felt such a heady mix of emotions; never discovered such a well-defined sense of purpose and adventure. I may have stopped flying, but I feel like I have finally started travelling.

What started as a New Year's resolution – to avoid flying for twelve months – has become a whole new way of life. I thought finishing this book would be where my flight-free journey ended; and yet, as it turns out, it feels like this is just the beginning.

Carbon comparison
560kg of CO2e for a return flight London Heathrow–Tangier[2]

26.8kg of CO2e for a return train London St Pancras–Marseille;[3]
433kg of CO2e for a return ferry Marseille–Tangier[4]
= 459.8kg of CO2e

Carbon emissions saved: 100.2kg of CO2e

Total carbon emissions saved for all flight-free journeys: 785.3kg of CO2e

Notes

Chapter 1: Is Flying All That Bad? Stacking Up the Stats

1   'Statistical information on air passenger numbers and characteristics
    collected for the House of Lords Science and Technology Committee
    inquiry into the Air Cabin Environment', Parliamentary Office of Science
    and Technology (www.parliament.uk/documents/post/e3.pdf).

2   'Terminal and Transit Passengers 2018', CAA (www.caa.co.uk/
    uploadedFiles/CAA/Content/Standard_Content/Data_and_analysis/
    Datasets/Airport_stats/Airport_data_2018_annual/Table_09_
    Terminal_and_Transit_Passengers.pdf).

3   IATA data, 2018 (www.iata.org/en/pressroom/pr/2019-07-31-01/).

4   'Holiday Habits Report 2018', ABTA (www.abta.com/sites/default/
    files/2018-10/Holiday%20Habits%20Report%202018%20011018.pdf).

5   Statista (www.statista.com/statistics/564769/airline-industry
    -number-of-flights/).

6   'Animal Agriculture's Impact on Climate Change', Climate
    Nexus (https://climatenexus.org/climate-issues/food/
    animal-agricultures-impact-on-climate-change/).

7   Niko Kommenda, 'How your flight emits as much CO2 as many people
    do in a year', *The Guardian*, 19 July 2019 (www.theguardian.com/
    environment/ng-interactive/2019/jul/19/carbon-calculator-how-
    taking-one-flight-emits-as-much-as-many-people-do-in-a-year).

8   IATA World Air Transport Statistics, 2018 (www.iata.org/en/
    pressroom/pr/2018-10-24-02/).

9   'Ryanair one of Europe's top polluters, EU data suggests', BBC News,
    2 April 2019 (www.bbc.co.uk/news/business-47783992).

10 'Climate change: Should you fly, drive or take the train?',
BBC News, 24 August 2019 (www.bbc.co.uk/news/science-
environment-49349566); 'Greenhouse gas reporting: conversion
factors 2019', Department for Business, Energy and Industrial
Strategy, 4 June 2019 (www.gov.uk/government/publications/
greenhouse-gas-reporting-conversion-factors-2019).

11 Jocelyn Timperley, 'Explainer: The challenge of tackling aviation's
non-CO2 emissions', Carbon Brief, 15 March 2017 (www.carbonbrief.
org/explainer-challenge-tackling-aviations-non-co2-emissions).

12 Hannah Ritchie, 'Cars, planes, trains: where do CO2 emissions from
transport come from?', *Our World in Data*, 6 October 2020 (https://
ourworldindata.org/co2-emissions-from-transport).

13 'Facts & Figures', ATAG (www.atag.org/facts-figures.html).

14 Simon Evans, 'UK's CO2 emissions have fallen 29% over the past
decade', Carbon Brief, 3 March 2020 (www.carbonbrief.org/analysis-
uks-co2-emissions-have-fallen-29-per-cent-over-the-past-decade).

15 Jocelyn Timperley, 'Explainer: The challenge of tackling aviation's
non-CO2 emissions', Carbon Brief, 15 March 2017 (www.carbonbrief.
org/explainer-challenge-tackling-aviations-non-co2-emissions).

16 'Carbon Calculator', Carbon Footprint (www.carbonfootprint.com/
calculator.aspx).

17 Emissions are often expressed as either CO2 or CO2e. The former is
just a measure of carbon dioxide; the latter literally means 'carbon
dioxide equivalent' and includes other greenhouse gas emissions too,
allowing them to be expressed in terms of CO2 based on their relative
global warming potential.

18 'These countries have the largest carbon footprints', World Economic
Forum, 2 January 2019 (www.weforum.org/agenda/2019/01/chart-
of-the-day-these-countries-have-the-largest-carbon-footprints/).

19 Stefan Gössling, 'The global scale, distribution and growth of
aviation', *Global Environmental Change* 65 (2020) (www.sciencedirect.
com/science/article/pii/S0959378020307779).

20 David Banister, 'Heathrow's third runway is expensive, polluting and
unequal – why the poor will lose out', *The Conversation*, 25 June 2018
(www.theconversation.com/heathrows-third-runway-is-expensive-
polluting-and-unequal-why-the-poor-will-lose-out-98781).

21 Simon Calder, 'Coronavirus: Two-Thirds of China Flights Cancelled
Due to Virus Fears', *The Independent*, 21 February 2020 (www.
independent.co.uk/travel/news-and-advice/coronavirus-china-
flights-cancelled-virus-symptoms-covid-19-a9350911.html).

22 Mark Kaufman, 'The carbon footprint sham', Mashable (https://
mashable.com/feature/carbon-footprint-pr-campaign-sham).

23 'Sweden sees rare fall in air passengers', BBC News, 10 January 2020 (www.bbc.co.uk/news/world-europe-51067440).

Chapter 2: This Green and Pleasant Land: Mastering the Art of the Staycation

1 'The GB Tourist 2019 Annual Report', Kantar (www.visitbritain.org/sites/default/files/vb-corporate/gb_tourist_annual_report_2019.pdf).
2 Calculated using ClimateCare's Carbon Calculator (https://climatecare.org/calculator/), based on a flight from London Gatwick to Inverness.
3 Calculated using Trainline's Carbon Calculator (www.thetrainline.com/trains/carbon-calculator), based on a train from London Euston to Inverness.
4 Simon Calder, 'Luxembourg Makes All Public Transport Free from Midnight', *The Independent*, 28 February 2020 (www.independent.co.uk/travel/news-and-advice/luxembourg-travel-free-public-transport-traffic-congestion-trams-trains-buses-a9364686.html).
5 Calculated using ClimateCare's Carbon Calculator (https://climatecare.org/calculator/)
6 Calculated using the EcoPassenger tool (http://ecopassenger.org/)
7 Calculated using Travel and Climate's Climate Impact Calculator (https://travelandclimate.org/). Please note, general emission calculators have been used to calculate ferry emissions as the companies involved are yet to carry out their own audits to calculate the carbon footprints of individual passengers.

Chapter 3: Why Would Anyone Do This to Themselves? Tips and Tricks from the Flight-Free Experts

1 'European Railway Station Index 2020', Consumer Choice Center (https://consumerchoicecenter.org/european-railway-station-index-2020/).
2 'Use of aviation by climate change researchers', *Global Environmental Change* 65 (2020) (www.sciencedirect.com/science/article/abs/pii/S0959378020307676).

Chapter 4: At a Rail's Pace: All Aboard a Train Tour of Europe

1 Calculated using ClimateCare's Carbon Calculator (https://climatecare.org/calculator/).

2   Calculated using the EcoPassenger tool (http://ecopassenger.org/).

Chapter 5: Carbon Guilt: Does Offsetting Actually Work?

1   'Paris Agreement', European Commission (https://ec.europa.eu/clima/
    policies/international/negotiations/paris_en).
2   'Voluntary Carbon Market', Corporate Finance Institute (https://
    corporatefinanceinstitute.com/resources/knowledge/other/
    voluntary-carbon-market/).
3   Sabrina Weiss, 'Carbon offsetting isn't a cure-all for your filthy
    flying habit', *WIRED*, 25 August 2019 (www.wired.co.uk/article/
    carbon-offsetting-uk-flights).
4   John Vidal, 'Offsetting carbon emissions: "It has proved a minefield"',
    The Guardian, 2 August 2019 (www.theguardian.com/travel/2019/
    aug/02/offsetting-carbon-emissions-how-to-travel-options).
5   'The Oxford Principles for Net Zero Aligned Carbon Offsetting',
    Smith School of Enterprise and the Environment, September 2020
    (www.smithschool.ox.ac.uk/publications/reports/Oxford-Offsetting-
    Principles-2020.pdf).
6   'How additional is the Clean Development Mechanism', Öko-Institut
    (2016) (https://ec.europa.eu/clima/system/files/2017-04/
    clean_dev_mechanism_en.pdf).
7   'Invasive pests kill so many trees each year, it's equal to 5 million car
    emissions', Purdue University, 13 August 2019 (www.purdue.edu/
    newsroom/releases/2019/Q3/invasive-pests-kill-so-many-trees-
    each-year,-its-equal-to-5-million-car-emissions.html).
8   Giulia Realmonte et al., 'An inter-model assessment of the role of direct
    air capture in deep mitigation pathways', *Nature Communications* 10
    (2019) (www.nature.com/articles/s41467-019-10842-5).
9   Simon Evans, 'Direct CO2 capture machines could use "a quarter
    of global energy" in 2100', Carbon Brief, 22 July 2019 (www.
    carbonbrief.org/direct-co2-capture-machines-could-use-quarter-
    global-energy-in-2100).
10 Roger Tyers, 'Nudging the jetset to offset: voluntary carbon offsetting
    and the limits to nudging', *Journal of Sustainable Tourism* 26 (2018)
    (www.tandfonline.com/doi/abs/10.1080/09669582.2018.1494737?j
    ournalCode=rsus20&).
11 Camilla Hodgson, 'Carney task force confronts concerns over carbon
    credits market', *Financial Times*, 27 January 2021 (www.ft.com/
    content/de5e8631-bdf2-4c2e-8b7f-83c0c80cdea8).
12 'Aviation 2050 Goal and the Paris Agreement', Aviation Benefits,

March 2019 (https://aviationbenefits.org/media/166838/
fact-sheet_4_aviation-2050-and-paris-agreement.pdf).

13 'The UK's Net Zero Target: Is Aviation In or Out?', Aviation
Environment Federation, 17 December 2019 (www.aef.org.
uk/2019/12/17/the-uks-net-zero-target-is-aviation-in-or-out/).
14 Brandon Graver et al., 'CO2 emissions from commercial aviation,
2018', ICCT, 19 September 2019 (https://theicct.org/publications/
co2-emissions-commercial-aviation-2018).
15 'CO2 emission and compensation price per destination', KLM (www.
klm.com/travel/gb_en/images/CO2-emission-and-compensation-
price-per-destination-2019_tcm638-995022.pdf).
16 Patrick Greenfield, 'Carbon offsets used by major airlines based on
flawed system, warn experts', *The Guardian*, 4 May 2021 (www.
theguardian.com/environment/2021/may/04/carbon-offsets-used-
by-major-airlines-based-on-flawed-system-warn-experts).
17 'Climate Change 2007: Impacts, Adaptation and Vulnerability', IPCC
(www.ipcc.ch/site/assets/uploads/2018/03/ar4_wg2_full_report.pdf).

Chapter 6: Drive Me Crazy: Learning to Hitchhike vs. Learning to Drive

1 'CO2 emissions from cars: facts and figures (infographics)',
European Parliament, 11 March 2019 (www.europarl.
europa.eu/news/en/headlines/society/20190313STO31218/
co2-emissions-from-cars-facts-and-figures-infographics).
2 'Transport and environment statistics: Autumn 2021', Department
for Transport, 19 October 2021 (www.gov.uk/government/
statistics/transport-and-environment-statistics-autumn-2021/
transport-and-environment-statistics-autumn-2021).
3 'Climate change: Should you fly, drive or take the train?', BBC News, 24
August 2019 (www.bbc.co.uk/news/science-environment-49349566).
4 '2021 set to be second "staycation" summer, RAC research reveals', BBC
News, 16 June 2021 (www.rac.co.uk/drive/news/motoring-news/2021-
set-to-be-second-staycation-summer-rac-research-reveals/).
5 Based on 82kg CO2e per passenger (x 4) flying London Heathrow–
Newquay (www.atmosfair.de/) compared to 19.4kg per passenger
(x 4) driving London–Newquay (www.bbc.co.uk/news/
science-environment-49349566).
6 Joseph Stromberg, 'The forgotten art of hitchhiking – and why it
disappeared', *Vox*, 10 June 2015 (www.vox.com/2015/6/8/8737623/
hitchhiking).

7   Ginger Strand, 'Hitchhiking's Time Has Come Again', *The New York Times*, 10 November 2012 (www.nytimes.com/2012/11/11/opinion/sunday/hitchhikings-time-has-come-again.html?_r=0).

8   'California Crimes and Accidents Associated with Hitchhiking', California Highway Patrol, 1974 (http://bernd.wechner.info/Hitchhiking/CHP/body.html).

9   'Hanger Lane: from country road to malfunction junction', Footprints of London, 13 February 2020 (http://footprintsoflondon.com/2020/02/hanger-lane-from-country-road-to-malfunction-junction/).

10 G. Chesters and D.B. Smith, 'The neglected art of hitch-hiking: risk, trust and sustainability', *Sociological Research Online* 6.3 (2001) (www.research.lancs.ac.uk/portal/en/publications/the-neglected-art-of-hitchhiking--risk-trust-and-sustainability%28c957316d-5777-4871-9ee8-3ee6800eb26f%29/export.html).

Chapter 7: But ... What about Tourism? The Dark Side of Going Cold Turkey

1   Vicky Karantzavelou, 'Travel and Tourism in 2018 contributed $8.8 trillion to the global economy', TravelDailyNews, 28 February 2019 (www.traveldailynews.com/post/travel-tourism-in-2018-contributed-88-trillion-to-the-global-economy).

2   Anurag Kotoky et al., 'Jobs Are Being Wiped Out at Airlines, and There's Worse to Come', BloombergQuint, 23 July 2020 (www.bloombergquint.com/business/400-000-jobs-lost-at-airlines-during-coronavirus-pandemic).

3   'Tourism-dependent economies are among those harmed the most by the pandemic', International Monetary Fund, Winter 2020 (www.imf.org/external/pubs/ft/fandd/2020/12/impact-of-the-pandemic-on-tourism-behsudi.htm).

4   Asif Khan et al., 'Tourism and Development in Developing Economies: A Policy Implication Perspective', *Sustainability* 12.4 (2020) (www.mdpi.com/2071-1050/12/4/1618).

5   Ibid.

6   Haroon Rasool et al., 'The relationship between tourism and economic growth among BRICS countries: a panel cointegration analysis', *Future Business Journal* 7 (2021) (https://fbj.springeropen.com/articles/10.1186/s43093-020-00048-3).

7   Franklin I. Ormaza-González, 'COVID-19 Impacts on Beaches and Coastal Water Pollution at Selected Sites in Ecuador, and Management Proposals Post-Pandemic', *Frontiers in Marine Science* 8

(2021) (www.frontiersin.org/articles/10.3389/fmars.2021.
669374/full).

8 'Cornwall tourists urged to "stay away" as cases rise', BBC News, 24
   August 2021 (www.bbc.com/news/uk-england-cornwall-58318695).

9 'Fly Responsibly', KLM (https://flyresponsibly.klm.com).

Chapter 8: I Love to Ride My Bicycle: From Commuter to Explorer in Amsterdam

1 'Number of overnight tourists up to 46 million in 2019',
   CBS, 9 March 2020 (www.cbs.nl/en-gb/news/2020/10/
   number-of-overnight-tourists-up-to-46-million-in-2019).

2 'Tourism in Amsterdam – Statistics and Facts', Statista, 10 November
   2021 (www.statista.com/topics/6025/tourism-in-amsterdam/).

3 Senay Boztas, 'Best case scenario: tourists to Amsterdam around half
   of 2019 peak this year', Dutch News, 23 April 2021 (www.dutchnews.
   nl/news/2021/04/best-case-scenario-tourists-to-amsterdam-
   around-half-of-2019-peak-this-year/).

4 'Redesigning the Visitor Economy of Amsterdam',
   amsterdam&partners (www.iamsterdam.com/media/pdf/corporate/
   brochure-redesigning-the-visitor-economy-of-amsterdam.pdf).

5 'National Travel Attitudes Study: Wave 3', Department for Transport,
   5 August 2020 (https://assets.publishing.service.gov.uk/government/
   uploads/system/uploads/attachment_data/file/905887/national-
   travel-attitudes-study-wave-3.pdf).

6 Calculated using ClimateCare's Carbon Calculator (https://
   climatecare.org/calculator/).

7 Calculated using the EcoPassenger tool (http://ecopassenger.org/).

8 Calculated using Travel and Climate's Climate Impact Calculator
   (https://travelandclimate.org/). Please see note 7 on page 280 for
   more information on the figures used for ferry emissions.

Chapter 9: Get on Your Soapbox: Infrastructure Changes to Save the World

1 'Amsterdam's cycling history', I Amsterdam (www.
   iamsterdam.com/en/plan-your-trip/getting-around/cycling/
   amsterdam-cycling-history).

2 Abbie Meehan, 'Edinburgh flights to London are five times cheaper
   than getting a train', Edinburgh Live, 9 August 2021 (www.
   edinburghlive.co.uk/news/edinburgh-news/edinburgh-flights-
   london-five-times-21261046).

3   'Are UK train fares the highest in Europe?', BBC News, 14 August
    2019 (www.bbc.co.uk/news/uk-49346642).

4   'Should train operating companies be brought back into public
    ownership?', YouGov (https://yougov.co.uk/topics/politics/trackers/
    should-train-operating-companise-be-brought-back-into-public-
    ownership).

5   '2020 UK Greenhouse gas emissions, provisional figures', Department
    for Business, Energy and Industrial Strategy, 25 March 2021 (https://
    assets.publishing.service.gov.uk/government/uploads/system/
    uploads/attachment_data/file/972583/2020_Provisional_emissions_
    statistics_report.pdf).

6   Philip Alston et al., 'Public Transport, Private Profit: The Human
    Cost of Privatizing Buses in the United Kingdom', CHRGJ, July 2021
    (https://chrgj.org/wp-content/uploads/2021/07/Report-Public-
    Transport-Private-Profit.pdf).

7   'Railway Restored: regular trains to run on the Dartmoor Line for
    first time in 50 years', Network Rail, 17 November 2021 (www.
    networkrailmediacentre.co.uk/news/railway-restored-regular-trains-
    to-run-on-dartmoor-line-for-first-time-in-50-years).

8   'Restoring Your Railway Fund', Department for
    Transport, 27 October 2021 (www.gov.uk/government/
    publications/re-opening-beeching-era-lines-and-stations/
    re-opening-beeching-era-lines-and-stations).

9   'Decarbonising the Scottish transport sector', Transport Scotland,
    23 September 2021 (www.transport.gov.scot/publication/
    decarbonising-the-scottish-transport-sector/).

10 Alex Chapman et al., 'A Frequent Flyer Levy: Sharing Aviation's
    Carbon Budget in a Net Zero World', New Economics Foundation
    (https://neweconomics.org/uploads/files/frequent-flyer-levy.pdf).

11 'The Climate Consensus: The Public's Views on How to Cut Emissions:
    Results from the Climate Calculator', Demos, September 2021 (https://
    demos.co.uk/wp-content/uploads/2021/09/Climate-Consensus.pdf).

12 Ross Lydall, 'London cyclist deaths increase as more people take
    to two wheels', *Evening Standard*, 24 June 2021 (www.standard.
    co.uk/news/london/london-cyclist-deaths-increase-during-covid-
    pandemic-b942378.html).

13 Duncan Dollimore, 'Highway Code proposals: a simple rule for
    junctions', Cycling UK, 11 August 2020 (www.cyclinguk.org/blog/
    highway-code-proposals-simple-rule-junctions).

14 Steve Westlake, 'A Counter-Narrative to Carbon Supremacy: Do
    Leaders Who Give Up Flying because of Climate Change Influence the
    Attitudes and Behaviour of Others?', SSRN, 2 October 2017 (https://
    papers.ssrn.com/sol3/papers.cfm?abstract_id=3283157).

15 'Minority rules: Scientists discover tipping point for the spread of ideas', Science Daily, 26 July 2011 (www.sciencedaily.com/ releases/2011/07/110725190044.htm).

Chapter 10: *Walk the Walk: A Real-Life Pilgrim's Progress*

1   Kerry Walker, 'Could pilgrimages be the next post-pandemic trend?', *National Geographic*, 1 May 2021 (www.nationalgeographic.co.uk/ travel/2021/05/could-pilgrimages-be-the-next-post-pandemic-trend).
2   Calculated using ClimateCare's Carbon Calculator (https:// climatecare.org/calculator/).
3   Calculated using the EcoPassenger tool (http://ecopassenger.org/).
4   Calculated using Travel and Climate's Climate Impact Calculator (https://travelandclimate.org/). Please see note 7 on page 280 for more information on the figures used for ferry emissions.

Chapter 11: *Whatever Next? Introducing the Sustainable Travel Tech of the Future*

1   Dan Rutherford, 'Size matters for aircraft fuel efficiency. Just not in the way that you think', ICCT, 27 February 2018 (https://theicct.org/ blog/staff/size-matters-for-aircraft-fuel-efficiency).
2   'Waypoint 2015', Aviation Benefits (https://aviationbenefits.org/ environmental-efficiency/climate-action/waypoint-2050/).
3   Brandon Garver et al., 'CO2 Emissions from Commercial Aviation', ICCT, October 2020 (https://theicct.org/sites/default/files/ publications/CO2-commercial-aviation-oct2020.pdf).
4   Alex Dichter et al., 'How airlines can chart a path to zero-carbon flying', McKinsey & Company, 13 May 2020 (www.mckinsey. com/industries/travel-logistics-and-infrastructure/our-insights/ how-airlines-can-chart-a-path-to-zero-carbon-flying).
5   'IAG to power 10 per cent of its flights with sustainable aviation fuel by 2030', IAG, 22 April 2021 (www.iairgroup.com/en/newsroom/ press-releases/newsroom-listing/2021/sustainable-aviation-fuel).
6   Tom Otley, 'Airlines pledge 10 per cent sustainable aviation fuel by 2030', *Business Traveller*, 23 September 2021 (www. businesstraveller.com/business-travel/2021/09/23/ airlines-pledge-10-per-cent-sustainable-aviation-fuel-by-2030/).
7   'US airlines pledge huge increase in use of sustainable aviation fuel by 2030', Fastmarkets, 14 September 2021 (www.fastmarkets.com /article/4007630/us-airlines-pledge-huge-increase-in-use-of- sustainable-aviation-fuel-by-2030).

8   'BA in SAF pledge during COP26 conference', Biofuels
    International, 8 September 2021 (https://biofuels-news.com/news/
    ba-in-saf-pledge-during-cop26-conference/).

9   Christine Akrofi, 'A Guide to Sustainable Aviation Fuels',
    ADS, 17 April 2020 (www.adsgroup.org.uk/sustainability/
    sustainable-aviation-fuels/).

10 'Developing Sustainable Aviation Fuel (SAF)', IATA (www.iata.org/en/
    programs/environment/sustainable-aviation-fuels/).

11 'What is sustainable aviation fuel (SAF)?', BP, July 2021 (www.
    bp.com/en/global/air-bp/news-and-views/views/what-is-sustainable-
    aviation-fuel-saf-and-why-is-it-important.html).

12 'Benefits from Sustainable Aviation Fuels Must Not Be Over-Claimed,
    AEF Highlights in Response to SAF Consultation', AEF, 21 September
    2021 (www.aef.org.uk/2021/09/21/benefits-from-sustainable-
    aviation-fuels-must-not-be-over-claimed-aef-highlights-in-
    response-to-saf-consultation/).

13 'Government Proposals for a Sustainable Aviation Fuels Mandate: Key
    Questions Still Need to Be Answered', AEF, 11 August 2021 (www.
    aef.org.uk/2021/08/11/government-proposals-for-a-sustainable-
    aviation-fuels-mandate-key-questions-still-need-to-be-answered/).

14 'The trouble with SAF', Flight Free UK, 12 October 2021 (https://
    flightfree.co.uk/post/the-trouble-with-saf/).

15 Jane O'Malley et al., 'Estimating sustainable aviation fuel feedstock
    availability to meet growing European Union demand', ICCT, 2021
    (https://theicct.org/sites/default/files/publications/Sustainable-
    aviation-fuel-feedstock-eu-mar2021.pdf).

16 'Hydrogen-powered aviation: A fact-based study of hydrogen
    technology, economics, and climate impact by 2050', FCH, May 2020
    (www.fch.europa.eu/sites/default/files/FCH%20Docs/20200720_
    Hydrogen%20Powered%20Aviation%20report_FINAL%20web.pdf).

17 'Mandating the use of sustainable aviation fuels in the UK', Department
    for Transport, 13 July 2021 (www.gov.uk/government/consultations/
    mandating-the-use-of-sustainable-aviation-fuels-in-the-uk).

18 'Government Proposals for a Sustainable Aviation Fuels Mandate:
    Key Questions Still Need to Be Answered', AEF, 11 August 2021
    (www.aef.org.uk/2021/08/11/government-proposals-for-a-
    sustainable-aviation-fuels-mandate-key-questions-still-need-to-be-
    answered/).

19 'Hydrogen-powered aviation: A fact-based study of hydrogen
    technology, economics, and climate impact by 2050', FCH, May
    2020 (www.fch.europa.eu/sites/default/files/FCH%20Docs/
    20200720_Hydrogen%20Powered%20Aviation%20report_
    FINAL%20web.pdf).

20 'Hydrogen: An important pathway to our zero-emission ambition', Airbus (www.airbus.com/en/innovation/zero-emission/hydrogen).

21 Caspar Henderson, 'The hydrogen revolution in the skies', BBC Future Planet, 8 April 2021 (www.bbc.com/future/article/20210401-the-worlds-first-commercial-hydrogen-plane).

22 Ibid.

23 Alex Dichter et al., 'How airlines can chart a path to zero-carbon flying', McKinsey & Company, 13 May 2020 (www.mckinsey.com/industries/travel-logistics-and-infrastructure/our-insights/how-airlines-can-chart-a-path-to-zero-carbon-flying).

24 Chris Baraniuk, 'The largest electric plane ever to fly', BBC Future Planet, 18 June 2020 (www.bbc.com/future/article/20200617-the-largest-electric-plane-ever-to-fly).

25 Duncan Walker, 'Electric planes are here – but they won't solve flying's CO2 problem', *The Conversation*, 5 November 2019 (https://theconversation.com/electric-planes-are-here-but-they-wont-solve-flyings-co-problem-125900).

26 'Sustainable synthetic carbon based fuels for transport', Royal Society, 2019 (https://royalsociety.org/-/media/policy/projects/synthetic-fuels/synthetic-fuels-briefing.pdf).

27 Peggy Hollinger, 'Hydrogen-powered planes: pie in the sky?', *Financial Times*, 15 March 2021 (www.ft.com/content/7099d84c-07b8-4970-b826-ac28b4e59841).

Chapter 12: The Big One: Just How Far Can I Get at Zero Altitude?

1 Halligan Agade, 'Nearly 13 million tourists visited Morocco in 2019', CGTN Africa, 3 February 2020 (https://africa.cgtn.com/2020/02/03/nearly-13-million-tourists-visited-morocco-in-2019/).

2 Calculated using ClimateCare's Carbon Calculator (https://climatecare.org/calculator/).

3 Calculated using the EcoPassenger tool (http://ecopassenger.org/).

4 Calculated using Travel and Climate's Climate Impact Calculator (https://travelandclimate.org/). Please see note 7 on page 280 for more information on the figures used for ferry emissions.